D0371895

The
ANGRY
HEART

An Interactive
Self-Help Guide to
Overcoming
Borderline and
Addictive Disorders

Joseph Santoro, Ph.D.
WITH EXERCISES BY RONALD COHEN, PH.D.

MJF BOOKS
NEW YORK

Publisher's Note: This publication is designed to provide accurate and authoritative information in regard to the subject matter covered. It is sold with the understanding that the publisher is not engaged in rendering psychological, financial, legal, or other professional services. If expert assistance or counseling is needed, the services of a competent professional should be sought.

Published by MJF Books
Fine Communications
Two Lincoln Square
60 West 66th Street
New York, NY 10023

The Angry Heart
LC Control Number 01-130259
ISBN 1-56731-439-2

This edition published by arrangement with New Harbinger Publications, Inc.

"Breathe" lyrics by Roger Waters © 1973 Pink Floyd Music Publishers Limited for the World excluding USA and Canada; ©1973 Hampshire House Publishing Corp., New York, NY. Used by permission. "Time" Lyrics by Roger Waters ©1973 Pink Floyd Music Publishers Limited for the World excluding USA and Canada; ©1973 Hampshire House Publishing Corp., New York, NY. Used by permission. "In the Flesh?" by Roger Waters ©1979 Pink Floyd Music Publishers Limited. "Greedy Fly" Lyrics by Gavin Rossdale. Reprinted with permission.

Text design by Tracy Marie Powell.

Manufactured in the United States of America on acid-free paper

MJF Books and the MJF colophon are trademarks of Fine Creative Media, Inc.

10 9 8 7 6 5 4 3 2 1

To my grandmother and nanny, Julie Santomauro, who inspired and nurtured my education. All my love and thanks.

—J.S.

It is one of the most beautiful compensations in life that no man can sincerely try to help another without helping himself.

—Ralph Waldo Emerson

Who then can so softly bind up the wounds of another as he who has felt the same wounds himself.

—Thomas Jefferson

Contents

I would like to thank several people for the assistance they provided me. Their help was invaluable and much appreciated.

Michael Katsarakes, Program Director and VP at Supervised Lifestyles, Inc., provided keen feedback on the style and clarity of the chapters as well as valuable advice for chapter exercises based on the mentorship therapy groups that ran under his supervision.

Michael Tisbe, M.D., Medical Director at Supervised Lifestyles, Inc., provided me with guidance and advice concerning the medication choices available to assist people with BPD. His many years of psychiatric experience were of great assistance to me.

My thanks and love go to my wife, Jeanne, and daughter, Nicole, for their patience and under- standing while I devoted hours and hours of my time to this project.

Finally, and most importantly, I thank Samuel, who, though he chose to remain anonymous, is really a co-author of this book. May his journey be blessed with the results that he desires.

—J.S.

Introduction

Our starting point in life is never our own choice. Our genetic code is pieced together through a miraculous microcosmic dance. Our family environment is our gift or our curse. A supportive family environment composed of love, security, progressive learning, and discipline helps to nurture a healthy and successful person.

But what happens when these critical ingredients are deficient? A dysfunctional family environment, which I term *psychotraumatizing*, creates a person whose heart is wounded by fear and anger and whose mind is often confused and impulsive. This is someone, who, because of his or her family environment, develops a personality disturbance and is at risk for addiction, failure, and even self-destruction.

This self-help guide can help you change the behavioral cycle that keeps you trapped in a zone of mental agony. It's a book for people whose unhappy childhoods have made them victims of their own behavior. It's for people who are stuck in a lifestyle that they hate. It's for people whose moods and actions are ever changing contradictions and who find that they are addicted to self-injurious pleasures and pains.

This guide was inspired, in part, by the struggles many young men and women have experienced as they felt and expressed their personal pain. I hope that it inspires you to create a new way of living. It can serve as the compass that guides your journey of healing. It does not provide any easy or quick answers. It does provide a way to understand what happened. It does provide skills you can use to change dysfunctional behaviors. It does provide emotional and motivational support to press forward and never give up. And lastly, it does offer a point of light to lead you out of the darkness of a self-perpetuating hell.

The book describes the experiences of Samuel, who suffered at the hands of his caregivers and then at his own hands. His experiences and the experiences of people I have treated and learned from over the last seventeen years are used to illustrate how borderline and addictive behaviors are created. Dr. Cohen and I offer advice and recovery exercises (based on over thirty-five years of combined clinical experience and practice) that deal with how these patterns can be altered. Samuel shares the emotionally traumatic experiences of his childhood and recent life. He also shares what it is like to try to alter one's own behavior (the successes and the failures). Each chapter is constructed from a tapestry of personal experience, clinical insight, self-help skills, and emotional encouragement. This unique combination can empower you to alter your feelings, thoughts, and actions for the better. It can help to calm your rage and fear. It can help you to break free of addictive behaviors. It can help, but it cannot make it happen. You will need willingness, an openness to change, and some determination.

A Word of Caution

This book was designed to help those who are burdened by borderline and addictive problems to overcome the psychological causes of these problems. The contents of this book can be psychologically powerful.

Readers afflicted with these problems may be actively blocking their feelings and will view the book's stories and commentary as irrelevant to their lives.

Readers who are "ready" will find the narratives, commentaries, and Recovery Exercises emotionally stimulating. They may experience surges of painful emotions accompanied by intense crying spells and strong anger. But these emotional experiences will pass and, while unpleasant, will help readers overcome the emotional walls that separate them from a happier life.

If these emotional experiences become too intense for you to bear on your own, seek out the support of someone you can trust, or of a behavioral health care professional. Feel free to contact me for further advice. I'll tell you how at the end of this introduction.

What Is Borderline Personality Disorder?

The term *borderline personality disorder* (BPD) suggests the image of a person who is on the edge or border of something. During the first sixty years of the twentieth century, the border in borderline was located between neurosis and insanity (officially called *schizophrenia*). In fact, the diagnostic term that preceded the use of borderline personality disorder was *pseudoneurotic schizophrenia*. This term was used because, at that time, all psychiatric problems were viewed as falling along a single continuum that ranged from neurotic, at one end, to psychotic (another term for insane), at the other. Today, most professionals have abandoned this single-continuum concept of behavioral health problems. We now know that borderline personality disorder does *not* progress to schizophrenia or psychosis. It is an independent, albeit complex, disorder with its own origins and prognosis.

The official diagnostic criteria of the American Psychiatric Association's *Diagnostic and Statistical Manual* (DSM-IV 1994) require that five or more of the following be present before a diagnosis of BPD can be made (these are a paraphrased version of the actual criteria):

1. Frantic efforts to avoid real or imagined abandonment

2. A pattern of unstable and intense interpersonal relationships

3. Unstable sense of self and identity

4. Impulsive actions that are ultimately self-damaging such as drug abuse, excessive spending, reckless driving, or unsafe sex

5. Recurrent suicidal actions, threats, thoughts, or self-injury behaviors (such as cutting)

6. Unstable, intense moods or emotions that can be triggered by events and may last hours or days

7. Chronic feelings of emptiness, boredom, or loneliness

8. Inappropriate or intense anger that is difficult to control

9. Temporary, stress-triggered paranoid ideas ("I feel threatened by others") or severe dissociative symptoms ("I don't feel real")

Not everyone who has BPD experiences all of these symptoms. Nor do they experience the symptoms they do have all of the time. Most people with BPD find that their symptoms change based on who they are with and the environmental demands they face. As their stress level increases, they often find that the intensity and frequency of their BPD thoughts, feelings, and behavior also increase.

Approximately 2 to 4 percent of adults have a clinically significant degree of BPD. This means that at least six million people nationwide have BPD. It is generally thought that females outnumber males by four to one in prevalence of BPD. In our practice, however, we see about equal numbers of each. I believe that male BPD is often underdiagnosed.

As is the case with many problems, no two people's BPD is exactly alike. Professionals have for many years sought to identify subtypes of

BPD. For example, some people with BPD will show psychotic symptoms when under stress. Others tend toward depression, intense anger, and suicidal thinking and actions. Still others are overly demanding, manipulative, and self-centered. These observations have led to attempts to classify people with BPD into subtypes such as psychotic, depressed/suicidal, manipulative/egocentric, and so forth.

My clinical experience suggests that fixed subtypes are not as helpful in treatment planning as they may appear to be. For example, fixed subtypes encourage treatments to be symptom focused, as opposed to cause focused. If someone with BPD has psychotic symptoms, should the primary target of treatment be the psychosis? If so, should that be the primary diagnosis? In addition, recent evidence suggests that traumatic stress, particularly stress exposure early in life, appears to play an important role in the development of BPD (Perry et al. 1996; Kroll 1988; Famularo 1991). In this regard, Kroll (1988) has challenged the definition of *psychotic* as it is applied to people with BPD. He argues that when people with BPD are placed under stress, their behavior can become highly agitated, confused, and dysfunctional—a reaction that can appear as if it were a psychotic process. Kroll put it this way: "I am suggesting that many borderline symptoms, especially the ones that have the appearances of 'brief psychotic episodes' and which I have included under the heading of cognitive disturbances, are no different from the symptoms seen in post-traumatic stress disorder." If early traumatic stress plays the critical role in the development of BPD, this should be reflected in any diagnostic subtyping scheme.

Two Possible Causes of BPD

BPD is a complex disorder whose causes are only starting to be more fully understood. Studies of people with BPD have shown that about 70 to 79 percent of people with BPD (e.g., Famularo et. al. 1991) report a history of serious abuse or psychological trauma. However, this also means that about 25 percent of people with BPD do not report such a history. This data suggests that two theoretical paths to BPD are emerging: one involves early exposure to psychotraumatic events and the other involves the presence of a biologic vulnerability. These statistics, other studies (e.g., Perry et. al. 1996; Silk, et. al. 1995; Stone 1990) and my clinical practice have led me to an *equifinality model of BPD* that provided the theoretical framework for this book.

Equinfinality (Miller 1978) is a systems concept that means "that a final state of any living system [borderline personality disorder] may be reached from different initial conditions [Factor I, Factor II, or both] and in different ways [antecedent or consequent dysfunctional family interactions]." As indicated, there are two sets of initial conditions labeled Factor I (psychotrauma) and Factor II (biologic vulnerability). The equifinal model states that either factor by itself or in combination can initiate the development of BPD.

In Factor I BPD (about 75 percent of people with BPD have this factor), dysfunctional family interactions directly produce psychotraumatic childhood exposures that trigger a cascade of aversive experiences and brain changes that lead to BPD by late adolescence. A *psychotraumatic experience* is an aversive event that triggers a fear response capable of causing a person to become concerned about his or her psychological or physical safety while effectively inhibiting the person's ability to protect him- or herself by terminating or escaping the aversive event. The magnitude of the event must be intense and chronic enough to have a lasting effect on a person's psychophysiological functioning.

Chronic and intense early-life psychotraumatization appears to make a person hypersensitive to stress by modifying brain systems responsible for arousal and fight-or-flight responses, which may alter the production of neurotransmitters such as epinephrine and serotonin (Perry et al. 1996; Teicher et al. 1994; de Vegvar et al. 1994). This emerging stress hypersensitivity and the dysfunctional coping behavior conditioned by it *and* the child's environment shape and define the other BPD symptoms. In this model, Factor I BPD is essentially a complex and chronic form of posttraumatic stress disorder.

In Factor II BPD (about 25 percent of people with BPD have this factor), a biologic vulnerability (not psychotrauma), such as attention deficit disorder, childhood bipolar disorder (for a description see Biederman 1997), a genetic defect, or intrauterine toxin (e.g., maternal substance abuse), creates a neurologically dysfunctional, emotionally sensitive, and difficult child whose aversive behaviors initiate and condition dysfunctional family interaction patterns in a *previously functional* family environment. These dysfunctional interaction patterns escalate family stress levels, worsen the child's behavior patterns, and eventually lead to the child developing BPD.

Of course, a combination of Factor I and Factor II BPD is possible and people dually affected might be expected to have a more severe case of BPD. (You can read more about the Angry Heart Theory of BPD in chapter 13.)

This equifinality model of BPD is a tentative one. A more accurate answer to the question of what causes BPD will have to await the results of future research.

A Word of Understanding for Parents

Talking to parent about their BPD children requires, at times, the wisdom of Solomon. Some parents are themselves responsible for assisting in the creation of the psychotraumatic environmental conditions that shape borderline behavior (Factor I BPD). Sometimes it was their spouse, other family members, or outsiders who perpetrated the psychotrauma. But unfortunately the parent was helpless to stop or prevent it and may have even been a co-victims of the traumas.

Parents of Factor II BPD children did nothing other than try to cope as well as they could with a very difficult child. Under the strain and stress of such a child's behaviors even the best of us make mistakes. However, the biological vulnerability, and not the mistakes, initiate the process that conditions Factor II borderline behaviors.

For Factor I BPD parents this book will not be easy reading. If you are a parent of such a person, chances are that you played a significant role in the development of your son or daughter's problem. Parents who read this book often react to it with anger because they believe that the book blames them for their children's problems. *It is important to understand that, while you are responsible, you are not to blame.*

The worst thing anyone could say to a parent is that he or she is a bad parent. This book does *not* say that. I do not seek, and do not have the right, to blame anyone for anything. The forces that create dysfunctional family life are many. Society as a whole bears a large degree of the responsibility for creating many of the forces that condition people to treat one another in psychotraumatic ways.

Remember that *all parents were once children*. Their own parenting style was shaped by how they were raised. If you are a parent and are reading this book, read it first as a child, and then as a parent. Dysfunctional behavior is passed down through the generations and society's demands and stressors affect everyone's ability to be a good parent. A good parent is someone who loves his or her children without condition. A good parent wants to minimize his or her children's pain. By better understanding your childhood, your evaluation of how you raised your children may change. Such a change may help to heal everyone.

The story of why you did what you did (or did not do) is one that deserves to be told. Your readiness to tell your own story will determine your ability to tolerate this one.

For everyone involved with BPD, what has happened is over and what matters lies ahead. While the early chapters of this book place greater emphasis on Factor I BPD, this book can be a useful source of support for all parents and people with BPD if you let it be. Open your mind and let go of your negative emotions. If it can happen, let it.

Borderline Phases

I have observed three behavioral phases of BPD: a *direct self-harm phase*, an *indirect self-harm phase*, and an *inter-phase*. A person with BPD can move among these phases and, generally, does not remain exclusively in one phase. By my estimate, a person with BPD can be in one of the self-harm phases for anywhere from minutes and hours (most likely) to weeks, and in the inter-phase from hours to months or, perhaps, even years.

Phase switching seems to be controlled by consequences that affect the core feature of a person with BPD's self-image: self-hatred. Self-hatred is the opposite of self-love and is a direct result of childhood psycho-traumatization. Periods of elevated stress increase self-hatred and the probability that a person with BPD will switch into a self-harm phase. As self-hatred increases, so does the probability of self-harm. The presence of people who can provide positive support can reduce self-hatred.

When the self-hatred is *directly* expressed through behaviors such as depression, cutting, and suicidal thinking, gestures, and actions, the person is in the direct self-harm phase. At other times, when it is expressed *indirectly* through behaviors such as agitated boredom, substance abuse, sexual excesses, reckless driving, or other impulsive actions, the person is in the indirect self-harm phase.

During periods of supportive living or working situations, people with BPD can become increasingly free of self-harmful behaviors. I call the time spent in this period the inter-phase. During the inter-phase the acceptance-seeking behavior of people with BPD becomes more visible. At these times their need to be wanted, liked, and accepted by others is so strong that they will often go to great lengths to please others. Transient mood fluctuations, especially mild depression and anger outbursts, still occur, but they are brief and mild. If attempts to gain acceptance are met with rejection, they may switch back into a self-harm phase. In addition to rejection and elevated stress levels, I suspect that reduced social-emotional support can also trigger a switch back into a self-harm phase.

The diagram on the next page models the dynamic interactions of these phases. People with BPD can cycle between a self-harm phase and the inter-phase (illustrated by the smaller arrows), they can cycle through both self-harm phases (illustrated by the larger arrows), or they can cycle through both self-harm phases and the inter-phase. It is my clinical impression that the vast majority of people with BPD spend at least some time in each phase.

Misdiagnosis of BPD

People with BPD are often given incorrect, or incomplete, diagnoses. These include major depression, bipolar disorder, primary polysubstance abuse, eating disorders, attention deficit disorder (ADD), schizoaffective disorder, dysthymia, antisocial personality disorder (for males with BPD), and psychotic disorder not otherwise specified. They are diagnosed in so many different ways because they present a multiplicity of symptom combinations.

How people with BPD are diagnosed depends, in my view, on which phase they are in at the time the diagnosis is made. For example, during the direct self-harm phase they can appear depressed, as if they have an eating disorder, or psychotic. If they consult a professional during this phase, they are more likely to be diagnosed along these lines.

People who are heavy substance abusers may mimic borderline symptoms, especially impulsiveness and poor anger control. Many people with BPD also abuse drugs and alcohol and such abuse worsens their BPD. They often develop other types of addictive disorders as well (for example, cutting, reckless driving, sexual excesses). An addictive disorder is the use of an activity or substance beyond the point where the costs of use outweigh the benefits of use. When someone reaches this point they place their lifestyle and health in jeopardy.

On a clinical level, then, BPD people are *not* schizophrenic nor manic- depressive, nor a combination of both. They may have ADD, especially if they are male. They are often mildly depressed and suicidal. They often use addictive activities to cope with their emotions.

But what is BPD on a personal level? A woman on the Internet put it this way, "Being borderline is like being a caged animal, constantly being whipped by a trainer for behaving badly. As the animal, you don't

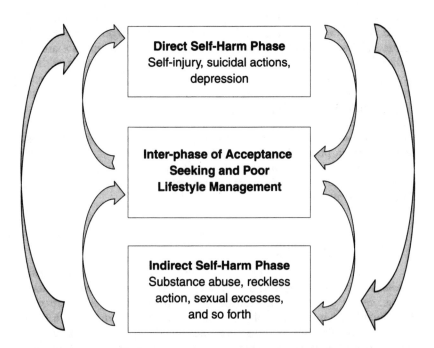

Figure 1: Borderline Personality Disorder's Phases

know the trainer's rules. But you are punished for not following them anyway.... The trainer wants you to shape up ... but your nature was never to act that way." Another woman wrote about her borderline identity with these words: "The fragments of my soul lie shattered within an empty shell.... Finally, a young man put it differently when he wrote, "I am working hard to believe in what I can become; to see possibilities and believe in some sort of future in which I can be happy and productive. This is not made easier by those who label me 'mentally ill' or 'borderline,' and refuse to recognize my individuality and potential to grow beyond what I am now." People with BPD are people who are struggling to overcome a psychotraumatized upbringing. They are people who, but for the workings of fate, could be any one of us.

How to Use This Book

This book is written from personal experience and professional knowledge. Tools will be presented in each of the following chapters; these tools will help you develop behavior-changing skills. Along with these skills, willingness, persistence, understanding, and positive support are the key ingredients for success. Together, they can help trigger a gradual process of day-by-day success.

For people who have what I call Factor II BPD (no history of childhood psychotrauma), chapters 2, 3, and 4 will have less relevance since they focus largely on childhood trauma. You can read chapter 1 and then skip to chapter 5 if you desire. In chapter 5 the PTES scale will help you to measure your level of psychotrauma. If you have Factor II BPD you should score zero. If you score above 10, then you may want to read the chapters you skipped.

You'll notice that a lot of text is set in italics; this is the writing of Samuel, a young man who is struggling with BPD and addictive activities. Samuel grew up in a dysfunctional family. His early psychotraumatizing experiences shaped his character and personality. His life never felt safe, secure, or consistent. Emotional thunderstorms were the norm in his childhood world, and naturally sunny days the exception.

I met Samuel a number of years ago. He was an intelligent and angry hell-raiser who could be quite charming and sensitive. The paradoxes of his personality and, I dare say, the stabilities in mine intrigued us both and we became friends. As we got to know one another I learned about his childhood, his stormy teenage years and early adulthood, his addictions, treatment attempts, and failures. My professional interests at that time were focused on personality disorders and addictions, and when I told him that I was thinking about writing a book on the subject, he offered to provide firsthand narratives about key events in his own life to use as illustrations. After much discussion, we agreed to collaborate. Samuel persisted in our collaboration despite his instabilities and the crises that took place in his life along the way. He also wished to remain anonymous, otherwise his name would be on the cover right next to mine.

Samuel's story isn't a success story. It isn't a failure story. It's a story about a life undergoing changes. It's about a person who, despite some very serious disadvantages, is trying to stabilize his life. My respect for Samuel is very great. Despite many setbacks, he remains determined to try to do it better next time.

Chapter Structure

Each chapter is composed of several parts: First there is the narrative material, which includes Samuel's writing and my explanations and suggestions. Throughout the narrative pages there are *Self-Help Skill* boxes and *Impact!* boxes. Self-Help Skill boxes describe a skill that can be used to develop more satisfying behavior. Impact! boxes describe a point that I think is especially important. They are best read as you come to them since the narrative material often refers to the information they contain.

The narrative part of each chapter closes with a summary (called *Chapter Milestones*) of the most important points to remember. The Milestones are there to help refresh your memory.

In order to be successful, you need to recondition the way you think. Your goal is to replace your negative thoughts with positive affirmations that will help you to feel better about yourself. The process of replacing your negative thoughts is a slow one. Practice and some persistence is needed. With a little of both you will begin to see results. In order to help you do this, each chapter includes a *Positive Affirmation* to memorize, rehearse, use, and, ultimately, believe in. Chapter 1 provides several Positive Affirmations and then each of the following chapters adds one more Positive Affirmation to your list.

Each chapter closes with several *Recovery Exercises*, designed by Dr. Cohen. You can use these exercises to gain insight and understanding into the complexities of your behavior. They will help you to develop the awareness and insight you need to alter your behavior. Each chapter is best read through at least once before you attempt to do any of the Recovery Exercises. Then the exercises can be done at any time you are so moved to do them. There are no rules to follow, so use your own judgment.

Our Web site at **www.slshealth.com** is an online resource you can also use to help support your recovery. As our site grows, you will be able to e-mail us (including Samuel), post your comments about the book, pick up some advice and tips, find out how Samuel is doing, and find links to other helpful Web sites.

The Angry Heart Map

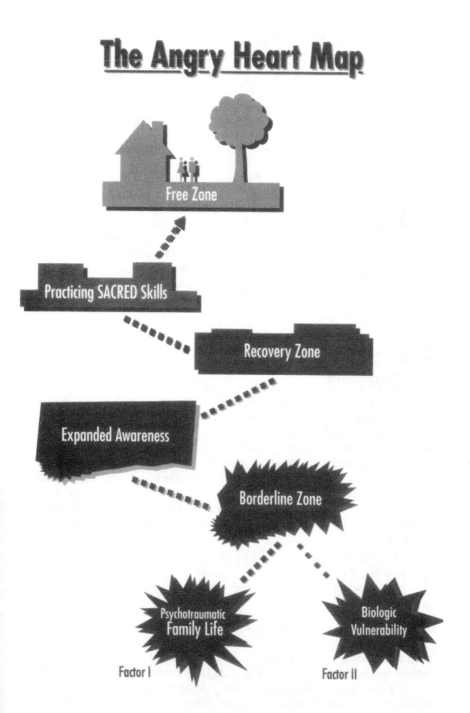

The Healing Journey

Healing the wounds of a dysfunctional childhood takes time. Some scars will always remain, but a better, freer life is possible. Your journey will proceed through three zones: the Borderline Zone (BZ), the Recovery Zone (RZ), and the Free Zone (FZ). The BZ is your starting point. You entered the BZ sometime during your childhood or teenage years. You will remain there until you face the effects your childhood has had upon you. Once you have done this you will enter the Recovery Zone. In the RZ, you spend less time in one of the BPD self-harm phases and more time in the inter-phase. Here is where the skills in chapter 7 of this book (I call them SACRED skills), and any therapy support you choose to access, can help you develop greater stability and more satisfying behavior and results. Once you make changes in your behavior that virtually eliminate self-harmful behavior *and* you begin to stabilize your lifestyle with productive activity, you will be ready to enter the Free Zone. In the FZ, the full possibilities of life and your full potential as a person can be actualized and enjoyed. The Angry Heart Map on the previous page illustrates the journey ahead. It is a demanding journey, but the results are well worth the effort.

Getting Our Feedback and Support

I would like to offer you the opportunity to get our feedback and support. Dr. Cohen and I welcome the opportunity to read your responses to any of this book's exercises. We will share with you our thoughts and ideas as well as words of encouragement. You can also send us any questions you may have about anything in the book. We would be happy to mail you a reply or you can send us an E-mail at www.slshealth.com. You can also call me at 1-914-279-5994.

To receive feedback about your Recovery Exercise answers by postal mail send them (or your questions) to me with a self-addressed, stamped envelope at:

The Angry Heart
P.O. Box 758
Croton, NY 10520

I will reply as quickly as I can. Remember, we are fully invested in your successful use of our book, so count on our support.

Dr. Cohen, Samuel, and I hope to reach out to you and touch your mind and your spirit. Our thoughts and our prayers go with you as you explore the meaning of your life as you have come to experience it. We welcome the opportunity to hear your own story. We wish you the best of luck in your quest toward a happier life.

I

Beginnings

A beginning is a very delicate time. . . .
—Frank Herbert, *Dune*

There are things to be said. No doubt.
And in one way or another
they will be said. But to whom . . .
—Cid Corman, *The Voice That Is*
Great Within Us

It's so hard to sit down and try to write down my past. The past is such a dark place to me. Every time I think about the past, it changes. Waves of piercing emotions overwhelm me, as though I am still there. "There" was not a happy place for me. Anger and distrust seemed to be a way of life for everyone around me, but as a young child I wasn't quite sure why.

The biggest problem for me as a child was not knowing why— not understanding why, why everyone around me was always yelling and screaming. If only I would figure this out, I thought, maybe I could make it better. I eventually realized that it was going to take many years for me to put this puzzle together. Being so young and having to deal with something so complex and confusing was very scary. To this day, I still remember my frequent thoughts of "Why me? Why me? Please, someone get me out of here!"

The journey towards recovery, as you may fear, is a tough one. Its difficulty is not to be underestimated, and the experience will never be forgotten. By sharing my true life experiences—the good and the bad—with you, I will hopefully be able to give you the strength and courage necessary to develop the skills needed to change your life.

Facing What's Happened

Facing a painful past is a task we want to avoid forever. The problem is that we cannot run from what we have been *made* to feel. The pain lives in our subconscious mind from microsecond to microsecond. As we interact with the world around us, our subconscious conditions our day-to-day decisions. It uses the pain and hurt we carry inside to influence our actions. And it often causes us to choose behavior that is self-destructive and harmful to our well-being. Furthermore, and all too often, overwhelming emotions penetrate our conscious minds, changing our moods in a flash and putting us in conflict with those we know and love. For better or worse, we carry what we learned from our childhood interactions with our family into adulthood.

Every word is a struggle. I've done so well blocking and hiding my feelings that it is hard to remember a lot. The one thing I never forget is the fear. Day in and day out, fear was always present in my life. I hated being scared all the time, never quite sure what to say or not to say. Not knowing what kind of mood my family members were in. Not knowing the impact my words or actions would have on them.

Every day the thoughts of the past haunt me, they still scare me. I remember when I was seven or eight, my mother and stepfather, the raging alcoholics that they were, gave me an ultimatum. To this day I don't remember exactly what I did wrong, but I do remember the consequences. My mom said to me, "You know you've been bad and you have to make a choice. Either your father or I will slap you in the face twice. You decide." I frantically ran around the house for nearly two hours trying to make my choice, not realizing at the time that I was just making things worse—because the longer I took, the more they drank. Finally, not knowing why, I chose my stepfather. With a "Be a man and take your punishment," he proceeded to slap me in the face twice as my brother giggled in the background. Sixteen years later, I sit here and write this and I have tears in my eyes; tears that I shed because I feel so bad for my stepfather and mother. I now know that they were acting the way they were taught to act, the way that I would be acting if I hadn't changed the course I was on.

The Way It's Supposed to Be

Dr. Erik Erikson, a psychoanalyst, wrote extensively about how human beings grow psychologically. He described eight growth stages that each of us pass through on our way to adulthood. Throughout this chapter I will refer to Dr. Erikson's work to help you understand what went wrong for the person who develops borderline/addictive behavior patterns. As you begin to understand what went wrong in your development, you will be freer to accept yourself as a good person and freer to take responsibility for changing your borderline/addictive behaviors. You will know who is responsible for allowing things to go wrong, and who is responsible for changing what's wrong. You will discover that the former person is *not* the same as the latter person.

The Stages

Each of Dr. Erikson's eight stages affects the growing child (and the future adult). Failure to receive the proper support at a stage can cause psychological harm. Since each stage builds on the one that came before, the damage that is done is cumulative. Here are the eight stages of human development and the approximate ages at which each stage occurs.

1. Basic Trust versus Basic Mistrust (zero to one and a half)

2. Autonomy versus Shame and Doubt (one to three)

3. Initiative versus Guilt (three to six)

4. Industry versus Inferiority (six to twelve)

5. Identity versus Role Diffusion (twelve to twenty)

6. Intimacy versus Isolation (young adult)

7. Generativity versus Stagnation (middle-age adult)

8. Integrity versus Despair (senior adult)

The degree of success we have in passing through each of Dr. Erikson's stages determines our level of adult maturity.

In the first stage, a child's mother heavily influences whether or not the infant develops a strong sense of basic trust. Trust is a feeling that grows from experiencing a mother as dependable and predictable. Mothers create a feeling of basic trust through the quality of their concern for their infant's needs. As Dr. Erikson (1950) wrote, "This [trust] forms the basis in the child for a sense of identity which will later combine a sense of being 'all right,' of being oneself, and of becoming what other people trust one will become."

The child who grew up in a dysfunctional family does not learn much about basic trust. This loss causes the child to doubt the validity of his or her own existence and distorts the child's sense of identity.

Samuel developed little basic trust of others during his infancy. His mother's problems blocked her ability to show deep and sensitive concern for his needs. This damaged his developing identity and created the basis for his later feelings of fear, anger, distress, and depression. It also made it difficult for him to feel love from others or to love others. This is the first impact of a dysfunctional family.

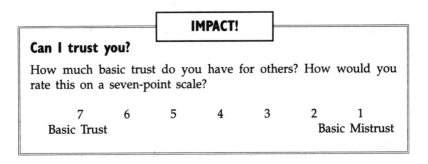

IMPACT!

Can I trust you?

How much basic trust do you have for others? How would you rate this on a seven-point scale?

7	6	5	4	3	2	1
Basic Trust						Basic Mistrust

Between the ages of one and three, children start to assert themselves with their parents. A struggle for control begins between mother and child. This struggle is a normal part of human growth. If handled properly, the child will learn the beginnings of autonomy with a minimum of shame and guilt. But if the child comes from a dysfunctional family, the balance will not be achieved. Instead, the child will *doubt* his or her ability to function independently. ("Can I do things on my own?") The child will also question whether he or she should do things independently, that is, the child will feel *shame*. Shame comes, according to Erikson, when the child questions whether they *should* (versus can) do somthing on their own. According to Dr. Erikson, shame occurs when a person turns his or her rage inward. When you do this, you feel small, inferior, exposed, and weak. Eventually, the child reaches a limit, and the shame can turn into defiant shamelessness. Dr. Erikson (1950) wrote, ". . . there is a limit to a child's and an adult's endurance in the face of demands to consider himself, his body, and his wishes as evil and dirty, and to his belief in the infallibility of those who pass such judgement." Such a child will try to get away with things in secret, until a chance to escape from those who torment him or her comes. Erikson continued, "This stage, therefore, becomes decisive for the ratio of love to hate, cooperation to willfulness, freedom of self-expression to its suppression. From a sense of self-control without loss of self-esteem comes a lasting sense of good will and pride; from a sense of loss of self-control and of . . . overcontrol comes a lasting propensity for doubt and shame."

Between the ages of three and six the child goes through the next stage, Initiative versus Guilt. A child who is succeeding at this stage (because of a supportive family) ". . . appears 'more himself,' more loving, relaxed and brighter in his judgement, more activated and activating. He is in free possession of a surplus of energy which permits him to forget failures quickly and to approach what seems desirable with undiminished and more accurate direction" (Erikson 1950). When parents react to a child's questions with indifference or irritation and when they consider fantasy and imagination a waste of time, a subconscious sense of guilt begins to form that will rob the child of the joy of living.

Dr. Erikson's fourth stage, Industry versus Inferiority, takes place from ages six through twelve. During this stage, the child who has developed sufficient trust, autonomy, and initiative, learns to use his or her abilities and skills to accomplish things in the world through healthy play and through schoolwork. The child's productivity builds self-esteem as he or she takes pleasure in the accomplishment of goals. A child whose family has not prepared him or her for this stage of life will feel isolated from peers. The child will begin to see him- or herself as a failure, as someone who does not have any good qualities, as someone who is a loser. The child will seek out the company of other "losers" and, thereby, fulfill his or her family's low expectations.

By the age of twelve, the impact of a dysfunctional family is low self-esteem, depressive rage, and a profound sense of inferiority that can be temporarily numbed through self-injurious pleasure seeking or introverted withdrawal.

During the fifth stage, Identity versus Role Confusion, the twelve- to twenty-year-old is faced with the task of forging an adult identity out of childhood experiences and newly awakened sexual energies. The young person is eager to try out different ways of acting and thinking. Clothing, social activities, and sexual experiences are used to clarify identity and define future goals about career and lifestyle. Children from a dysfunctional family lack adequate trust of themselves and others. They have not been allowed to explore their capabilities in a supportive environment. They feel ashamed, defiant, or selflessly compliant, and they lack positive self-control and initiative. They are confused about who they are and what they want. Their identity confusion is intensified by their sexual feelings. During this stage the strongest feelings from childhood become aligned with sexual feelings. If love is one of those feelings, than the road to healthy relationships is open. But if the strongest feelings are pain, anger, and resentment, then the road to the Borderline Zone beckons.

This intensely confused mix of behavioral energy fuels a chaotic search for identity. The search often leads to addictive activities and painful results. New pain then blends with childhood pain, which fuels an even more chaotic, and desperate, search.

In stage six, Intimacy versus Isolation, young adults from supportive families are able to love others. In possession of clear identities, these young adults are eager to commit themselves to others—in work, in play, and in love. They are now ready to start families of their own. Young adults from a dysfunctional family are in danger of isolation. They often feel lonely, empty, and afraid of being abandoned by others.

The final two stages, Generativity versus Stagnation and Integrity versus Despair, build on all of the prior stages. Generativity is the capacity to guide the next generation, to be productive, and to be creative. Integrity is the capacity to feel fulfilled and satisfied by one's life experiences. It also involves seeing the cycle of life as a whole and thereby understanding and accepting that death is a natural part of the life cycle. Those who fail to successfully negotiate this stage "fear death: the one and only life cycle is not accepted as the ultimate of life" (Erikson 1950).

The Ball and Chain of Denial

As you confront the past that shaped your characteristic behavior patterns, your inner resistance to such confrontations will grow strong, but if you persist, it will gradually weaken, and you will begin to feel the first signs of true relief.

However, like Samuel, your survival instincts will first tell you to avoid, distract, escape, deny, ignore, repress, and explode. These familiar alternatives will have to be overcome one by one. They may help you numb the pain, but they can never help you heal it. There is an alternative that does help: a gentle, private confrontation of your past and the pain it causes you, through structured journal writing.

Before I explain Recovery Journal writing in detail, consider the importance of the *childhood womb*. Humans need a long childhood to grow into healthy and successful adults. It takes nine months for a fertilized egg to become a full-grown human infant. It takes another eighteen years to reach adulthood. The biological quality of the infant's womb has a major impact on its growth. The use of medications, the mother's health, her use of alcohol and drugs, her nutrition, and her emotional health can all affect the developing fetus in ways that science continues to learn about. The biological womb of the fetus transforms itself into the psychological womb of the newborn. The quality, stability, and security of the newborn's family environment profoundly affect that innocent infant's development. Can anyone doubt that a loving family womb creates a happier and healthier adult than an angry family womb? Can anyone doubt that a family womb in which the child can predict the caregiver's behavior creates a more secure and confident adult than the family womb created by caregivers whose actions often are capricious and unpredictable whims of their moods?

The adult (and inner child) who grew up in a dysfunctional family does indeed doubt both of these views! How is such a thing possible? In a single word: *denial*. The dysfunctional family womb teaches its members to deny what is really happening. It invalidates the experiences and the feelings of its innocent children. It teaches mistrust of others and of self. It teaches them that they are at fault. It teaches them that they are not wanted (if they were wanted, their caregivers would be happy). It teaches them that they are bad seeds. It teaches them that they are not in pain. It teaches them that they are not scared. It teaches them that they are not seeing, hearing, and feeling what they are seeing, hearing, and feeling. The reality of their experiences is denied. The world is the way their caregivers say it is, even if it isn't. They feel bad because they are told they are bad. They learn to hate themselves. They learn to hate their lives. They may even learn to hate being alive.

As the children master the art of denial, feelings and memories are "forgotten" through repression. Emotional pain is numbed. At first it is numbed through fantasy and later it is numbed through anger, acting out, alcohol, drugs, and even self-injury. As the years roll by, more and more pain is accumulated and repressed. The brain stores the pain deep inside itself. Rage and depression emerge from this cauldron of numbed agony. Moods change without notice. Relationships become stormy. Success in school and work is impaired. All of these experiences keep the children's self-esteem low and fragile.

Despite this trauma, children from a dysfunctional family will often look for someone to help them out of their nightmare, but their basic mistrust of others and their lack of credibility, leads, more often than not, to failure. The painful memories then get buried ever deeper as helplessness, hopelessness, depression, and rage take greater command of their inner world.

"I am in pain but I can never admit this to myself or others." This is the cognitive command conditioned into the subconscious mind of the child from a dysfunctional family. And this is why confronting the past is such a struggle—"If I start to face the past, I will be overwhelmed by all of my buried emotions." But as an adult you suspect the truth. You sense the road you are on and where it will lead. Is a marginal existence (marked by loneliness, addiction, and ever changing, stormy moods and relationships) all you can hope for in your life?

I hope I know your answer. The time has come to put denial aside. The time has come to *slowly* dig up the buried emotions. The time has come to resolve the causes of your rage, your depression, and your addictive behaviors. Indeed, the time has come time for something better, before time runs out.

> In the past five years, I've wasted so much time doing negative
> things toward myself and others. If only I knew then what I know
> now, things would be so much different for me. I have covered up
> my feelings so deeply that it's going to take years for me to get in
> touch with all of them. It hurts so much to sit here and know who
> taught me how to feel this way. I never wanted to be a "bad"

person or to hurt anyone else in any way, but no matter what I said to myself I just continued to hurt myself and others. If I had a nickel for every minute I wasted on feeling angry, resentful, jealous, or rageful toward others, I'd be a wealthy man today.

When I was growing up, there wasn't a day that went by where I didn't wish that things were different. I loved my parents. I don't think I necessarily wanted different parents. I just wanted my parents to be different, to have different standards of conduct and different attitudes. Time is a very precious thing. It seems that most of us take it for granted, not realizing how fast it disappears.

An important part of my recovery is the amount of time and energy I put into convincing myself that I am a good person and deserve better than I had. As long as you feel that you're worthless and no good, you act like a worthless and no-good person. This has been the single, toughest thing for me to honestly say: I am a good person. When I was young, my embattled family consistently told me that I was a bad boy, that I was too hyper, and that I was no good. I came to believe it and I acted accordingly. Now, I'm starting to feel differently about myself. There are still times when I'm so down and depressed that the old feelings of being bad and no good return. But more often than not, I can feel positive and I can say to myself that I am a good person.

Don't get me wrong. There is nothing easy about this whole process. But once I started consistently putting the energy I used to manipulate and hurt others toward positive actions, the pieces of a better life started to fall into place.

Contradiction and inconsistency are hallmarks of people with BPD's upbringing. Their dysfunctional family fails them at each developmental stage. Because of this, their psychological development is impaired and they learn to blame themselves for their failures. Consequently, their self-esteem is low or easily depleted by life's challenges and disappointments. And deep in the core of their being they are incredibly depressed and wounded. But they, like everyone else, must survive. So they develop defenses to cope with an agonizing and painful family environment. These early coping behaviors form the basis of their adult mask. Ironically, however, they never really escape from the traumas of their childhood. They do daily battle with its demons.

My mom always used to say to me, "You say you are sorry but you never mean it." There were times when I didn't mean it, but most of the time I really did. I always felt that saying I was sorry would stop my parents from becoming very angry with me, but most of the time it made things worse because they insisted I was lying. Granted I did lie a lot, but I was taught to hide the truth and protect myself anyway I could.

One of the things that really hurt me a lot is that my

parents never said they were sorry for anything they did to me.
It's like they were in complete denial about their own problems.
I can just imagine what they thought: "How can we tell a young
child that we're sorry? It would give the child the upper hand.
It would be an admission that we did wrong. It would undermine
our power." My parents yelled at me, beat me, ignored me, mocked
my nervous facial tics and taught me to feel like I was an
unwanted, piece of dirt. But we always said we loved each other.
      We weren't very good at facing the truth, I guess. Denial
was easier.

Starting Your Recovery Journal

Samuel's childhood, adolescent, and adult experiences may help you to
explore your own inner pain. You are not alone. With this in mind, at
your first opportunity, buy yourself an attractive notebook in which to
record your thoughts, feelings, and experiences. The notebook should
have at least two hundred pages. Next, divide the notebook into these
five sections: Childhood Experiences (birth to age twelve), Adolescent
Experiences (age thirteen to seventeen), Current Life (from the start of
your journal and going forward), Recovery Exercises, and Future Plans.

In the Childhood section, record your memories and feelings about
your psychotraumatic experiences. Record your positive memories and
experiences here as well—particularly, those that recall people who cared
for you.

In the Adolescent section do the same, but also include the things
that you did that were self-harmful, dangerous, or illegal.

In the current life section, keep a diary of the work you are doing
to get your life more balanced. Identify what you are doing that is positive. What's working for you? What are the healthy things that are making
you feel better about yourself and your life?

In the Recovery Exercises section, record your answers to the book's
exercises.

In the Future Plans section, sketch out the changes you would like
to make in your life in such areas as career, schooling, people, where
you live, your recreational interests, and your relationship with family
and friends. You don't have to write in each of these sections every time
you write. Just write what feels appropriate.

Before you begin to write in your Recovery Journal, you need to
think through the following: Where and when will you feel safest writing?
Where will you safely store your notebook to keep it secure and confi-
dential? Is there anyone with whom you will want to share your writings?
How many minutes per day will you spend writing in your Recovery
Journal?

Expect the writing process to be slow and difficult. That's how it should be. Years of repressed feelings emerge slowly from their poisonous repose. Patience and encouragement are needed. In order to encourage your thoughts to flow, you need to suspend all critical self-judgment. Avoid abusing yourself. Don't tell yourself, "I can't write. I can't spell. I don't know the right grammar." If you can talk, you can write. Simply write the way you talk. If it helps, use a tape recorder to get your ideas down at first. Tell yourself that whatever you write is good because it comes from inside you. Your writings are your personal experiences. You are writing to free yourself from the grip of your painful emotions, not to create a best-seller. Perfect grammar, perfect spelling, or perfect style is irrelevant! Your only objective is to express what you have been repressing in *your own words*.

The Recovery Journal writing steps are summarized for you in the following Self-Help Skill.

Self-Help Skill: Recovery Journal Writing

1. Buy a two-hundred-page, divided notebook.

2. Make five sections and label the sections: Childhood Experiences, Adolescent Experiences, Current Day, Recovery Exercises, and Future Plans.

3. Plan where, when, and how often you will write. Try to write at least twice per week.

4. Can you share your writing with someone you trust and who is good for you? If you can, discuss it with him or her and be as open and honest as you can.

5. Expect the writing to be slow and painful. Remember, it is very difficult to express your deepest pain.

6. Whatever you feel is okay! If you feel disoriented by your writings, know that the feeling will pass. Learn to tell yourself that everything will be all right. You might want to record this positive message, so you can play it back to yourself whenever you are feeling scared or enraged.

7. Reread what you have written until it no longer evokes strong emotions in you. This process is called *extinction*. It will help to heal your wounds. Be sure to reread each of your entries until you feel little or no pain or discomfort.

8. If you find that you become too overwhelmed to write in your Recovery Journal and you do not have anyone who can support you through the rough times, consider seeing a professional therapist for assistance. Bring this book with you and explain to the therapist what you want to do.

9. If your writing stresses you out too much, follow the instructions in Recovery Exercise 1.6: Breathing to Relax at the end of this chapter.

As you read the next entry from Samuel's writings, allow it to reso-
nate with your own memories and feelings. You may even feel the urge
to jot down a few of your own recollections.

Facing Painful Memories

*While I was growing up, I was always very jealous of my friends.
The reason for my jealousy was the fact that my friends' families
seemed to be so much nicer than mine. Even if I liked a friend a
lot, I still always sabotaged the relationship because of my jealousy.
I would go over to their homes and see what a big difference there
was between the way my family treated each other and the way
their families interacted. My jealousy would soon turn into anger
and resentment. When I was ten, I had a good friend named Bob.
He came from an affluent, well-structured, and happy family. It
was obvious to me that his family did not have my family's
problems. As the years passed, I resented Bob's good fortune more
and more. Instead of telling Bob how I felt about his family, I set
Bob up to get in trouble with his parents by convincing Bob that
it was cool to smoke cigarettes. A couple of days after Bob started
smoking, I anonymously called Bob's parents and told them that
their son was seen smoking cigarettes at school. They grounded
him for a month. Part of me felt great to hear this and part of me
was upset because I also set myself up to be alone. A couple of
month's later, Bob found out that I was the one who informed on
him. He was really upset and hurt and told me that he never
wanted to speak to me again. To this day Bob and I have not
spoken and I dearly regret it. If I could have only told Bob the
truth about my jealousy of his family life and how I really did care
about him, I think he would have understood and forgiven me.
Someday, I will summon the courage to tell Bob that I'm sorry.*

Write to Feel Better!

As you start to record what you are thinking, feeling, and remem-
bering, you will begin to put to rest early traumatic experiences. It requires a willingness on your part to feel what you dread, so you can
confront the monster and destroy its power to cause you more pain. To
do this, you must reach a point in your life where the chaos of your
lifestyle has become intolerable. When the pain and discomfort of your
present life exceed your dread of what you hold inside, you are ready
to confront your past and grow healthier.

*For me this book is my journal. I've always grossly underestimated
just how positive it would be to write down my feelings. By
contributing to this book, I have opened up avenues of emotions*

and feelings that I never thought existed. It was a pleasant surprise how helpful it was writing things down. I know it sucks and it seems like the worst thing in the world, but it's really a wonderful way of starting to feel better. You have to get past the feelings of "How can something that feels so bad be so helpful?" It's true that when you first start writing it hurts deep down inside, but when you walk away from the writing and think about what you wrote, you realize it is for the better and you will grow stronger. Knowing that I wasn't a good writer always gave me the excuse I needed to avoid writing. The real thing that stopped me, though, was the fact that I was completely scared of getting in touch with my true feelings about my childhood.

You see, writing is like talking. It is a form of relief and release. I wish I knew this when I was a young child, if I did I would have kept a journal. I never had anyone to talk with, and a journal would have been my friend—a friend that only listens and does not make judgments. There was a time when I was twelve that I was writing poems. I thought that they were great. I never showed them to anyone because I was insecure about what others would think. One day my brother was snooping around my bedroom and found my poems. He ridiculed me and called me a faggot. He made fun of me in front of a bunch of kids at school. After that experience, I couldn't find it in my heart to write anymore. When I told my mother what my brother had done to me, she simply said, "Boys will be boys." That really bothered me a lot because I was looking for someone to understand my feelings. It felt like the end of the world to me. If my own mother couldn't and wouldn't understand me than who would? If I could go back in time, I would have endured my brother's belittling, torturous ways and continued to write my poems. Like they say, hindsight is twenty-twenty.

A word of advice for anyone out there: Go with your heart. Go with your instinct; if it feels right, don't stop because of the ridicule of others. Most times people act the way they act because they are jealous. It takes inner strength to be honest with yourself about your feelings. Never give up on yourself. Always remember that you are doing this to secure a better life for yourself.

To all of you people out there who are going through or have been through what I've been through, don't forget it's only over when you throw in the towel. I know it is hard and it seems like the end of the word, but it's not. It's just the beginning. The only way things will get better is if you get off your ass and stop feeling sorry for yourself. Day in and day out, you must brand in your mind, "I am a good person and I will prevail."

Measure Your Starting Point

How many borderline behaviors do you currently have? How far into the Recovery Zone are you? To measure this fill out the Angry Heart Compass on the next page. Check off in each box (Free, Recovery, and Borderline) the items that describe your current behavior and feelings. To score yourself, add up the number of items checked in each box and place that number next to Score.

If your highest score was in the Borderline Zone and it was at least 4 out of 10, then you can certainly benefit from the book. If your score in the other zones is 0 or 1, that's okay. It is to be expected at this point in your recovery. If you scored less than 2 in the Borderline Zone and above 4 in the Free Zone, you are not showing much indication of borderline problems. For additional scoring information see chapter 12. I will ask you to measure your progress again in that chapter.

Chapter Milestones

1. The failure to deal effectively with emotional pain can lead to negative thoughts and dysfunctional behavior.

2. A dysfunctional (or more powerfully, poisonous) family environment causes a child's psychological development to fall behind that of other children.

3. Deficiencies in basic trust are acquired in the first years of life. They will persistently undermine relationships until they are addressed.

4. Denial is the single biggest obstacle to recovery. Resolve that you are going to face your pain, as well as any pain you have caused others.

5. Start and keep writing in your Recovery Journal. Measure your starting point.

Positive Affirmations

This chapter has six Positive Affirmations in it. These six Positive Affirmations will help open your mind to the concept of changing your behavior and life.

Change requires a commitment before it can happen—a commitment forged by your mind and heart. A mind that says with an angry heart, "I can't change, the world must change instead!" is closed to change. The world never changes for anyone. It is your responsibility to adapt your behavior to the world. You can protest all you like about this. Your rage changes nothing and you'll remain unhappy about your life.

Self-Help Skill: The Angry Heart Compass

Free Zone   Score: /10
Early Stage
Late Stage

- [ ] able to openly talk about past pain with loved one
- [ ] able to hold on to close relationships
- [ ] able to hold steady employment
- [ ] able to tolerate stress without resorting to addictive activities
- [ ] comfortable being affectionate toward a loved one

- [ ] word and actions are more consistent
- [ ] you know what you want from life
- [ ] you can love another without fear
- [ ] able to laugh about the past
- [ ] you feel optimistic about the future and you are more at peace with the past

Recovery Zone   Score: /10
Early Stage
Late Stage

- [ ] able to write about pain
- [ ] able to cut short temper outbursts
- [ ] able to cut back addictive behaviors
- [ ] able to slow stress-accelerated mind
- [ ] able to accept your deficits without anger

- [ ] able to tolerate feedback without anger
- [ ] able to show others appreciation for help given
- [ ] willing to follow the advice of a mentor
- [ ] able to accept the help of a therapist
- [ ] the defensive "wall" is down more than up

Borderline Zone   Score: /10

- [ ] addictive activities used (drugs, sex, cutting, etc.)
- [ ] poor control over your temper
- [ ] bouts of depression
- [ ] suicidal thinking or suicidal actions
- [ ] angry, rebellious, inconsistent

- [ ] moods change a lot and you feel bad
- [ ] stormy relationships
- [ ] feel as if you can't trust anyone
- [ ] feel as if you don't know who you are
- [ ] racing thoughts, impulsive actions

Your Location:

Free Zone [ ]   **By Recovery Zone** [ ]   **By Borderline Zone** [ ]

Self-Help Skill: Positive Affirmation Practice

Here is your Positive Affirmation (PA) practice routine. Twice daily, once in the morning just after you wake up and once at night, sit down in a comfortable place where you will not be disturbed. Take several slow deep breaths to calm yourself. Then close your eyes and repeat each PA ten times. After you have repeated all of them, say to yourself, "I believe in who I am and what I think." Repeat this ten times and take several slow deep breaths.

Repeat ten times each:

1. I am not to blame for being the way I was.

2. I am responsible for changing myself.

3. I want to change.

4. I feel better when I face my inner pain.

5. I can change. I will change. I will never, never, never, never give up!

6. I am a good person and I will prevail.

To experience positive results, do this routine twice per day for at least six weeks.

You can use the set of six Positive Affirmations to open up your mind to changing. Carefully follow the instructions in the Self-Help Skill box. Practice as prescribed and you will experience positive results.

In each of the following chapters you'll find one new Positive Affirmation. Use the affirmations during PA breaks throughout the day. For example, you can plan a PA break with lunch that uses PAs to help you focus more on your recovery.

Recovery Exercises
Recovery Exercise 1.1: Beginnings

Objective
To focus on other times in your life when you started something new, and what it means now to start a self-help program.

Background
Terms such as "fresh start," "clean slate," and "new beginning" may all characterize where you are in your life now. Take a moment to give some thought to the meaning of these terms for you.

Expanded Awareness

Write a brief entry into your Recovery Journal entitled, "Beginnings." (According to Samuel, *You don't even have to call it that, call it whatever you want.*) In this entry, talk about some of the significant beginnings in your past. Talk about what reading this book means to you, including what you hope to achieve and how you hope you might change.

Recovery Exercise 1.2: My Genes and Me

Objective

To help understand the role of genetic inheritance in who you are.

Background

In this book, the piecing together of one's genetic code is described as a *microcosmic dance.*

Expanded Awareness

Imagine that the microcosmic dance that created you was placed under a high-powered microscope. What would that dance look like? Try moving around the room interpreting how that dance would look.

Write down your impressions of your dance movements. Then answer these questions as well: To what extent do you think genetic inheritance affected who you are today? To what extent do you see yourself breaking free of any of the negative influences?

Recovery Exercise 1.3: Defending Your Life

Objective

To understand the role of denial and other defenses in daily living.

Background

Feelings and memories are sometimes "forgotten," "numbed out," or "buried" when they are too painful. Painful feelings and memories may directly or indirectly cause various forms of negative thinking and behavior including anger, addictions, and even physical self-harm. Painful feelings and memories may be replaced by fantasies.

Expanded Awareness

Write about the pain you have experienced in your life and how you have defended yourself from even more pain. Give specific examples of how you defended or numbed out painful situations through overeating, drugs, alcohol, anger, self-injury, or withdrawal and isolation. Write about how you would like to be able to cope with the pain in the future.

Recovery Exercise 1.4: Needs

Objective

To understand something about what you needed in the past and how your needs have changed over time.

Background

Beyond food, water, air, and other physical necessities, people have a wide variety of psychological and emotional needs. Sometimes a psychological need, such as a need to escape, has a way of transforming itself into a physical need such as a physical addiction.

Expanded Awareness

List some of the physical and emotional needs that are particularly important to you. Discuss your needs with regard to other people. Focus in particular on your caregivers or guardians. How did they overlook or ignore your needs as a growing child?

How are you trying to satisfy your unmet needs today? How has this changed over the last few months? How do you think it will change over the next few years?

Recovery Exercise 1.5: Changes

Objective

To get in touch with how you have tried to change in the past.

Background

Changing one's behavior does not happen in a straight line. Change occurs in fits and starts. Two steps forward and one step back is the norm. Persistence separates those who succeed from those who are resigned to failure.

Expanded Awareness

Write down as many positive steps as you can that you have taken to change your life.

Which step or steps are you most proud of? How many other positive steps can you list that you would like to take in the future?

Recovery Exercise 1.6: Breathing to Relax

Objective

To learn a breathing technique that can manage the stress of writing about painful feelings and memories.

Background

Many of the people who have worked with this book report that writing in their Recovery Journal is stressful at first. Managing this stress is easier if you know how to calm yourself with a breathing technique.

Expanded Awareness

Sit comfortably in a chair and close one nostril with your finger. Take a deep breath (to a count of ten) through the open nostril. Hold it for two seconds. Close the open nostril as you open the closed one and breath out through the newly open nostril. Repeat this technique until you feel noticeably calmer. This breathing technique is called the Nose Breath.

Use the Nose Breath whenever you feel stressed out by your writing: Calm yourself down, take a break, and then, if you want to, return to your writing. It works!

Remember to write in your
Recovery Journal today.

2

Do As I Say, Not As I Do

*The small world of the child, the family milieu, is the
model for the big world. The more intensely the family
sets its stamp on the child, the more he will be
emotionally inclined, as an adult, to see in the great
world his former small world.*

—Dr. Carl Jung, *Psychological Reflections*

Children who grow up in a dysfunctional family enter their preteen and
teenage years ill prepared for what is ahead of them. Their psychological
immaturity draws them into a cycle of failure and frustration. Their mistrust, low self-esteem, and lack of goals haunt them at each and every
turn. Their dysfunctional families cannot give them the support they
need to face the challenges of adolescence. Who do they turn to for help?
Who understands them? Who gives them the guidance they crave? Who
makes them feel safe? Who gives them the love they long for? These
questions beg, without success, for answers. These children are driven
by needs and emotions they do not understand and are confused by
questions that they cannot answer. They soon learn to take and do whatever they can to soothe their scary feelings and silence their troubled
minds.

> *As I entered my adolescence, things only seemed to get worse. No
> matter what I did I could never manage to appease anyone in my
> family. Looking back now, I certainly cannot blame my family for*

how they acted. But back then I didn't know any better. Who else was I going to blame and resent for all of the pain and suffering I experienced? You see, I learned to hate myself at a young age. I didn't feel loved by my family so how could I love myself? At best I can say that the majority of my actions were the direct effect of what I saw and lived. I did not live the normal life of a young boy, but instead the life of a scared and angry boy on the run from his emotions. My mind was like a pan of scrambled eggs. Most of the time I didn't know whether I was coming or going. Day in and day out I struggled to survive. Because my family was extremely volatile, one wrong word could set anyone off, even myself. I never liked living this way; but I didn't make the rules, I just played the game.

Young children learn to perceive the world through the eyes of their families. If they experience a high level of conflict and anger they assume that the world outside of their family is the same way. When they become the object of their caregivers' hostility they learn to hate the very people they "should" love. They also learn to think of themselves as "bad children." Why else would their caregivers be so angry all of the time?

Abuse is like a game the whole family can play. But the game never seemed fair to me. As the youngest of three I always got the brunt of it. My older brother and sister were more skilled than I at manipulating and stroking my parents. My brother was a master at priming the pump and getting out of the way only to let me endure my parents' wrath. I would beg and plead with them, but they never listened. The only time I was in the right was when my parents actually witnessed my brother physically abusing me. Only then would they punish him, but only in some minor way. I always felt that the pain he put me through warranted a greater punishment. My sister, on the other hand, was not a troublemaker like my brother and me—she had mastered the art of being invisible. No matter how much she hated the drunkenness and fighting, she rarely challenged my parents. Her means of survival was to seclude herself in her room. Many a time I would beg her to let me in her room, but she never did. I thought that I could find a sense of relief there, safety, sort of out of the way of all the anger. I don't blame her for not letting me in her room, because she was afraid of me—all she ever saw me do was get angry. I never really told her this. I now wish that I had. I guess I didn't know how to tell her then, but now I know that if I had told her she would have probably let me hide in her room with her. We were all victims of each other.

I was a young victim with a wicked temper who learned how to victimize others. There were many times that I became enraged

*at the drop of a hat. It never felt good to me or like the right
thing to do, but I just didn't know how to stop myself. I would
go to bed at night praying that I would become a different person,
a person who was good. But every morning I would wake up and
there I was, nothing changed and nothing mattered.*

*My parents, caught up in their own denial, always wondered
why I would go to school and get into so much trouble. But
that was an easy one, every day was the same for me. My parents
would get drunk every night, and every night a new and
different catastrophe would explode like wildfire through our home.
Yelling and fighting would lead to angry, hurtful words being
thrown around like they didn't mean anything. Nothing was ever
settled or resolved. All we ever did was just go to bed. The next
day we would all "forget" about what happened, that is, until that
nighttime. But I couldn't forget, that's why I got into trouble at
school, I could never forget how much those words really hurt. I
was so angry and upset.*

We Learn What We Live

We learn to be who we are, in part, by imitating the behavior of others.
Children naturally copy their caregivers' behavior. This tendency is part
of our natural survival instincts. Unfortunately, children are not selective
in what they learn from their caregivers. They will copy both good and
bad behavior. Dysfunctional caregivers, who model for their children dysfunctional behavior, often trigger a behavioral chain reaction that can have
explosive consequences for the entire family. The caregivers will invari-
ably blame their children for the children's bad behavior. Children will
subconsciously accept this blame and their self-esteem will be devastated
by it. By refusing all responsibility for their children's behavior, caregivers
compound their children's problems. After all, their children know the
truth about their caregivers, but their caregivers persist in pretending that
their secret is well hidden. This type of caregiver denial breeds rage and
self-hate in their children, whose emerging adolescence intensifies everyone's pain. The truth is that your caregivers acted the way they did not
because you were "bad," but because they were unhappy with themselves.

*Like the old saying about all monkeys doing what they see, it's the
same with young children. It's so damn true, and most
dysfunctional parents just can't or won't see that. Because of this,
nothing really ever changes. As I entered my teens, my means of
escape evolved into something totally new. I started to learn how
my parents numbed their fragile emotions: substance abuse—it
quickly became a way of life for me as well.*

I figured, if it worked for them, then it will work for me. It was also something that I had never experienced before, and, once I tried it, I discovered that it felt very good. By the age of thirteen, I was getting high on anything I could find. I didn't care what it was, as long as I could get away from my painful life for just a little while.

My parents were very messed up people but they were not stupid people. They quickly realized what I was up to. They did everything in their power to stop me, but there was no way to stop me. Even if I wanted to try to stop, I had no reason to do so. As far as I was concerned it was the right thing to do. My parents told me to stop but they never backed up their words with action. In one breath they would say drugs and alcohol were bad and self-destructive and, in another, they would take one more swig of beer, their liquid remedy.

To their credit, my parents never used any illicit drugs, just alcohol. My mother was basically a pleasant drunk, that is, until she and my stepfather decided that they were sick and tired of looking at and dealing with each other. My stepfather on the other hand was a mean, vindictive son-of-a-bitch when he was drinking. When he was sober, he was a totally different man. One too many beers, though, and he was your worst enemy.

My parents' alcoholism made me feel very sad. I really did love my parents a lot. I just hated what they became after just a few beers. Every day I felt completely powerless about what was going to happen between me and my family. I would desperately think and ponder ideas and ways in which I could change this horrible life that I was living. There were times when I would try to talk to my parents when they were straight, but all I would get from them was that nothing was wrong and everything was going to be okay. What a contradiction! I never understood what they meant by that. In a single breath, they would deny everything as they tried to soothe me with kind words of reassurance.

Learned helplessness is the opposite of empowering a child. It breeds resentment and failure. Samuel illustrates how twisted it made him feel. He could not sort out these contradictory experiences and how they affected him. The result was a growing sense of powerlessness and futility. How can a child grow into a successful adult with this type of "training"?

On the other hand there were my father and my stepmother. They were the two other people in my life that could not and would not make an effort to create a stable and safe life for us. When I was only two years old, my mother and biological father divorced. At the time it didn't make any sense to me. I can only assume that it did indeed affect my older siblings. My father met my

> ## Remember to write in your
> ## Recovery Journal today.

stepmother-to-be when I was four. She seemed to be a very nice person. They were married five years later. This, by the way, was when most of my family turmoil began. This is also when my brother, my sister, and I started to see a lot less of my father and stepmother. The visits became shorter and less frequent. This really hurt because I knew damn well that they both knew exactly what was going down. They were in the process of opening their second restaurant and it seemed as if they were tired of hearing us complain about Mom and Pop's abusive ways. There were times when we kids would beg to live with them. "Please, oh please get us out of there. We can't stand it anymore, it's not fair for us to be treated this way. We don't deserve this!" It had gotten to the point where my father would say, "Oh nonsense, it's not that bad, you kids can deal with it, you're strong just like your daddy." Even though I was only a young boy, I knew that this was just my dad's way of saying it wasn't his problem. As for my stepmother, she was simply saying I'm done raising my children and I'm not raising any more. You see, I have two stepbrothers and two stepsisters, all of whom are eight to ten years older than my oldest brother.

Feeling abandoned by all of the adults in his life, Samuel and his siblings did the best they could to cope with traumatic circumstances. At times, they tried to "fix things," but their efforts were doomed to fail.

Mission Impossible

I can recall only a few times during my childhood that my brother and I actually worked together on something. The one common interest we both had was to see my parents remain sober for a length of time. Every once in a while we'd join forces to overthrow our parents' nasty habit. I remember one time as if it were yesterday—we had this really good plan. My parents always kept a large supply of beer in the garage. When they ran dry, they would simply take out the empties and stock up on more. All of my friends and all of my brother's friends knew that my parents kept their beer in our garage. Our bikes and other toys were stored out in the garage as well. Anyway, one day my parents went out for the day and evening. We knew that they would be gone for many hours so we took full advantage of this. We set the whole garage up like someone had broken into it. It looked perfect, from the missing hedge trimmer to the purpose of our mission, the missing beer. We simply took the beer to a quarry by our house, drank some of it, and disposed of the rest. Neither of us really cared about getting caught, we just wanted to prove our point of how much we hated the drinking. I don't even know if it was the drinking that we hated as much as it was what drinking did to them and to us. Well to our surprise, my parents never found out that it was my brother and I who stole their beer. I don't know about my brother, since he and I never talked about this, but I was sort of upset about how our mission played out. The next day my parents simply replenished their beer stock and went on with their everyday routine. There were no new developments. Nothing changed except for the new garage door and the locks.

Demoralized, my brother and I went right back to our usual way of antagonizing and fighting with each other. In one sense it really sucks looking back at all of the bad things that happened to my family and me, yet it was my destiny and there was no way for me to change that.

To change anything takes participation from everyone involved and that just wasn't possible then. By the time I was fourteen years old, the hole was so deep that no one in my family could climb out of it. It was just all about dealing and surviving anyway that you could. There were no "Let's start overs", or a consensus from everyone to change—no one knew how. It's scary to say, but my parents, in fact, seemed to be very content with their situation. My parents were "functioning alcoholics." They went to work every day and, besides immediate family, no one had any idea of the magnitude of their problems.

As it is with any growing child, you start to develop worries and fears of how to conform to what society thinks is right and wrong. You pick a certain peer group to be with, to act like. But I had no idea what right and wrong was nor did I care what peer group I would enter. I lived for the moment, day to day. Good or bad, if people accepted me, they were my friends, or so I thought.

In the latter part of eighth grade I was kicked out of the public school that I was attending. There's really no reason to go into why, you can just imagine why. I acted like a fool and had no respect for anyone. It was a tough time for me. I wasn't old enough to be emancipated so I had to go to a residential school. Part of me was excited to go to a school with a group of kids who were just like me. Well, that didn't last very long. Once in my new school I challenged anyone who had authority. I was always scared of authority. I felt like whoever was in charge would hurt me. It was all I knew. My parents had authority over me and they hurt me more than anyone.

As soon as I turned sixteen, I dropped out of the residential school. I begged my parents to give me a chance—a chance to live at home and a chance to show them that I could be a good boy. By this time my brother was long gone, I didn't even know where he was and that was okay with me. I figured that without my brother around I could successfully live there and do whatever I wanted to do. I quickly learned that I was dead wrong. It was worse without my brother there because now I was the center of my parent's attention. Every move I made was critiqued and analyzed by them, and I hated this with a passion. I just wanted to be left alone.

A Downward Spiral

As all of this was taking place, I developed a peer group consisting of drug-abusing, out-of-control kids who were looking for only one thing: an escape from their horrible, deeply hidden feelings. Like me, these kids hated what their families were like and needed the escape. As far as my parents were concerned, I was a waste of time and any time they spent on trying to help me get out of the nasty rut I was in was a waste of their time. My self-esteem was at an all-time low. I had now given up on any chance of getting better.

So out of anger and a sense of hopelessness I tried to exploit my parents' indifference by becoming a bully at home. If I wanted something, I would simply take it. I was not physically stronger than my stepfather and I knew this but I didn't care. I would always push the envelope to get as much as I could. Violence and anger had become my only means of release. I wish that this wasn't true but it is and I can't get better by denying anything. There were many times that I pushed my mother around, trying to scare her into doing what I wanted her to do. I had become a selfish, uncaring person. I believe deep down that my parents did grow to regret how they treated their children. They made their bed and now they had to sleep in it.

The day came, as it had to, when the camel's back was broken. One night I had come home after an evening of sex, drugs, and rock 'n' roll. I just wanted to be in my bed, the only place that I felt warm and secure. I was not surprised to see a little war going on between my parents when I walked in the door. It was typical for them to be arguing when I got home at night. This evening, however, was different. It was obvious to me that my stepfather had beaten up my mother. Even though I was angry at mother for being a drunk and doing what she had done to me, this, I felt, was uncalled for. I immediately jumped to my mother's defense. The fucked-up part of me thought that this might win my mother's love back finally. Little did I know that the events to follow would become the worst experience of my life.

I started to verbally abuse my stepfather in my mother's presence. She told me to shut up and to stay out of it, but I wouldn't hear her. All I heard was my anger getting louder and louder. Before I knew it, my stepfather and I were wrestling around on the floor trying to prove our manhood to each other. Although it was a short-lived effort on both our parts, the rage continued within me. I wanted my stepfather to regret the day he put his hands on my mother. I was feeling grandiose (thinking that my mom would, then, come to my defense). This fantasy powered me to take this fight even further. I started to break things around the house. By the time I was done, I had broken one window, a door, a couple of dishes, and a chair. I had never felt rage like this before and it really scared me. Yet it didn't stop me from doing what I did. The next thing I knew my stepfather had convinced my mom to call the police. Not to my surprise, she called them. It was the fourth or fifth time this happened. So I didn't think much of it until the police arrested me for destruction of private property and aggravated assault. It blew my mind that the police never even said a word about the bruises or marks on my mom. They were just there to take me away. I felt so lonely and betrayed that day, betrayed by my mom, the woman I tried to protect from a madman. I know now she was just as mad as he was. That's why it played out the way it did. When I got to jail and was stripped of all of my clothes and put into a gown, I had this hollow, heart-wrenching feeling inside of me. It was a feeling that I promised myself I would never ever feel again. For thirteen days I sat in my cell and thought about how much I hated the unfair situation I was put into.

My mom kept me in jail for thirteen days to punish me for activities they provoked in me. I did my time and paid my dues to my messed up family. When I walked out of jail I knew that I would now have to deal with the court and I did. I went there once to hear the judge tell me two things: one, that I was not in trouble now, and two, that if I ever stepped foot on my parents property, I would be arrested and I would then be in real trouble.

Seasoned Veteran

These are the events that welcomed me to the real world. On my own at sixteen and getting high on anything I could since thirteen, I had the will and courage of a seasoned veteran and the discipline and knowledge of a little boy. I was very fucked up and had no idea how to live like a normal person. *The only thing that changed was the game—it was now my game and I could make the rules. Good or bad, whatever was to happen now would be on my shoulders. There was no one else to blame anymore. One part of me loved this newfound freedom, and the rest of me hated it. Hated being alone to deal with whatever life threw at me.*

Chapter Milestones

1. Dysfunctional caregivers create feelings of fear, insecurity, and helpless rage in their children because they are absorbed by their own problems and are therefore unable to consistently give their children the support and guidance they need.

2. A psychotraumatized child hopes against hope that somehow his or her family will change.

3. Eventually, the family environment decays to the point where serious, sometimes violent, consequences result.

4. Lacking a firm foundation for meeting life's challenges, the psychotraumatized adolescent-turned-adult seeks out various and addictive forms of escape.

Positive Affirmation

Telling my story helps me ease my angry heart.

Recovery Exercises

Recovery Exercise 2.1: Emotional Support and Guidance—Past

Objective
To consider how a lack of support and guidance while growing up may have influenced development.

Background
Children growing up in dysfunctional homes seldom have access to the emotional support and guidance they need or want.

Expanded Awareness
Envision yourself at different key stages in your childhood. In your journal, write about the emotional support or guidance you may have needed or wanted but did not obtain.

When you were a child, who was available for you? Who wasn't available for you? Who nurtured you? Who failed to provide as much nurturance as you needed? How did you, as a child, adjust to any failure to receive adequate support or guidance?

What major life choices—right or wrong—do you think you made as a child as a direct result of such failures to obtain needed emotional support or guidance?

Recovery Exercise 2.2: Emotional Support and Guidance—Present

Objective
To consider how a lack of support and guidance resources while growing up may still be influencing present day behavior.

Background
The failure to receive needed emotional support and guidance in childhood has significant consequences in adolescence and adulthood.

Expanded Awareness
In what ways do you think failures to receive needed emotional support and guidance in childhood may be influencing current behavior patterns? Provide a specific example by talking about something you did within the last week or so and then link it back to some event in your childhood.

Recovery Exercise 2.3: Emotional Support and Guidance—Future

Objective
To consider how any lack of support and guidance during childhood will be overcome in the future.

Background
A lack of support and guidance during childhood does not necessarily sentence an individual to an unhappy adult life.

Expanded Awareness
In what ways have you been able to overcome or compensate for any lack of support or guidance during childhood? In what ways would you like to be able to overcome or compensate for any lack of support or guidance during childhood? What sources of support or guidance do you have in your life now? What additional sources of support or guidance might you have in your future?

What major life choices do you anticipate you will make in the near or long-term future? How do you intend to bring sound judgment to bear—and not past emotions—in making these choices?

Recovery Exercise 2.4: Maturity and Immaturity

Objective

To focus on the concepts of psychological maturity and psychological immaturity.

Background

At the beginning of this chapter, the term *psychological immaturity* is used. In this next exercise you will be asked to consider what this term means, and how it can be applied to you personally.

Expanded Awareness

How would you define the term *psychological maturity*? How would you define the term *psychological immaturity*? What kind of home environment encourages each? What kind of fun or pleasures do you associate with each?

Describe in as much detail as you can the nature of the psychological maturity you one day will reach.

Recovery Exercise 2.5: The Origins of Anger

Objective

To better understand the origins of the angry heart.

Background

Anger can be thought of as a hostile response to a real or imagined threat. It may be expressed in passive ways, such as sulking in withdrawal or isolation. It may be expressed in extremely aggressive ways, as when one human being renders physical harm to another as a direct result of the arousal of this emotion. Ways of experiencing and expressing anger can be learned.

Expanded Awareness

How and what did you learn about anger in your childhood? What effect, if any, has this childhood lesson had on the way you cope with or fail to cope with anger today?

How do you deal with and tend to express anger? How would you like to be able to deal with and express anger?

Exercise 2.6: Models—Caregivers and Other People

Objective

To better understand how caregivers served as models for various kinds of adaptive as well as maladaptive behavior patterns.

Background

Children learn from the behavior of their caregivers or other caretakers. Sometimes what they learn can help them in life, but not always.

Expanded Awareness

Think about the ways in which you are behaving that are very much the same way your caregivers used to behave. In what ways is it a good thing that you are following in their footsteps? In what ways is it a bad thing that you are following in their footsteps?

If you could choose anyone in the world to serve as a model for the way you would like to be, who would that person be? If that person doesn't exist in real life, create an imaginary person to write about. What would that person look like? What would he or she value and believe in? What would this person think was fair and just? How would he or she treat others? How would he or she handle stress?

Recovery Exercise 2.7: You've Got the Power

Objective

To explore thoughts and feelings related to the concepts of power and powerlessness.

Background

Many children who grew up in dysfunctional homes sensed an overwhelming powerlessness through much of their childhood; there were few empowering experiences.

Expanded Awareness

Think about the things that empowered you when you were a child. Were the things that gave you a sense of power good or bad for you?

Now, think about those times when you felt powerless. How did you cope with those feelings?

What did you as a child need to hear in order to be empowered? What do you, right now, need to hear or say to yourself in order to be empowered? What thoughts, feelings, and images contribute to your sense of mastery and empowerment?

3

Abused, Confused, and Out of Control: Entry into the Borderline Zone

He might rage and storm and howl against their verdict but it would do him no good. They had decided. Nothing could change them.

—Dalton Trumbo, "Johnny Got His Gun"

If you want to find out what's behind these cold eyes, You'll have to claw your way through this disguise.

—Pink Floyd, "In the Flesh?"

The transition from a newborn infant to an out-of-control adult progresses over the course of many years. The failure to develop basic trust as an infant leads to an inability to enter into close and meaningful relationships with others. When someone is unable to trust others, relationships are secretly used to fulfill desperate, unmet needs for belonging, love, and survival. Such people cannot give to relationships in the same measure that they take. So their relationships frequently become unstable battlegrounds where misperceptions, self-defeating manipulations, broken promises, and resentment are briefly interrupted by seductive truces.

Denied critical access to a supportive family environment, these children, now adolescents or adults, must learn to fight their own battles and get their needs met in any way they can. Regardless of their living situation, at home or on their own, twenty-four-hour survival becomes their primary goal. As they run from their traumatic past, they rob themselves of the opportunity to create a satisfying future.

At this point in my life, I had to seek other methods of survival. I had to quickly decipher who I could and could not trust. I had to act like I wasn't scared and that I knew what I was doing. Most of my friends were a bit older, and a lot of them were in the same situation as I was. The only difference was that they were more experienced at this way of living. It had nothing to do with emotional support. I really never had that growing up. It had to do with being on my own. I had to adapt to doing and obtaining anything I needed by myself. If I was hungry and had no food, I had to figure out how I was going to eat.

I was sixteen and on my own; money was obviously a problem. In one sense I was lucky to have a few close friends to help me along, yet it never seemed to be enough. I was the perfect example of a person with no self-control and no idea of what I was doing. There was nothing textbook about my persona. I didn't care about the responsibilities of being on my own. All I wanted to do was party. It was all I knew. It was my main method of escape. It was the way I numbed out the nasty feelings I had felt for so long. A lot of people I knew felt and acted the same way, but none of us were even remotely close to admitting this to ourselves, let alone someone else. It really hurt me to feel this way but I just wasn't ready to make the effort needed to change it. I did not know the steps I needed to follow, and this made it even worse. My life was so full of ambivalence. Part of me wanted a change to happen and the other half knew that it was completely out of my grasp.

Of course, my desperate pipe dreams of going back home and living a normal life never seemed to leave me. I knew deep down that even if I made the changes, my parents would still be the same. My parents were caught up in their lifestyle for so long that it would take a miracle for them to meet me halfway. A miracle I prayed for, but knew would never come true.

The longing Samuel experienced to return home has a deeper meaning to it. The home Samuel wanted is not the one that rejected him but the one he never had. He wanted to be the center of his mother's love and attention. He wanted the love and encouragement of a proud father. He wanted to be part of a family that wanted, loved, and taught him. He wanted what the healthiest among us received as our birthright. Resentfully, he had to settle for a lot less than his dream.

Self-Defeating Manipulation

During this period of time, I learned another way to escape my pains and fears. Women—sexual relationships with them—became a new method for me. It was sort of like a drug, a bit taboo and very exciting for me. I soon learned how to take full advantage of these types of relationships. I can truly say that I have never been in a relationship that I did not manipulate and eventually destroy. There were a few women that I was involved with whose memories cause me, to this day, to regret the way I treated them. They were genuinely good people. That scared me, because I never felt that I was a good person and that I deserved them. So I abused them until they abandoned me.

But alcohol, drugs, and sex never really helped to numb my pain for long. In fact, life for me continued to be an uphill battle, never seeming to get any easier. Day in and day out, it got more difficult and seemingly more impossible. I could not hold a job, even at things I was good at. I didn't have one ounce of discipline and, more important, I lacked the courage to be a winner. I didn't know what it was like to feel good and to do good things for myself. I was always concerned, and this will sound odd, with making other people happy over myself. I would do anything to make someone happy, even if it took making a fool out of myself, just for a laugh of acceptance. All my life I just wanted to be liked or loved and I would do anything for it. I never set out to hurt anyone but it always seemed to happen. It was like I would try to make someone like me even if they chose not to. I now know that this was a very negative part of my life. If only I could have stepped back and shown people the real me. My overaggressive needs of wanting to be a part of someone's life hindered and dismantled most of my relationships—with males and females. My stepfather would always say to me, "Easy on the whip, don't tire the horse." Only now does it make a helluva lot of sense to me.

Paradox as a Lifestyle

How can people who want to be liked by others abuse those whose acceptance they want until relationships with them are dismantled? This paradox puzzles those who must live out its curious logic: "I want to be accepted by you. I want you to like me. I don't know what it feels like to be accepted and loved. Everyone that loved me hurt me. I don't want to be hurt. I must survive somehow. No one can love me because I hate myself. I don't trust you. If you say you love me, you are lying to me so you can exploit me. I'll exploit you first. I hate you (because I believe that you will treat me the way my family treated me). But I need you to survive. I'm confused."

These thoughts make up a *borderline twister* of swirling thoughts and accompanying emotions. It pushes its sufferers toward any and all actions that will help them escape from its deadly path. Its logic can be brain numbing in its twists and turns. An understanding of it might go like this: "If I look for your acceptance while subconsciously fearing that you will not accept me and will in fact use me, I will pick up on even the slightest signs of nonacceptance (or use) of me. I will then react with anger and misuse our relationship. My anger (and use of you) will confuse and anger you and you will eventually reject (or use) me. After this happens time and again, I learn to take what I can from my relationships because I have come to expect that they will all end badly for me."

The borderline twister creates a *cycle of failure*. Failed relationships, jobs, and living situtations increase mental agony and the need to escape from its pain. This in turn leads to more addictive activity, including suicidal thinking and actions, which produces further lifestyle failure. The borderline cycle of failure, crisis, agony, escape, and failure continues until help is sought and *accepted*.

Home Again?

As I turned eighteen, desperation really started to set in; I felt completely lost and had no idea where my life was heading. The realization that I needed my parents' help pissed me off. They were the last people I wanted to ask for help, but I had no choice. From what I can remember I had to dig really deep inside of myself to find the courage to ask them for help. I had to be very humble and I could show no anger or resentment toward them because I knew that it would turn them right off. I can't remember what I said to them but they reluctantly said I could come home.

Shortly after coming home I started right up with my typical behaviors. I was going out all of the time, I couldn't hold a job, and I still lacked respect. As far as I was concerned, they also made little or no efforts to change. I know now that back then I subconsciously knew that I would do the same shit but I had to go home because my life was getting so bad. Even though nothing had changed, I still felt a little better being at home with three square meals a day and the comfort of a warm bed.

Once again it all came to a head and we were all frustrated and enraged with each others' behaviors. There had to be a solution and it had to come from me. My parents certainly weren't going to leave, so I had to make another difficult decision. Either I would go back out on my own and make another go of it (which we all knew was not likely to happen) or I needed to put myself into a treatment program. I made the decision to enter a program. It was the lesser of all evils.

A Starting Point

Program *was such a scary word for me, becuause I didn't want anyone telling me what to do. I entered one facility and made a go of it for a short time. After about three weeks, I was completely fed up with people telling me what to do. I'd entered this program voluntarily, and after my three weeks of pretending to be a good boy I tried to leave. The thing I did wrong was that I tried to leave in the middle of the night and the nursing staff did not like this. I quickly became belligerent and angered by their attempts to stop me. Without delay they restrained me and tied me to a bed. I was then injected with some type of tranquilizer. I woke up to my doctor telling me that I was 2PC (committed against my will) and would be going to another program. I hate so very much talking about this because it brings back the feelings I had during those few days. I felt completely powerless. It was like I had no say in what I could do. I was always scared of this feeling and now it was right on top of me. There was nowhere to run and no way to numb the way I was feeling. I was so used to medicating myself until I felt better. Now I had to learn to do it through talking and getting real with myself, or so they told me.*

I had now put myself smack dab in the middle of a situation that I, at that time, really regretted. This was a hard-ass program with serious-minded, recovery-oriented staff. They took no shortcuts and none of my shit. Desperately, I tried to fool them but it was an unsuccessful fight. I was there for ten months, which to me was a lifetime. For the first five to six months I did as little as possible, just enough to appease them, but not quite enough to make a difference in my life. Each day was regimented by groups and meetings. It was very weird and I truly cannot say as to why, but one day I did make a conscious effort to change. It was nothing spectacular. It was only that I tried a little harder. The more I talked the better I felt. The better I felt the more in control of my actions I became. For the first time in my life I could say to myself, "I am a good person who deserves a better life." Don't get me wrong, I was not cured by any means but I was starting to take my first positive steps forward instead of taking my usual negative leaps backwards.

I was always a nonbeliever. How could talk help when it hurt so much to do? It never made any sense to me until I tried it on for size. But it's not something you do once in a while. You have to do it consistently. The people at this program taught me how to do it and I will remember them forever. It was a very special gift that they gave me. I am human and sometimes I don't want to talk about how I feel—but I never forget that eventually I will have to talk or else I will regress.

Samuel's life was full of confusion. Confusion about what to think, feel, and do. Confusion about where to turn for help. Confusion about what his future would throw at him next. What he learned, despite tremendous resistance and fear, was that only by talking could he feel better without the use of drugs, alcohol, sex, or any other type of self-injurious addictive activity. Talking about what you really feel makes up the first, second, and third steps of recovery.

Remember to write in your Recovery Journal today.

Chapter Milestones

1. Inability to trust leads to unstable relationships.

2. Running away from pain never makes the pain go away.

3. A person cannot work productively as long as he or she is driven by painful self-hate.

4. Sometimes you must be forced to face your feelings.

Positive Affirmation

Talking helps me feel better.

Recovery Exercises

Recovery Exercise 3.1: In Whom Do You Trust?

Objective

To consider the role of trust in one's life as well as the people who are, and are not, trusted.

Background

Trust is at one and the same time belief, feeling, and ability. People come to trust other people as a result of relying on them, and seeing that this reliance has predictable and consistent payoffs. From early on in life, some children learn the hard lesson that they cannot rely on their caregivers. Compounding this tragedy is the fact their ability to trust other people both in childhood and later in life may be severely affected.

Expanded Awareness

How would you characterize the level of trust you place in other people? List the people you trust most and discuss why you trust them.

List the people and the kinds of people you trust least and discuss why you don't trust them.

What early childhood experiences do you think contributed to your present ability to trust others, as well as your choice of who you trust?

Recovery Exercise 3.2: Relationships—Then and Now

Objective

To consider how early relationships with caregivers may influence current relationships with peers and lovers.

Background

Early, dysfunctional relationships with caregivers and siblings may have lasting effects in terms if one's ability to bond with friends or make lasting and loving attachments with others.

Expanded Awareness

What are some of your earliest memories relevant to your relationship with your caregivers?

What were some of the primary "events" in your relationship with your caregivers that led you to the relationship you have with them today (or if deceased, the relationship you had prior to their death)?

How do you think aspects of this relationship might be affecting you today in terms of both your ability to make lasting friendships and your ability to enter into a loving and lasting attachment with another person?

Recovery Exercise 3.3: Declarations of Financial Independence

Objective

To consider the role of money in one's life and the extent to which desire for it has been served in adaptive or maladaptive ways.

Background

Independent living requires funds sufficient to maintain independence. There are many obvious and hidden costs related to common expenditures such as food, clothing, shelter, telephone, and recreational expenses. While many people, for example, adolescents, desire to be financially independent, they do no yet have the means to do so. Some people have the means for achieving independence, or have actually achieved it in the past but have somehow self-destructed along the way. In either case the likely result is criminal or other maladaptive behavior as a means of earning enough money to assert their financial independence.

Expanded Awareness

What role does money, or lack of it, play in your own life?

In what ways, legally as well as illegally, have you earned money in the past?

How do you think you learned to use money the way that you use it? In what ways in the past would you describe your money-related behavior as maladaptive?

How do you earn money? Are you proud of how you earn money? Why or why not?

Describe the satisfaction you experienced as a result of purchasing or owning physical possessions. What kind of things did you spend the most money on? What kind of things did you not spend enough on?

In what ways do you hope that your money earning and spending behaviors will be more adaptive in the future? How do you anticipate your spending habits will change as your behavior becomes more adaptive?

Recovery Exercise 3.4: Part of Me

Objective

To get in touch with the sane, rational, and adaptive part or side of you that knows what is right.

Background

You read in this chapter about Samuel's mental conflict with an irrational side of him that knew it was out of control, and a saner, more rational side striving to adaptively change what was happening. Many people report some similar phenomena in terms of a mental conflict between adaptive and maladaptive forces.

Expanded Awareness

Draw a picture of the irrational side of yourself. Use as much creative energy as you can. Allow your imagination to roam free. When you have done this, write a brief, twenty-five-word description of your "dark" side.

Next, draw a picture of your rational side. Be as creative and energized as you can be. Avoid being judgmental. When you have completed your drawing, describe in twenty-five words your "bright" side. How are your two drawings different from one another? How are they similar?

Recovery Exercise 3.5: Untwisting the Twister

Objective

To halt a maladaptive swirl of thoughts and beliefs.

Background

In this book the term *borderline twister* has been used to describe a particular variety of maladaptive thinking. The borderline twister begins with a thought like, "I want to be accepted by you, but I can't accept myself" and it spins into "I hate you for liking me because I hate me, but I blame you for how I feel" and ends with "I reject you, but please don't reject me."

Expanded Awareness

Look at yourself in the mirror and make eye contact for as long as you can tolerate it. Then take out a picture of someone who cares about you. Look at that picture for a few minutes and try to imagine how that person feels about you. Now, compare and write about how you felt looking at yourself in the mirror and how you felt about looking at that person who cares about you. In what ways are those feelings similar and in what ways are they different?

Recovery Exercise 3.6: Getting with the Program

Objective

To feel comfortable going into a treatment program.

Background

For Samuel, even the word *program* was scary. He entered one treatment program and followed a coping strategy of pretending to be a "good boy." When he eventually attempted to escape from that program—that is, have more liberty and control of his own life—the consequence was confinement in a setting in which he actually had less liberty and control of his life. His life circumstances only really began to improve once he "got with the program."

Expanded Awareness

What are your resistances to entering a treatment program that may prepare you to better cope with all you are dealing with?

What forces are operating in your life that might prompt you to pretend to be "good," rather than making an earnest effort to improve?

What rewards do you see for yourself at the successful completion of a treatment program?

4

Borderlining to the Edge

If only people could realize what an enrichment it is to find one's own guilt, what a sense of honour and spiritual dignity! . . . Error is just as important a condition of life's progress as truth.

Dr. Carl Jung, *Psychological Reflections*

At an earlier age than most, adolescents with BPD are forced to confront the world outside of their families. They are not ready for the rules, structure, and demands of that world. They are driven by fear, sadness, and anger. They are mature beyond their years in some ways (raw survival skills), but as naive as toddlers in other ways (frustration and lack of tolerance). This combination of maturity and immaturity creates its own stresses. An adult appearance, some very battle-hardened survival skills, and unmet emotional needs are bound together by an unpredictable rage that guarantees an explosive introduction to the adult world.

At the borderline, crisis becomes the rule and calm the exception. Relief from an ever present sense of mental agony is the unconscious mantra and power source that motivates their search through society's pleasure and pain alleyways. They search, hoping that their next pill, hit, drink, smoke, hairpin turn, cut, burn, or fuck will make everything feel different.

> *Undoubtedly, what I'm about to share with you was and still is the hardest part of my recovery. For the rest of my life I will have to keep a close eye on where I'm at. I can never lose touch with myself. Things in my life are at a decent point now, but I can't forget where I have come from and what I was like.*
>
> *When I was about nineteen years old, life started to take some positive turns for me. I had a wonderful girlfriend, a good job, and I started to learn how to love myself. I'm not saying that life was all that good. I still had a lot of the old-time attitudes and traits. But I was trying hard to do the right thing. The one part of my life, at this time, that gave me a big problem was how I lacked the qualities needed to be a responsible adult. I was always a stubborn person and that didn't help at all. Susan, my girlfriend, always told me to slow down but I never listened much. She would beg and plead with me to stop going out, stop partying, and to pay more attention to her. If only I had listened to her, we would still be together.*

An Attitude of Need

Borderline behavior makes it difficult for people to make positive use of their skills and abilities. A fear, bred of mistrust, of others and of relationships makes people with BPD very "selfish" and unable to give to a relationship. Their unmet childhood needs lead them to demand and to take. They are possessed by what is best described as an attitude of need.

Their mistrust leads them to fear being controlled and abused by others. Their loneliness and emptiness make it hard for them to feel loved even by those who do love them very much. They regret the consequences of their borderline actions, but seem unable to stop. They want to do things differently. Unfortunately, the explosive momentum of their painful childhood makes it difficult for them to take control of their lives. They just can't slow down enough to change things.

The Power of Addiction

> *Here is where it gets hard to be honest and up-front with myself. I kick myself in the ass just about every day when I think about Susan and how much I still love her. I also had another friend at this time and I cared for this person a lot. Since I'm being honest here, I'll tell you that I didn't treat these friends of mine with much respect. I used them as much as I possibly could. I certainly did love them both, but I still needed to learn how to show that to*

them. It really sucks to sit here and write about this. It hurts me
very much. I wish it could have been different. If only I knew
what it was that I had to do I would have done it. Well, maybe.
I'm not even sure if this would have been enough, just knowing,
I really can't say. It's just so confusing!

One thing was for sure: deep inside of me was a lot of anger
and pain. I was now turning twenty-one and I still lacked the
control I needed to move on to a better and more productive
plateau in life. Susan and I were still together but it was a
struggle for me to keep her happy. She certainly deserved, if
anyone deserved, to be treated better than I treated her. I just
could not do it. I hadn't a clue as to how to love her or how to
make her feel that being with me was the right choice. We both
knew that nothing was perfect and that hopefully time would help
us, or should I say it would help me, grow up.

Soon after my twenty-first birthday, I was introduced to yet
another vice—the nastiest vice to date. It was cocaine; at least
that's what the people call it to make it sound better. The die-hard
street name for it is crack. The first time I did it I was very
scared and had no idea what to expect. The first hit made me
throw up profusely and I didn't like this at all. "Luckily" for me
I had a good friend there to tell me that after the first hit or two
it would be much better. NOT. I wish that I could have just
walked away. After that I had the taste of the devil in me. And
the devil it was. It made me do things that I thought I would
never, could never do. I stole money from anyone that I could.
I completely stopped caring about anything except for the one
thing I did care about—getting high. After a while, and before
I knew it, I had a full-speed-ahead crack habit and I didn't have
a clue as to where it was leading me. The devil had enabled me
to hide my habit from Susan for about one year. I wanted crack
so badly that I would do and say anything to get it including
covering it up from her.

The one difference that Susan noticed was that I wasn't
going out as much as I was before. She actually liked this.
Obviously, it was because I was using coke, and she still didn't
know. She was simply happy to see me spend more time at home
and less time in the bars. What she didn't know was that I stayed
home more because I had become a seclusive, paranoid crackhead.
I was so paranoid that I couldn't even look in the mirror. I used
to be able to snort coke and go out, but after the devil got me,
there was no more cocaine snorting and bar hopping. Without a
doubt things got worse. I wanted so badly to reach out and ask
for help but I couldn't, and even if I had tried, I still didn't know
how. I started to lose a lot of my friends, my money, respect from
others, and my self-worth.

The power of an addiction is largely a mystery to those who have never been addicted to something or have not had a loved one who was. The ability of the addictive substance or activity to change the behavior of its addict is unsurpassed. Some addictive substances or activities are powerful *positive reinforcers* for behavior. They directly activate the brain's reward centers that are stimulated whenever we learn something new or successfully complete an action. Cocaine is one of the most potent chemical reinforcers. It, more than many other substances, produces powerful behavior control. Rats will work in a cage pressing a bar for cocaine injections until they die of exhaustion. They will ignore food, opportunities to have sex, and sleep. They will even walk across electrified grids to get their fix. People, unfortunately, will do the same.

Instead of becoming addicted to positive reinforcers such as drugs, alcohol, gambling, sex, or fast driving, some people become addicted to negative reinforcers. Such people, who've undergone borderline conditioning as children, learn to injure themselves by cutting, burning, banging, or otherwise harming their bodies. This type of addiction relieves intense emotional pain as well as serving as a means of controlling others. A woman in a treatment program wrote about her cutting in this way:

> I love you Dad. I love you Grandma. I don't feel good. I
> feel sadness. Pain. You are always going to be a failure. You
> are gonna be in mental hospitals all your life. Cut, Cut!!!
> Blood. Scary. Love it. Blind me. Hate you. Why is everyone
> leaving me? Please don't leave me Mommy.

Another woman connected hurting herself with a need to feel alive:

> I cut to release the pain buried deep within. Sometimes it
> feels like it's the only way to extract it. I found the blood
> comforting; reassuring myself I was alive when I felt alone
> and dead. The scars are an everyday reminder of a brutal
> youth.

When the action of injuring oneself relieves emotional and psychological pain, it is called a *negative reinforcer*. It is so named because the activity stops something unpleasant from continuing. People who cut do so because cutting stops the psychological pain they feel. Their acts of cutting are then negatively reinforced by the relief they experience.

For people who choose cocaine (or other chemicals), the use of the drug produces a positive feeling (a "high") and this positively reinforces their drug use behavior. In addition to these positive feelings, the drug stops or numbs the emotional pain and withdrawal symptoms ("the jones") of its user so its use is also negatively reinforced. This dual reinforcing effect locks the addiction in place and makes escape all the more difficult. Samuel chose alcohol, pot, and cocaine as his escapes from emotional pain; others choose cutting, burning, or sex. Still others combine many types of addictive activities, using whatever works at the moment.

Addicted and still feeling the same powerful self-hatred I'd been running from since childhood, I found myself on the road to NO success. It—the drug abuse—became the center of my attention. I weaved it into my life to fill my emptiness. I used it any way I could. But somehow something unexpected happened to me. The cocaine brought back some old emotions from my past. From the time I was sixteen until I starting using I had done everything in my power to disguise and hide my past. It was like the chemicals in the drug destroyed every disguise I put up to protect myself from my past.

This chemical-induced breakthrough made things really suck. I was so confused. I felt waves of emotion running throughout my body, and none of these piercing waves made much sense to me. It was as if some pissed-off terrorist had bombed the railroad station in my head. I felt so angry, and at the same time I was sad and hurt and confused by the reasons why I was such an asshole to Susan. I would steal from her when I was "jonesin'" for that very special toke that would break me away from my sad reality.

When I was high, I didn't care about anything or anyone—only my desire. And I'm telling you, it was one motherfucker of a desire. Once I came to the conclusion in my mind that I wanted to dance with the devil, I would and I did. I thought I was even good at getting high, one really smooth operator. I was what you would call a binge smoker. A day or two here, a day or four there, it didn't matter to me, I didn't even care where. There always seemed to be a point of premeditation with me before I smoked crack: a get yourself together, check your finances, make travel plans, and, then, go off and running type of thing.

Most of the time my finances would be Susan's paycheck and, after I lost my license for speeding, my travel plans would involve sneaking her car out of the driveway. The more I talk and write about this, the more I realize how truly badly I treated her. No person would ever deserve this kind of harsh, cruel, and unloving treatment. The funny thing is that the same emotions and painful feelings I caused her to feel, my parents made me feel years before. Yes, the time and place were different, but the abuse and the addictions were the same. It was a relentless pursuit to get high, get drunk—whatever you want to call it—without regard for the effect it had on others or on me.

I'll tell you one thing, it's been a weird road for me. I know that there are a lot of you out there just like me. We are the bunch of people that have experienced both ends of this stick, and a nasty stick it is. For as long as I can remember, I've always said to myself "I will never be like my parents" or "I will never hurt someone the way I was hurt." Well that short-lived thought obviously had no long-term effect. I had become a product of my environment. I can't really say when but one day I got so fed up with the bullshit I decided that if I was going to be treated this way and feel this bad all of the time, then everyone around me should feel the pain I was feeling. Plain and simple, I just stopped caring—for myself and for anything or anyone around me.

I know it may seem to you that I am jumping all around with my story. Well, I am. Please bear with me and understand that it takes every ounce of courage and strength for me to tell my story. I also know that by reading this story you might start to feel saddened and hurt by your own troubles and heartaches. If so, that's good. We all need to feel these emotions. They will truly help you on your road to feeling better. If it becomes too much to bear, put the book down for a while. If you come back for some more, then you will know it's working.

Persistence and courage are required to confront and accept the painful feelings from which your life was molded. I recommend a slow approach. Read as much as you can and stop when it becomes too much. I have said this before and will continue to remind you of this. It is that important. I don't want you to run away from this book. I want you to use it for all it's worth to help soothe your pain.

I feel like crying every time I think about how I destroyed the best thing that has ever happened to me—Susan, my ex-girlfriend. I must tell you something that I've neglected to tell you: Susan and I had decided to get engaged. We had all these grandiose ideas that everything would work out. Well, do you think things worked out? Obviously things didn't work out so well. I really wish they had but I was just too caught up in my pain and the drugs. Instant gratification will destroy anyone. I always tell people that we just grew apart but that was bullshit. I know for a fact that subconsciously I purposely destroyed our relationship because I was so ashamed of myself for what I was doing to her and to myself.

There were two straws that broke this camel's back. The first was the day I took her engagement ring and sold it for a hundred dollars' worth of crack. I tried to convince her that I had lost it. You see we'd gotten into a big fight, and she told me to take the ring. So I did. I really wish she'd never given that goddamn thing to me, not that it would have changed much of anything. It would have just prolonged the pain I was causing each of us. The second thing occurred a couple of days later when I was jonesin' to get high. I took the new TV that she had bought for us and her car and I took off for five days. (I forgot to tell you that the reason we'd needed that new TV was because the low-life drug addict in me sold the other TV for crack. Of course, I tried to rationalize

*that I had bought it and it was mine. If you could only imagine
what an asshole I was.)*

*It is now July and I'm writing to you about my life. It's also
my twenty-sixth birthday and I'm very lonely. Every inch of my
body longs to be with Susan because she is still my one and only
true love. Believe me when I say this, I did, and still do, love
Susan with all of my heart. I have not seen her since October of
last year and I miss her. I think about her every day. The day she
left me, or should I say the day I abandoned her, was the last time
I enjoyed getting high. I know that she will never forgive me for
what I did to her. Nobody deserves the kind of treatment I gave
her. Trust me, I know how that feels.*

*For all of these memories and regrets, I cry inside, always
and forever, but I must move on, and moving on means forgiving
myself. . . .*

Why couldn't Samuel accept Susan's love? Why did he prefer the
company of crackheads and lowlifes over her loving embrace? Why did
he push his relationship with her over the edge? How did Susan experience what Samuel was doing to her? Why did she tolerate his horrible
behavior for so long? Why couldn't Samuel, despite his statements of
love for her, show his love? Does anything he has written about touch
something in you? Can you understand, if even on a nonverbal level,
why he did what he did?

**Remember to write in your
Recovery Journal today.**

Chapter Milestones

1. Children who grow up in a psychotraumatic environment develop borderline behavior patterns that are driven by fear, anger,
and incredible sadness.

2. As these children grow into young adults, they seek out ways
of coping with their intensive and unstable feelings and behavior.
Some will turn to "pleasure" addictions such as alcohol, pot, cocaine, or sex and others will turn to "pain" addictions such as
cutting, burning, or putting themselves at risk with reckless driving and so forth.

3. Self-destructive behaviors damage, and eventually destroy, the good in their lives. In time, they are left alone and hurting in the Borderline Zone.

Positive Affirmation

"Ugly" truth heals better than "soothing" denial.

Recovery Exercises

Recovery Exercise 4.1: The Maturity/ Immaturity Paradox

Objective

To understand how the maturity/immaturity paradox may be at work and to gain insight into resolving this paradox.

Background

Some people find themselves to be mature beyond their years in some ways, such as with regard to survival skills. These people may find themselves to be relatively naive in many other ways, such as with regard to dealing with outside frustrations or their own anger.

Expanded Awarenes

In the past, in what ways do you think you were mature or experienced beyond your years?

Today, in what ways do you see yourself as more mature or experienced than most people who are the same age as you?

In the past, in what ways do you think you were relatively naive in the ways of the world?

Today, in what ways do you think you remain relatively naive in the ways of the world?

Recovery Exercise 4.2: How Do You Spell Relief?

Objective

To explore and understand the mechanisms used to achieve a sense of relief, calm, or freedom from stress, worry, or pain.

Background

Relief of emotional and physical pain can be sought and achieved in many ways, some of them adaptive, and some of them maladaptive.

Expanded Awareness

Discuss the ways that you have attempted to relieve emotional or physical pain in the past. In what ways do you think these attempts were mature or immature?

Taking another look at the situations that caused the stress or pain, in what ways do you think the pain could have been relieved more effectively?

Recovery Exercise 4.3: "When Things Are Too Good" or "Time to Self-Destruct"

Objective

To understand self-destruction mechanisms that may become active when things seem too good.

Background

Some people seem to have a low tolerance for things going too well in their lives. Just when they seem to have met the right person, started the right job, or in some way begun a meaningful experience, they seem to sabotage the positivity and somehow replace it with negativity.

Expanded Awareness

Have you ever sabotaged something good in your life? How? Why?

Is there a part of you that feels that you do not deserve to have good things happen to you? How did these feelings arise?

What needs to happen in order for you to feel that you deserve good things to happen to you?

Recovery Exercise 4.4: Of Emptiness and Nothing

Objective

To understand how a void in one's life may be filled in some maladaptive way.

Background

Some people experience a gaping void or emptiness in their lives that they try to fill in some way.

Expanded Awareness

Have you ever experienced a void or emptiness in your life? How would you describe that void? How would you describe your attempts to fill that void? How successful have you been in filling that void? What will it take to genuinely fill that void?

Recovery Exercise 4.5: Not-So-Instant Replay

Objective

To understand how feelings experienced at the hands of someone in the past may be replayed by others in the future.

Background

Samuel recalled that, *the same emotions and painful feelings I caused her* [his girlfriend] *to feel, my parents made me feel years before.*

Expanded Awareness

Can you identify with the notion of experiencing some emotion or feeling at the hands of one person, only to have another person experience much the same emotions or feelings as a result of your own actions? Explain.

What memories does the experience of these emotions or feelings call up in you? Why might you have a conscious or unconscious need for others close to you to experience these same emotions or feelings?

Do you think it is possible for you to allow someone to get close to you without pushing him or her away?

5

Taking Responsibility

> "Mom, do you remember when you broke my ribs?"
> Katie asked in a hard, steely voice ... Her mother
> whirled around to her face. "What are you talking
> about?" she demanded.
>
> "When I was six ... I was learning to do a
> jump—it was a toe loop—and I fell and I didn't want to
> get up, and you said I had to. And then when I said my
> ankle hurt, you got so mad you pulled me up off the ice
> and you threw me against the barricade of the rink. And
> you broke my ribs."
>
> ... "It wasn't that way!" Her mother's voice was
> getting louder now and shrill. "I had to be strict with
> you. You were so lazy."
>
> —Steven Levenkron, *The Luckiest Girl*
> *in the World*

You are at the point in your journey when it is time to make a leap of faith. Why faith? Because what I am about to explain doesn't make a lot of sense the first couple of times around. You will need faith to help you suspend criticism of these ideas. This way you can let them settle in for a while and then you will understand something crucial to your recovery.

The Existential Paradox

I have already discussed how early psychotraumatization creates mistrustful, hurt, confused, and angry children and adults. Paradoxically, the caregivers or others who helped to create the environment that made you this way turn around and curse you for what you have become. Their failures become your fault. You are blamed for your intolerable behaviors. You are even cast out of their lives. But wait, isn't it really their fault? They made you this way. They failed to nurture and support you. They were abusive, controlling, indifferent, or consumed by their own addictions. It's not your fault. It's their fault!

Well, then again, maybe it isn't. Your behavior is dysfunctional. Your life can be very unstable. Your thoughts, emotions, impulses, and behavior are hard to control. Let's be honest for a moment. You are often out of control. Your actions damage your life, even your very body, more than you dare admit. So, your screwed-up lifestyle, then, is your fault after all?

Hold on, don't throw this book across the room yet.

Both points of view are simultaneously correct and incorrect. This is the *Existential Paradox*. If you seek a life that you can feel good about, you must come to terms with the Paradox:

> **We are not responsible for how we came to be who we**
> **are as adults. But as adults we are responsible for whom we**
> **have become and for everything we do and say.**

As promised, this doesn't seem to make a lot of sense. It's like a Chinese finger puzzle, the more you struggle with it, the harder it is to get out of. But relax, and let it float through your mind. Your developmental environment, which includes all of your childhood experiences, and your genetic code made you into the person you find yourself to be. Since you did not have any control over either of these influences, the first part of the Paradox is easier to accept: "We are not responsible for how we came to be who we are as adults."

The second part is harder to accept, but here is an explanation that can help you do so: Because you are gifted (or cursed) with the capacity for self-awareness, the universe empowers you to accept responsibility for your way of living and being. Your self-awareness as a human being, and the empowerment it provides you, enables you to change how you do things. This means that you are not condemned to live out the script written by your genetics and your conditioning. This means that you can choose your destiny by changing the behavioral choices you've made. In order to make better choices, you need to accept responsibility for who you are today (borderline behavior and all). You must courageously accept responsibility for your dysfunctional behavior despite the fact that it was "forced" upon you. This is the harder, but powerfully transforming, part of the Existential Paradox. Its acceptance, however, is the key to escaping from the borderline twister of enraged failure.

Accepting responsibility for our own behavior is never an easy task. Most of us try to avoid doing so at least some of the time, and some of us try doing so all of the time. Our motivation for this is simple: refusing responsibility prevents us from making changes in our behavior. "If I'm not responsible, then I can't do anything to change things. I'm just a victim." We learn to accept being a victim, rather than trying to be happy, once we lose hope for the future.

People with BPD carry a heavy burden of dysfunctional behavior—behavior that was "taught" to them (whether through psychotrauma or a biological vulnerability), and that hurts them more than anyone else by preventing them from taking responsibility for their lives.

As you read in chapter 1, children need to feel safe and secure before they can learn to trust adults. If basic trust isn't fully developed, their personality will not develop normally. Healthy people develop trust early in life and, therefore, learn to accept a large measure of responsibility for their successes and failures. Their caregivers help them to do this by being supportive, loving, empathic, and patient teachers. And most important, they create a deep, almost unconscious feeling of security and safety in their children.

When these ingredients are missing in a developmental environment, children grow into adults who have a difficult time trusting and loving (and being loved by) others. Instead, they grow up afraid and insecure, but the mask that hides their fear and insecurity is formed from a molten cast of anger. Anger that is often driven by hidden self-destructiveness. Consequently, they do not understand how to take responsibility for their lives. They do not know how to care for their own physical and psycho-

---

IMPACT!

It's fate—I just have bad luck.

Many people in the Borderline Zone (BZ) develop a fatalistic attitude about life. They believe that the good and bad things that happen to them occur randomly. They believe that their efforts and actions do not influence the results they experience. It's all just luck—good and bad. How they act does not matter.

This attitude grows out of their psychotraumatic childhood experiences. As children they learned to believe that they could not influence how they were treated. It didn't seem to matter how they behaved. Sometimes they were good, and they were treated badly. At other times they were bad, and treated well. It was fate, not their actions, that determined what kind of day they had.

This attitude needs to be overcome in order to accept the Existential Paradox.

logical well-being. Poorly thought-out actions lead to roller-coaster lives with endless stormy relationships and experiences.

They try to comfortably numb their painful feelings with self-injurious, addictive activities. Too often, they do unto others (and to themselves) what was done unto them as children. They run scared. They run hot. They run away. They blame others. And most troubling of all, they cling to the person or thing that promises freedom from responsibility for the fluctuating agony of their daily lives.

Victor Frankl, a psychotherapist and survivor of three years in the most psychotraumatizing environment ever created by man, a Nazi death camp, wrote in his 1959 book, *Man's Search for Meaning,*

> Ultimately, man should not ask what the meaning of his life is, but rather must recognize that it is he who is asked. In a word, each man is questioned by life; and he can only answer to life by answering for his own life; to life he can only respond by being responsible.

It is time to move the healing process to the next level.

IMPACT!

The First Five Steps into the Recovery Zone

Here are you first five steps into the Recovery Zone:

Step 1: Figuring out how much psychotrauma you absorbed

Step 2: Learning about how you can begin to heal by burying the past (Is there a ritual you can use to initiate your grieving process?)

Step 3: Understanding how you've coped with psychotrauma and how it affects you now (Do you act out or act in?)

Step 4: Understanding the process of psychotrauma (Is the past really the past, or do you relive it daily?)

Step 5: Coming to terms with your family or caregivers (How will your relationship with them change once you face what's happened?)

Entering the Recovery Zone: Step I

Self-love is the opposite of self-hate and self-destructiveness. Let's begin to create the basis of self-love—feelings of personal security—by measuring your exposure to the psychotrauma of your family environment. A psychotrauma is an aversive environmental event that is stressful enough to make you feel fear, anxiety, or that your personal safety is being threatened. Being robbed at gunpoint is a psychotraumatic stressor. So is humiliation by a caregiver on a regular basis.

Samuel has already shared a number of his psychotraumatic developmental experiences with you: the addictions of his caregivers, the daily fighting that took place in his family, the abuse and mistreatment he experienced, and the fear all of this instilled in him. His story has been repeated millions of times in the United States and worldwide. Sadly, it isn't the worst set of childhood experiences either. Research surveys indicate that up to 75 percent of people with borderline disorder have experienced physical or sexual abuse before the age of eighteen. However, these traumas are not the only types creating the poisonous womb that fosters borderline behavior.

On page 70 you will find a scale that will help you to classify your family environment's degree of traumatic stress. It is the Psychotraumatic Exposure Scale, or PTES. Take a moment to read through the scale and familiarize yourself with it. Be prepared to feel uncomfortable while reading it as it may bring back some unpleasant memories or feelings. If this happens, be patient with yourself and try not to overreact to any of the feelings and memories you may experience. If you find that you cannot manage your feelings (for example, you feel very angry or self-injurious), take a time-out and relax with some music or a soda. When you feel more in control, you can return to the book.

In completing the scale be aware of the fact that while psychotraumatic experiences can be created by caregivers, siblings, peers, strangers, teachers, prejudice, or natural disasters, this scale excludes psychotrauma caused by natural disasters. All of the other potential sources are relevant and should be considered as you are completing the scale.

Once you have read through the PTES, follow the instructions for filling out your PTES so you can calculate your total number of psychological years of traumatic exposure.

How to Fill Out the PTES

1. Think back through your childhood years. Try to remember your first memories—when you started school; when you played with your mother, father, or stepparent; how you were disciplined; what you were praised for; when your caregivers were proud of you and so forth. Review your journal entries. Under the "Yes" column, check off each psychotraumatic event that you experienced prior to the age of eighteen.

2. Then, for each item you checked, under the "Months" column, record the number of months you think you were exposed to the psychotrauma you checked off. Most people will not be able to accurately

recall how many months they were exposed to each trauma, so you will need to estimate it. Try to underestimate your exposure. DO NOT over-estimate it.

3. After you have gone down the list, you will need to get a cal-culator so you can score your scale. Starting with Level V, add up the total number of months of exposure and multiply this total by 1. Then record this number in the column labeled "Score." For example, if the total number of months of exposure to Level V trauma was 62, you would record 62 in the score column.

Next go to Level IV. Add up the total number of months and mul-tiply it by 0.8. For example, if your total number of months was 96, multiply 96 by 0.8 and put 76.8 in the "Score" column.

Next go to Level III and multiply your total number of months by 0.6 and put this number in the "Score" column.

Do the same thing for Levels II and I. For Level II multiply by 0.5 and for Level I by 0.4.

4. Add all the totals in the "Score" column and divide this total by 12 to get your final score. This is the number of *psychological years* you were exposed to traumatic stress. Samuel's score was 29 psychological years. His highest level of psychotrauma was Level IV. Since he took this test at age 24, this means that for 121 percent (29 divided by 24) of his life he was exposed to psychotraumatic stress.

If your total PTES score exceeds your actual age, you are probably experiencing some of the more severe borderline symptoms, such as urges to cut or burn yourself or serious addictions to alcohol, drugs, or sex. You are also probably finding it difficult to complete school or keep a job for more than a few months. You can interpret your PTES score as a rough index of the amount of psychotrauma you absorbed as a child. Since it is not a standardized score (that is, a score that would allow you to compare yourself to other people), it does not give you a relative meas-ure of how much psychotrauma you absorbed as compared to someone else. If your score was more than Samuel's, it does not mean that you absorbed more psychotrauma than he did. The higher your score as com-pared to your age, the more trauma you absorbed.

If your total score is a zero, then read on. *If it is not zero, you can skip this paragraph and go on to the next section.* A zero score may indicate one of two things: First, it may indicate that you are not be fully in touch with recollections of your early childhood. Denial may be at work here. If this is the case, you may wish to reread the first two or three chapters to see if this helps you to recall your childhood experiences more clearly.

The second possibility is that you belong to the group of one in four people who have BPD, but who do not have a history of psychotrau-matic exposure in childhood (Factor II BPD). If your PTES score is zero, you may wish to consult a behavioral health professional to determine whether you have bipolar disorder, attention deficit disorder, or an atypical depression. The symptoms of these disorders overlap with BPD. If you had either of the first two disorders as a child, then it could be the biological vulnerability that contributed to the development of BPD. If this is the case, it is important to get it treated as well.

If your PTES score is zero then the final possibility is that you do not have borderline personality disorder. If you have an addiction problem and your childhood was pleasant, then addiction may be your problem. If this is the case consider reading chapter 9 on addiction. If you have not done so, try out a self-help group such as AA or NA. Look in your local yellow or white pages for the number to call to get information on meetings in your area. If you do not have an addiction problem and scored zero on PTES, but feel very dissatisfied with your life, you may wish to consult a behavioral health professional. Chapter 10 provides guidelines on how to select a therapist.

IMPACT!

All was not traumatic.

A psychotraumatic family environment isn't traumatic all of the time. In Samuel's family there were times when everyone did enjoyable things together. They weren't always in conflict with one another. They also shared good times. Rarely, in fact, is a psychotraumatic family always in a state of crisis and stress. The usual rhythms of life are followed: holidays, birthdays, family gatherings, chores. The normal things, the good things, are mixed with the painful, traumatic things. The bond between parent and child, though damaged, survives. As Samuel writes, *I loved my parents. I don't think I necessarily wanted different parents. I just wanted my parents to be different . . .*

Entering the Recovery Zone: Step 2

Now that you know how much psychotrauma you have absorbed, the next question you need to address is what can be done about healing its effects? The first understanding you need to reach is that *what happened is over*. The past cannot be modified. You need to accept this. As obvious as this is, many people in the Borderline Zone try to relive the past and end up re-creating situations from their childhood over and over again.

Psychotraumatic Exposure Scale (PTES)

Level	Psychotraumatic Event	Yes?	Months	Score
V	Sexual and physical abuse (from parent, peer, sibling, other)			x 1 =
	Sexual abuse only (from parent, peer, sibling, other)			x 1 =
IV	Physical abuse only (from parent, peer, sibling, other)			x .8 =
	Viewed physical or sexual abuse between parents			x .8 =
	Viewed severe physical or sexual violence to others			x .8 =
	Parents were addicted to alcohol, drugs, gambling, sex			x .8 =
III	Parent, peer, sibling, or other verbally belittled you on a regular basis			x .6 =
	Parents emotionally manipulated you on near daily basis			x .6 =
	Viewed severe, near daily verbal fights between parents			x .6 =
	Both parents resented your birth/adoption (and needs to care for you)			x .6 =
	Parents went through a bitter, harsh divorce			x .6 =
	Either parent resented your birth/adoption and having to care for you			x .6 =
	You lived in more than eight places by age seventeen			x .6 =
II	Same-sex parent avoided close relationship with you			x .5 =
	Any parent aloof, disinterested, unaffectionate toward you			x .5 =
	Any parent controlling, demanding, unaffectionate toward you			x .5 =
I	Parents divorced before you were twelve (not bitter or harsh)			x .4 =
	Severe family financial problems (couldn't meet bill payments)			x .4 =
	Very little hugging, kissing, or other types of healthy physical affection in your family			x .4 =
0	None of the above applies to you in any way			0
	Weighted Number of Years of Exposure			

This makes their relationship with others unstable and unhappy. As a child you learned that you could not depend on your caregivers to care for you. As an adult you fear depending on others and you fear others depending on you.

It is essential that you begin to find meaningful ways to "bury the past." To do this you need to take an inventory of what was lost and what needs to be let go. BZ losses include childhood happiness, caregivers lost to divorce or addiction, years of lost time, and the lost opportunities a better upbringing would have opened. You need to let go of pain, sadness, grief, anger, and self-blame.

People have always created rituals to mark transitional periods of their lives. Familiar rituals include marriage, funerals, engagements, dating, religious confirmation and baptism, and graduations. One of the better ways of coping with your losses and need to let go is for you to create a meaningful ritual that will help you do this. Your ritual should be something you will remember for the rest of your life. It should produce a sense of closure and relief. It should be a private ritual for your eyes only. It should reflect your personality. Here's an example of such a ritual: Joe wanted to make a break with his past. He decided on a burial ritual. He drove off to a wooded and sparsely populated area and he hiked into the woods. When he knew that he was all alone, he found a beautiful spot for his ritual. He dug a three-foot-deep hole and into it he placed a sealed container with several symbols of his psychotraumatic childhood—a picture of himself as a young boy, a picture of the homes he lived in, a poem he wrote about how he felt as a child, objects he used to cut himself with, his bong, and a prediction he made about how he will turn his future around. He placed this "time capsule" into the hole and buried it. He camped at the site that night to cleanse himself further.

There are no right or wrong rituals. They may even seem silly to others, but that is irrelevant. If you allow yourself to consider what type of ritual you need, you will, much to your surprise, come up with a good one. A ritual is not a miracle; it is a very human way to cope with life's transitions and hurts.

Entering the Recovery Zone: Step 3

This step involves explaining to yourself what your psychotrauma is doing to you now. In general, psychotraumatic stress makes people afraid. It puts us on alert to protect ourselves from impending danger. Typically, there are two innate protective mechanisms that all humans have: we run from a threat or we prepare to fight back. If a tornado warning is issued for our town, we take steps to escape from its path and protect ourselves from its destructive force. If someone attacks us on the street, we may fight back to save our lives. If your caregivers were frequently drunk and abusive toward you, the same alert messages flashed through your brain. Unfortunately, as a child you did not have the ability to directly escape or counter their threats. Often, children have to absorb the stress as well as the fear it invokes. Sometimes children even "forget" that their caregivers were abusive to them in order to survive living with them.

Acting In and Acting Out

The effects of psychotraumatic stress, particularly when exposure is chronic, have a cumulative impact on a child's behavior and brain development. Some exposed children develop an *acting-out* coping style and others develop an *acting-in* coping style. These styles roughly parallel our inborn fight-or-flight self-defense behavior.

The children who develop an acting-out style will counterattack by developing conduct problems in school or at home. In their teen years, they will seek the support of their peers and thrill-seeking forms of escape. They may get into drugs and high-risk activities to numb the traumatic fear they have been conditioned to feel. Participation in such activities also gains them the support of their peer group "family."

Their acting out is fueled by their tremendous anger (the flip side of fear). Their type of counterattack behavior puts them in head-to-head conflict with their caregivers. Tit-for-tat battles ensue over the course of many years. Typically, such adolescents end up explosively leaving home early, and become persistently addicted to substances and high-risk activities.

> When I was a young child, my house was a nightly war zone. There was always fighting and mass confusion going on. Everyone expected it to happen, but no one did anything to prevent it. It was as if none of us cared, but deep down inside I did care. I just didn't know what to do to stop the insanity. The way I handled things was by acting out in school. All my teachers would say, "What's wrong with you? Why are you acting this way?" I could never answer them. I would seek out the acceptance of my peers by taking any dare. I tried to be the center of their attention by acting as the class clown. I remember one time when one of my peers dared me to walk out on the second floor window ledge from one classroom to another: I took the challenge and after I did it everyone clapped "for" me. I thought that I was the coolest guy in the school. But truthfully they were clapping and laughing at me, not for or with me. Later that day I was suspended from school for a couple of days for my actions. When I got home I was

beaten by my stepfather. The beatings never stopped me from doing things. They seemed to encourage me to act out more because of the anger and resentment I felt toward my parents—toward my stepfather because of the physical abuse and toward my mother because she would stand there and watch without doing anything about it.

As an adult, I found myself acting in similar ways. I would do things that the average person would never consider doing. The reason was the same: acceptance. I've always needed to feel a part of something even if it meant looking like the fool.

The acting-in children withdraw inside of themselves. They learn to space out. Mentally, they travel far from their present reality and pretend they aren't really the person who is in pain. This is called *dissociation.* This protective mechanism allows them to numb the effect of the psychotraumatic stressors. This acting-in form of escape is fueled by fear and anxiety and may eventually lead to self-injury in the form of cutting, burning, bruising, or banging one's body. Those who injure themselves say that the physical pain of the injury helps them to numb their emotional pain. In fact, surveys of people who injure themselves reveal that 67 percent do not feel any physical pain at all (Favazza and Conterio 1988). What they want is relief from their emotional agony and emotional pain; they do not want to feel physical pain. It is just the means to an end. Most of the time they know just how much injury to cause themselves to get that relief. However, studies have shown that frequent use of self-injury increases the likelihood that these individuals will think about and attempt suicide (Dulit et al. 1993).

Combinations of the acting-in and acting-out strategies for coping with trauma are more often the rule than the exception. However, preferences are eventually established. Which style best describes your preferred method of coping?

Entering the Recovery Zone: Step 4

At this point you might be thinking, "All of this trauma happened a while ago, why does it still affect me?" This question gets at the toxic essence of psychotraumatic stress: There is no resolution or closure for the affected person. In the case of borderline behaviors, the long-term nature of the exposure combined with a lack of closure leaves the person replaying those traumatic memories and emotions over and over again in his or her head and, most troubling, in his or her daily life.

People with BPD often learn to dread calm and successful periods of their lives because they have been so conditioned to psychotraumatic crisis. They learn to re-create crisis and stress. For some, success in life breeds anticipatory anxiety because they see it as the calm before the storm. For others, success is "boring," it lacks the adrenaline rush of exposure to psychotraumatic events. Recent research has even suggested that the brain chemistry of those exposed to early and severe psychotraumatic stress appears to undergo modifications (Perry et al. 1992). Numerous studies have documented a potential connection between abnormal neurological functioning and early psychotraumatic stress. A group of researchers led by Dr. Martin Teicher (1994) found that people with a history of psychotrauma such as physical, sexual, or psychological abuse were much more likely to have abnormal electrophysiological brain waves than people of the same age who were not subjected to early psychotraumatization (47 percent for psychotraumatized versus 19 percent for not psychotraumatized). Keep in mind that these results are preliminary and may change with further study of the problem.

Eventually a person exposed to a traumatic developmental environment will develop a *relationship control phobia*, which is a *generalized* (spreads out of the family environment) and irrational (spreads to people who have done no harm) fear of being abusively controlled by other people. People with this phobia fear relationships with other people because they fear being controlled (and, therefore, hurt) by others. (You'll read more about relationship control phobia in chapter 6.) They attempt to manage their fear by either overcontrolling the relationship or getting away from it. However, all of us have strong social, economic, and sexual needs for other people. Consequently, there is no psychologically healthy way to avoid or to control all relationships. Because of this a painful dilemma develops: How do you get what you need from others without falling under their abusive control? The behavior you use to cope with this dilemma creates some of the borderline and addictive problems that make your life an insecure and unhappy experience. Typically, you find yourself ping-ponging between controlling and staying versus avoiding and leaving a relationship. It is a very confusing and stressful place to be. Understanding this process is the first step in changing it for the better.

Entering the Recovery Zone: Step 5

Coming to terms with your caregivers can be a hard step to take for many reasons. For starters, you need to have reached the point in your recovery where you are in touch with your feelings and have a good understanding of how your family life has affected your behavior. Once you are in touch with your feelings, you will realize that much of your anger is directed toward what your caregivers did to create a psychotraumatic family life. As you become more aware of this, you will also become more aware of the guilt and shame that you feel. As the guilt and shame take hold you may discount your feelings and fall prey to the magical belief that maybe your caregivers can change and maybe your relationships with them will spontaneously improve.

Your feelings will differ for each of your caregivers, because each caregiver played a different role in your family life. One may have been the addict, the other the victim or enabler. Or perhaps they were both addict and enabler. Or perhaps neither were addicted, but one was controlling and emotionally distant and the other was emotionally hungry and angry. They may have been perfection freaks who gave little in the way of love or emotional nurturance. Or perhaps they were so involved with themselves that they had little time or concern for you, which made you feel as if you didn't even exit. There are many ways to sing the same song. Samuel had four caregivers. Each played a slightly different role in making his a psychotraumatic childhood. Samuel's biological father played a crucial role in his upbringing ...

My relationship with my father has always been a one-sided relationship. No matter what I said to him, he was always right. As they say, father knows best. Well, that's bullshit; he certainly didn't know best and he still doesn't. He did everything possible not to get his hands dirty. To this day my father and stepmother think they know me, but they don't. They never had the time or the patience to understand me. As far as he's concerned he had no responsibility for my upbringing and that's where it ended for him. There is still a lot of anger deep inside of me. I've tried hard to deal with this, but I can't do it alone. If only my father would say to me, "Yes, I was wrong for letting you kids grow up that way, I should have done something about it but I didn't know what to do." The more I write the more my anger is right there in front of me, and the more it pisses me off and hurts me at the same time. But every time I confront my father with my feelings, he has a new way to invalidate them. He gets angry because of his deep-seated guilt, and I get angry because of his unemotional denial.

Like they say, the apple doesn't fall far from the tree. For my father and me nothing could have been truer. You see my father was a hell-raiser when he was a young boy. He was also kicked out of high school. His parents thought that a military school would be good for him so they enrolled him in the local military academy. He did well for a while, but eventually he was asked to leave. It seems that he had become too disruptive for them, and there was no controlling him. As far as I know, my father never got his high-school diploma.

As a young man my father was off and running. But he was, and still is, a very talented chef, so he followed that road.

My grandparents owned a restaurant, and eventually, my father took it over. Around that time he started to get into coke and other drugs. Doesn't this sound so very familiar? It's like déjà vu. What I am trying to get at is that my father and I are very much alike. Almost to a T, I did the same things that my father had done. The really weird thing is that I found out about my father's past only a short time ago. It wasn't like I knew what my father was like all of these years and was using that as a reason to act the way I was acting. When I found out, it didn't come as a complete surprise, but it did certainly make me think a lot more about how my father treated me.

There were times when my life was on a good path, and there were times when I was self-destructive and out of control. My father, in some weird way, seemed to go with my flow. The times I needed him the most were the times when I was lonely and hurting. These are the times we all have experienced, the times when it would've been nice to have a loved one there to help us through it. As for my father, I could count on him for one thing: when the going got rough for me, he was nowhere to be found. It was like I didn't exist; or maybe I should be real honest with myself and say that he just didn't have the capacity to care. He was a lost child just like me.

There was one other thing that I could count on. When I was doing well, Daddy always seemed to be around for me. The times when I didn't need any help and felt secure about my life, he was right there to give all of the fatherly advice that a young man needed.

The way I see it now is when things are going well for me, my father felt less guilt for his past sins. I don't care what my father says, he does feel guilt from the past, he has to. And when things weren't going well, I can only say that my father felt more guilt than he could handle. It burned him so badly that he couldn't stand to be around me. I never understood this until a couple of weeks ago when I was talking to a dear friend of mine. I was feeling quite sad and I needed to talk. That's the great thing about true friends, no matter how you feel or what you're doing, they'll always make the time to talk to you. I only wish that my father was one of my true friends; maybe someday he will be.

The pain all of this causes me is common. Many people, just like you and me, feel these seemingly endless waves of hurt. In a sense it's the same for all of us, yet in a lot of ways it's very different. For me the pain has been a controlling factor in my life. It has been a source of many negative feelings and actions that have only stopped me from living the life that I deserve. My parents still don't seem to understand what they put us kids

*through. When I think about it, I often feel the pain curdling
in my stomach.*

*For now, the hurt I feel from my parents will no longer
dictate my life or my actions. I wish that I could say that I'm
totally free of the pain and suffering, but then I'd be lying,
and I've done enough of that. The truth is that the process of
recovery, however slowly, is healing my pain.*

Your feelings toward your parents are very complex. You need to
think through how those feelings are affecting you today. If the pain you
feel is driving your dysfunctional behavior, then it is time to break this
connection. If you still harbor the fantasy that somehow your parents
will treat you the way you wanted them to, think again. This may never
happen, and you may waste your life waiting for it to occur. This issue
is discussed further in chapter 10.

Once you begin to understand how your family environment made
you behaviorally vulnerable, you can begin to separate yourself from what
you have been and what has been done to you. Accepting the Existential
Paradox, can help you imagine a Recovery Zone that surrounds you
wherever you go. You can use that image to forgive your parents and
yourself, and accept responsibility for what you do. As you take these
steps, you too can begin to "be apart from what you've done." As Samuel
wrote, *For all of these memories and regrets, I cry inside, always and forever,
but I must move on, moving on means forgiving myself . . .*

Chapter Milestones

1. To create feelings of personal security you need to begin to understand and accept the Existential Paradox.

2. You must start to accept the fact that past trauma cannot be undone; but know that you can move on.

3. Discovering how your past traumas affect you now can lead you into the Recovery Zone. What is your preferred coping style? Acting out or acting in?

4. A relationship control phobia can prevent you from establishing healthy relationships.

5. It is important to think about how you would like to come to terms with your caregivers.

Remember to write in your Recovery Journal today.

Positive Affirmation

I seek the safety of my own Recovery Zone.

Recovery Exercises

Recovery Exercise 5.1: Paradox
Part 1—Not Responsible

Objective

To explore in-depth the first part of the Existential Paradox discussed in this chapter.

Background

The first part of the Existential Paradox discussed in this chapter says, "We are not responsible for how we came to be who we are as adults."

Expanded Awareness

Critically evaluate this statement. Thinking about your own life, in what ways do you think you were or were not responsible for how you came to be who you are as an adult?

Recovery Exercise 5.2: Paradox
Part 2—Responsible

Objective

To explore in-depth the second part of the Existential Paradox discussed in this chapter.

Background

The second part of the Existential Paradox discussed in this chapter says, "As adults, we are responsible for whom we have become and for everything we do and say."

Expanded Awareness

Critically evaluate this statement. Thinking about your life to date, in what ways are you responsible for whom you have become? In what ways are you not responsible for whom you are today? In what ways do you reject responsibility for everything you say and do? Have you tended to blame others for your actions or their results?

In what ways have you accepted that responsibility? Do you think the Existential Paradox is a fair burden for humans to carry? Why or why not? How would you rewrite it?

Recovery Exercise 5.3: Past Tense

Objective

To appreciate that it is not possible to modify any of the tension, anger, frustration, and pain experienced in the past.

Background

Unfortunately, time machines exist only in the works of science fiction. It is not possible to go back in time and modify any of the tension, anger, frustration, or pain experienced in the past. It is, however, possible to heal the consequences of such emotions.

Expanded Awareness

Make a list entitled, "The Ten Most Provoking Things That Ever Happened to Me." The list should include only the most frustrating, painful, and anger-provoking things that have ever happened to you.

Then, for each item on the list, write a paragraph or two that acknowledges that it is impossible to go back and change the past, and explores what will have to happen in the future for healing to occur.

How will you overcome the negative feelings aroused by each of the items on your list? Which items confuse you the most and will be the hardest to overcome?

Recovery Exercise 5.4: Runaway Fears, Runaway Anger, Run Away from Home

Objective

To reexamine the motivation in childhood to run away from home.

Background

Unable to cope with certain life circumstances, many children at one time or another fantasize about running away from home. Some children actually act on such wishes.

Expanded Awareness

As a child did you ever fantasize about running away from home? Did you ever act on such a wish? Did you ever run away mentally, not physically, from home? Draw a picture of how you "ran away" from home and then write a brief description of your picture and of what you would want your family to know about how you felt back then.

As an adult or near-adult, have you ever fantasized about running away from a relationship you were in with someone? Did you act on that wish? What motivated you to do so? Did it make things better for you? Did you regret running away (or conversely, not running away)? How did this adult fantasy or action differ from your childhood fantasies or actions about running away from home?

6

Life in the Borderline Zone

If I could keep myself from thinking! I try, and succeed:
my head seems to fill with smoke ... and then it
starts again: "Smoke ... not to think ... don't want
to think ... I think I don't want to think. I mustn't
think that I don't want to think. Because that's still
a thought." Will there never be an end to it?

—Jean-Paul Sartre, *Nausea*

In this chapter, you'll look at the decisions "forced" upon you in the Borderline Zone. What motivates your decision making? What kinds of situations do those decisions get you into? How can you begin to use the *power of choice* to change the course of your life? As Samuel indicated, this is not a simple task. However, learning about the key factors—the psychotraumatic developmental environment, the explosion into adulthood, and the person with BPD's attitude of need—has prepared you to understand the Zone and the decisions you make there.

Each factor plays a role in creating or maintaining the four major borderline behavior patterns:

1. Relationship control phobia

2. Distorted self-image

3. Hypersensitivity to stress

4. Excessive need for impulsive gratification

Together, these behavior patterns can leave you with a low level of *self-efficacy*. Self-efficacy is believing in your personal capabilities. It is being optimistic about the future and about your ability to be successful. People who lack self-efficacy expect that bad things will happen to them regardless of how hard they try to succeed.

IMPACT!

The Sunny Side of Life

Dr. Albert Bandura, a well-respected psychologist, is an expert in self-efficacy. He views self-efficacy as a fountain of human optimism. It empowers someone to meet life's challenges with determination and success. In the *Harvard Mental Health Letter* (March 1997), he wrote, "People with high self-efficacy . . . approach difficult tasks as challenges to be mastered rather than threats to be avoided. They are deeply interested in what they do, set high goals, and sustain strong commitments. . . . [They] attract support from others, which reinforces their ability to cope. . . . They guide their actions by *visualizing* successful outcomes instead of dwelling on personal deficiencies or ways in which things might go wrong." He goes on to point out that people with high self-efficacy blame their failures not on their personal inadequacies but on things that can be fixed: ignorance, lack of skill, or lack of motivation. By contrast, low self-efficacy people beat up on themselves, give up, and sink more easily into anxiety and depression.

Part of recovering from a psychotraumatic upbringing or biological disadvantage involves opening the door to the possibility of viewing yourself as someone who is effective and who can be successful.

The key to exiting the Borderline Zone is accepting the truth of the Existential Paradox. Its liberating potential can empower you to take true control of your decisions, and, thereby, set you free on the road to becoming a healthier person.

I have already introduced the person with BPD's relationship control phobia in chapter 5. Before you continue to read this chapter, be sure that you have completed the Psychotraumatic Exposure Scale and have been making your journal entries. If you have done so, you will get more out of this chapter than if you have not.

IMPACT!

Remember the Existential Paradox

We are not responsible for how we came to be who we are as adults. But as adults we are responsible for whom we have become and for everything we do and say.

Relationship Control Phobia (RCP)

Parents (and others) who create a family environment that exposes their children to prolonged traumatic experiences generate chronic fear in their children. This fear eventually coalesces into a relationship control phobia. This phobia initially protects the children from what is happening in the family environment. The phobia is the children's way of avoiding those who psychotraumatize them. As the children grow, this once defensive phobia, expands into a generalized fear of intimate and authority-based relationships that extends to people outside of the family.

A phobia is defined as an irrational fear of something. This phobia, however, has a very rational point of origin. The rational part of this phobia is that, as a child, it was your protective response to your parents' actions. It is only natural to develop a fear of those who are hurting you, even when those people are your parents or siblings. Unfortunately, this protective response can be irrationally extended to relationships with other people who have not mistreated you. You come to anticipate mistreatment so you do unto others before they do unto you. Children live what they experience. They assume that the people in the outside world are similar to their family members. Furthermore, their model for trusting others is based in large measure on the trust they feel for their parents. It is little wonder that people with BPD cannot easily trust others and, in fact, fear the abuse that, as they've seen in their prior experiences, closeness inevitably brings.

Keep in mind that you may not be experiencing your relationships as "phobic." That is to say, you may not feel afraid of your close relationships. Instead, you may be feeling angry, misunderstood, ashamed, or mistreated. These feelings are masking your fear. You need to gently put them aside and take a deep look into your heart of hearts so you can touch your core fear. Of course, it is easier to say this than it is to do it.

Another thing to keep in mind about relationship control phobia is that it has nothing to do with being shy around people. It doesn't impair a person's ability to make friends. In fact, you can be a very outgoing person and still be caught up in it. The phobia also doesn't affect all types of relationships. It usually "kicks in" only after a relationship moves out of the acquaintance or casual friendship category and into the employer/employee, close friendship, or intimate relationship category. If you take a close look at the relationships that fall into those categories, you will begin to connect the dots that form the outline of your relationship control phobia.

How RCP Affects Your Life

RCP has four major effects on your life.

1. *A relationship control phobia can block you from trusting others.* The cognitive script goes something like this: "If I can't trust my parents, I can't trust anyone. If my parents hurt me, then everyone will hurt me. My parents couldn't love me, so I don't know how to love another (or myself)." Relationships with others are seen as dangerous, but necessary. "If I get too close, the other person will try to control, abuse, and hurt me." People with BPD may perceive depending on others and having others depend upon them as psychologically threatening. They might "pretend" to trust others in order to get what they need, but they can never truly reciprocate trust. A young man on the Internet wrote, "Every now and then I hate my girlfriend and think she is a real bitch. The same thing with my friends. The closer a person gets to me, I find faults with them, I think they're taking advantage of me and are out to hurt me."

2. *A relationship control phobia blocks the development of a mutually loving relationship.* This is not a surprise. In loving relationships, people with BPD can say the words, but not clearly feel the emotions or "walk the walk." They desperately want to be loved by others and they want to love others! However, they cannot trust them. They don't know how to love them back and cannot negotiate the control issues that are a part of all relationships. Their inability to love others, and feel the love others try to share with them, makes people with BPD chronically afraid of losing those relationships. One Internet surfer wrote: "I think that borderliners are concerned with only one thing: losing love. When cornered I get very scared and I show that by getting angry: anger is easier than fear and less vulnerable. I strike before being struck."

3. *A relationship control phobia demands that you use any means at your disposal to keep control over the other person so you can get your needs met.* Since people with BPD feel as if they are battling for daily survival, any form of exaggeration, deception, manipulation, or seduction is considered a reasonable method for keeping the relationship going. This process is not entirely under their conscious control. It is motivated by a cruelly imposed need to survive on their own without help from others. It is a semiautomatic process that they learned as children. It is driven by the same emotional needs that drives addictive, self-injurious behaviors. It

started out as a way of getting needs met in a difficult environment. It ends up becoming a very unsatisfying way of life.

How do all of these "survival behaviors" make your relationship partners feel? In three words, they feel angry, hurt, and confused. They will often feel as if you are a selfish person who is using or manipulating them. They will feel betrayed by an inconsistency of purpose and affection. Finally, as your relationships with them develop, you become more and more of a mystery to them. Instead of understanding you better, they will become more and more confused by your behavior. Is this beginning to sound familiar?

4. *A relationship control phobia can make you chronically anxious about losing control of your relationships and of being abandoned.* Since people with BPD are rarely sincere and open with the people who care about them, they constantly fear abandonment. Do you fear that once others find out how screwed up and emotionally selfish you are, they will leave you? Or when they get sick and tired of being treated badly, they will give up on you and the relationship and walk? As one woman on the Internet wrote of her borderline behavior,

> No matter how hard my boyfriend tries to please me it is
> never enough. I demand this and that. I yell. I get jealous
> over stupid things. I never have enough. I'm just afraid that
> he'll leave me.

Few people will tolerate being manipulated and abused for an extended period of time. The natural instinct is to get out of such a relationship. People with borderline behavior fear that this will be the outcome of all of their relationships. The most frustrating fact of all is that even though they are often aware of what they are doing, they just can't seem to stop themselves from doing it anyway.

RCP makes relationships emotionally stormy affairs. If you are a social introvert, it makes you cling to others in a desperate fashion. If you are a social extrovert, you may find yourself driven to compulsively meet others whom you declare your instant friends. You collect as many friendships as you can so you will never run out of relationships. Either way, the phobia conditions you to strike out at those who care most about you and prevents you from learning to love them. The ending that you dread, and that you create, leaves you feeling alone, abandoned, and unloved. Another person on the Internet posted,

> I don't believe that anyone understands me. . . . I lead a very
> guarded life. Certain people see specific sides to me but I
> never allow anyone to see all of the sides. If I did, that
> would be lowering my defensive walls and I am petrified
> that this will lead to total criticism, something I can't deal
> with.

The image people with BPD present to the world is based on phobic feelings toward others. It hides their sensitivity and their love.

Can you risk letting go of your phobic mask? Can you allow yourself to truly trust and love another? Can you trust yourself? Can you love yourself? Can you rethink who you really are?

Distorted Self-Image

Your brain constructs your self-image from the raw experiences of your daily life. In constructing your self-image, your brain gives a lot of weight to your childhood experiences. If you were loved, nurtured, cherished, fairly and consistently disciplined, and given the opportunity to develop your talents, your brain will more readily generate a healthy and positive image of yourself. This internal image then forms the basis of the social image that you present to the outside world.

In a psychotraumatic family environment, however, children do not experience themselves in a positive way. This environment, as we know, creates children who feel insecure, fearful, and inadequate, and do not trust their caregivers. They are unable to form a healthy self-image. Their self-image forms, instead, around feelings of self-hatred that often border on suicidal. They learn to hate themselves for obvious reasons: their psychotraumatic experiences conditioned them to feel worthless and, sometimes, unworthy of living.

But most people cannot live for long hating themselves. And so a compensatory alternative to an image of self-hatred also develops. It is an idealized, grandiose self-image that allows its holders to arrogantly believe that they can be anybody or do anything without real, sustained action. This combination of self-hating and grandiose self-images makes it difficult to realistically assess their abilities and skills. The tendency is to flip-flop between believing that they are lowlifes incapable of successfully doing anything versus believing that they are gods and can do anything. This distorted self-image also impairs their self-efficacy.

The primary subconscious self-image is negative. It whispers its negativity: "I am not worth anything. Everything I do is evil. Nothing good will ever happen for me. It doesn't matter what I do. I will never succeed at anything. If I do succeed, it is only by accident." Consciously, people with BPD may experience periods of grandiose feelings that briefly counteract these negative refrains, but these feelings rarely last, and, ultimately, they make matters worse.

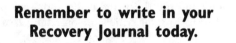

**Remember to write in your
Recovery Journal today.**

A woman in her twenties wrote of her distorted self-image,

When I look in the mirror I see a lot of different things, it all really depends on the mood I'm in at the time. Sometimes I see someone who is beautiful, intelligent, loving, honest, creative, and hopeful. Someone who has such a strong desire in the world to be happy and successful that nothing will stop her.... But, sometimes I see someone who is hurt and lost, ugly and stupid, shady and deceitful, vengeful and angry. Someone who will do whatever it takes to make someone else feel the pain she feels. Someone who's desire to be happy and successful is nonexistent, and everything that gets in her way she runs from or just lets it stand there.

Social image reflects self-image. Distorted by self-hate and its grandiose compensation, your social image is presented to others in confusing and contradictory variations. This confusing presentation leads other people to misperceive who you really are. Some people may perceive you as manipulative, selfish, phony, arrogant, angry, or crazy. Other people may see you as charming, sensitive, hurt, perceptive, or needy. Those who know you best eventually see you in all of these ways. Ironically, you are probably just as confused as everyone else.

A distorted self-image (and social image) can also make you vulnerable to stress. A positive self-image provides its holder with a reserve of good feeling to help him or her through tough, stressful events. By contrast, an image of self-hatred and arrogant grandiosity provides only minimal protection from what Shakespeare called the "slings and arrows of outrageous fortune." The reserves are limited and easily exhausted. Depression and anxiety can quickly take over. During times of heightened stress, you can even lose your grip on reality and retreat into psychotic fantasy or dissociation (total detachment from your environment and from your sense of self).

Stress Hypersensitivity

Closely connected to a distorted self-image is a tendency toward stress hypersensitivity and emotional overreaction. Chronic exposure to traumatic stress overloads the brain systems responsible for self-protection. An emotional numbness can emerge that blunts all feelings—good and bad. In addition, the emotional "breaking point" is lowered such that even minor stress can trigger a major behavioral reaction. These reactions typically take the form of outbursts of anger and hostility that, depending upon circumstances and the person's coping style (acting out or acting in), are directed toward others or toward oneself.

Once stress releases a "mood of self-hatred," its effects can expand at a frightfully powerful pace. It is at these moments that you are in the greatest danger. For it is then that thinking becomes disrupted: thoughts sizzle, race, flash, explode, or blur. Emotions become intensely confused or numbed. The mental agony builds and builds to nearly intolerable levels. Rational problem-solving, let alone helpful discussion with others, becomes very difficult. You hate anyone near you. You curse anyone who dares to offer help. You don't want to talk. You want immediate relief and you want it any way you can get it. It is at these moments, and when these moments are anticipated, that you turn to your addiction or distraction of choice. Getting stoned or drunk, driving recklessly, getting laid, or engaging in self-injury becomes an attractive form of relief from the mental agony. If you are "lucky," your addictive activity will buy you the relief you crave—at least for a little while. If you are not lucky, it will merely help you dig a deeper and darker hole. Forgotten is the first rule of being stuck in a hole: stop digging!

Worse yet is the observation that adults who were traumatized as children tend to re-create similar psychotraumatic environments for themselves in the present. Crisis, which was so much a part of their earlier life, becomes the norm, and its absence feels strange. They do not tolerate success very well either, and good times (that are not artificially induced by addictive activities) leave them feeling uneasy. They often mock their successes as an undeserved calm before the next storm. Caught between a rock and a hard place, they are driven to seek relief from all of these contradictory feelings through impulsive gratification.

Excessive Need for Impulsive Gratification

The combined effect of RCP, self-image distortion, and stress hypersensitivity are swirling mixtures of inconsistent actions. Low self-esteem, self-hatred, and hair-trigger anger (and panic) can set you up to develop the last behavior pattern in the Borderline Zone: an excessive need for impulsive gratification, i.e., gratification that is obtained through overindulgence in pleasure or pain.

Are there better ways than this to soothe agonizing feelings? Perhaps, but your feelings and needs can drive you hard. You may feel cheated by your childhood, tormented by your life. You seek quick relief. You've learned that impulsive actions can be effective soothers of agonizing feelings. But you'll find out later that it is a double-edged sword that becomes both cause and consequence of many of your difficulties.

Impulsiveness is doing something without taking the time to think through the consequences of your actions and how those consequences will affect you and your lifestyle.

Impulsiveness is choosing to do something that promises an immediate reward, relief, pleasure or distracting sensation over something that requires sustained effort to get an equal or larger reward or pleasure. Impulsiveness is also choosing to escape from a problem situation by indulging in pleasurable or painful activities that effectively distract you from that problem.

Gratification is the procurement of satisfaction or relief. It can take the form of pleasurable or painful (this includes fearful) activities. Often, the most gratifying actions combine both emotional sensations.

Examples of impulsive gratification include getting drunk to avoid dealing with the loss of a job, then ending up crashing your car and getting arrested for drunk driving; buying something you want with money needed to pay basic expenses such as rent or food and, later, ending up with an eviction notice; or cutting yourself because you are overwhelmed by your thoughts and feelings, then ending up hospitalized.

In each of these examples, a distracting pleasurable or painful action was used to either avoid facing an unpleasant situation or set of feelings or to satisfy an urge for something wanted immediately.

Impulsive gratification is caused by poor decision-making skills and an attitude of neediness. Effective decision-making skills are learned during the developmental years. And if childhood needs were reasonably satisfied, those children do not become excessively needy adults. Children who learn how to effectively delay gratification by making thoughtful decisions can become reasonably successful students, athletes, parents, employees, professionals, or business owners. The more demanding the goal, the more success depends on being able to work long hours for very little immediate reward. But children whose basic psychological needs have not been met will, as adults, experience an overwhelming but poorly defined sense of emptiness. As Dr. Carl Jung (1953) wrote, "A million zeros joined together do not, unfortunately, add up to one." Their inner emptiness (unsatisfied childhood needs) demands constant satisfaction and encourages them to make impulsive decisions in order to meet its raging demands. These impulsive decisions make success in life an impossible fantasy.

Parents who create a psychotraumatic developmental environment for their children generally are overstressed, deeply unhappy, poorly skilled, or addicted people. Consequently, in addition to exposing their children to chronic stress, they are not effective role models or teachers. They often lack the motivation or skill to be effective. They have difficulty teaching their children how to delay gratification and work toward time-delayed goals. Additionally, the aversiveness of family life makes everyone very much on edge. Research has shown that exposure to stimuli that produce emotions such as fear and extreme anxiety disrupt a person's ability to learn new skills (Perry et al. 1996). High levels of stress dull our mind's ability to concentrate and to learn.

It is little wonder, then, that many people in the BZ have not mastered the art of thoughtful decision-making. They suffer a double effect: they lack the skills needed to make a thoughtful decision, and they are driven by intense feelings that they have great difficulty soothing. These intense feelings, in turn, drive them to make impulsive decisions. Their inability to soothe those feelings in safer ways coupled with weak decision-making skills perpetuate this seemingly endless cycle.

IMPACT!

Addiction Statistics

It's been estimated that up to 69 percent of people with borderline behavior become addicted to drugs or alcohol versus 9.5 percent of the general population (Miller et al. 1993; Reiger et al. 1993).

If alcohol and drugs become your primary form of escape your behavior can quickly become enslaved by the reinforcement effects of these substances. As Samuel described earlier, setting up your next high (or self-injury episode) can become literally the only purpose of life. The seductive core of addictive activity is its ability to totally distract from the mental agony and unhappiness of your life. Life becomes getting what you need to fuel your addictive activities. This process applies to all potentially addictive activities. Sex can become very addictive, as can cutting or mutilation. Reckless driving or gambling can also be used to pathologically escape from agonizing inner pain or external reality. My clinical experience suggests that virtually 100 percent of people in the BZ become addicted to one of these activities. The specific choice of addictive activity (drug, alcohol, cutting, sex, etc.) is irrelevant. All that matters is the addiction.

Potentially Addictive Activities

The list of potential addictive activities is long. There are three criteria for membership on the list:

1. The effect of the activity must be powerful enough to distract a person from his or her mental agony.

2. The consequences of excessively doing the activity must be harmful to the physical or psychological well-being of the person.

3. The immediate effect of stopping use of the activity must create psychological or physical discomfort in its own right.

Addictive activities or reinforcers can create positive, pleasurable feelings or they can create painful, frightening feelings. They can even create both types of feelings at different points in their use. You'll find a list of addictive reinforcers used by people with borderline behavior in the following Impact! box.

NOTE: The addictive use of the following reinforcers generates additional problems, such as money problems, withdrawal symptoms, brain damage, and so forth.

IMPACT!

Potentially addictive reinforcers.

Pleasurable, Exciting Initially	*Painful, Frightening Initially*
Alcohol	Cutting your body
Cocaine	Burning your body
Heroin	Reckless, dangerous driving
Marijuana	Swallowing objects
LSD	Picking physical fights
Compulsive sex	Near-overdosing on drugs
Excessive spending of money	Unprotected sex with strangers
Bar hopping	Prostitution
Gambling	Starting arguments
Lying and fantasizing about who you are	
Bragging	
Deceiving others	
Fast driving	

As you may notice from the list, there is a fine line distinguishing pleasure from pain, fear from delight. The use of activities that generate both of these sensations are very addictive. Even apparently painful activities, such as cutting yourself, can produce a trancelike "high" that relieves mental agony without causing physical pain! The attention and medical care that are often triggered by a self-injury episode reinforce the use of that behavior.

The emotional sensation all addictive activities share is the intense feeling of "dancing with death" that, after all, is the ultimate terrifying thrill for someone who is filled with angry self-hatred. Chapter 9 addresses the question of what to do about your addictive activities.

Exiting the Borderline Zone

Each of the four behavior patterns created by the psychotraumatization you experienced as a child keeps you trapped in the Borderline Zone.

Relationship Control Phobia Trap

When people hate themselves, it makes it hard for them to trust or love others because they need to trust and love themselves before they can trust and love another. The readiness to trust and love others starts to develop at birth, and as I have been saying, early psychotraumatization slows or inhibits the development of the capacity to do this. The resulting relationship control phobia makes it hard to feel loved and trusted by the people who, in fact, truly love you. Instead of opening your hearts to them, you might behave in an inconsistent and confusing fashion because of your mistrust and suspicion and, sometimes even, paranoia.

Fully experiencing the love and trust of another human being is one of the primary ways a person can exit the Borderline Zone. But RCP blocks this exit.

Stress Hypersensitivity and Addictive Traps

The social agony of RCP combines with stress hypersensitivity to drive people with BPD toward making impulsive decisions to gratify their neediness and soothe painful feelings. The accumulating consequences of pleasure or pain addictions put the quality and stability of their lifestyle in jeopardy. This makes them even harder to love and to stay with, which, in turn, increases the fear of abandonment and loneliness.

Addictive activities also harm their physical well-being. Ultimately, addictive activities become new ways of abusing themselves, of doing to themselves what was done to them earlier. Their sense of personal effectiveness is, then, further undermined by the failure, instability, and social isolation that follows.

Self-caring and personal accomplishment is the exit from Borderline Zone that stress hypersensitivity and addictive behavior block.

The Mistrust Trap

If you decide to get help from a professional therapist, your RCP makes trusting that person and accepting help very difficult. Worse still, many professionals dread "borderlines" and "addicts" because of their reputation for being difficult patients. Angry and mistrustful actions toward therapists then reinforce this stereotype. The result is treatment failure.

Another exit from the Borderline Zone, *professional treatment*, is blocked by mistrust.

The Silver Lining

At about this point you might be feeling hopeless. Please remember that things are not hopeless. They are challenging, but they are never hopeless! This book's primary purpose is to explain what happened to you so that this painful knowledge can help expand your awareness and unlock these exits from the BZ. The rest of the book is devoted to this task. The knowledge and awareness you gain by reading this book will help you make all the changes that you choose to make.

These exits will become easier to open as you gain a better understanding and acceptance of the Existential Paradox. As you *willingly* accept responsibility for your behavior in the here and now, your impulses, rages, and addictive activities will become *your choices*. Once they become your choices, you will have the power to make *better* choices. Better choices will enable you to unlock the exits from the Borderline Zone.

The seeds of a more authentic you are still alive inside of you. Inside is the you that you would have grown to be if you had not endured what you did. You can build on this inner potential by making the choice to do so now. Your time is precious and delay is costly. You know this will not be easy, but what is your alternative?

Chapter Milestones

The following points summarize the behavior patterns that create the Borderline Zone:

1. The four borderline behavior patterns and their common point of origin (psychotraumatic developmental environment) exist between the social image you present to the outer world and your authentic self.

2. Your authentic self is overloaded by the task of processing a painful past into a healthy and predictable personality.

3. Borderline behavior inserts itself between your social image and your authentic self and corrupts these healthy aspects of your psychobehavioral functioning. Consequently, the world sees an inconsistent and unstable person.

4. Understanding and accepting the Existential Paradox frees your authentic self to use the power of choice to gradually alter the decisions you make. As your decisions mature from creating self-

destructive results to creating self-nurturing results the quality of your life will improve.

Positive Affirmation

The power of choice frees me from life in the Borderline Zone.

Recovery Exercises

Recovery Exercise 6.1: The Origins of RCP

Objective

To gain a firsthand understanding of relationship control phobia by thinking about it in terms of your own background.

Background

RCP arises from repeated psychotrauma in the family leading to a chronic state of fear in the child. This fear, originally associated with family members, generalizes to other people, and manifests itself in the form of distrust. Other feelings, such as anger, may mask the fear of being mistreated by others. RCP becomes evident in close, intimate relationships as well as other, noncasual relationships, such as that between an employer and employee.

Expanded Awareness

Do elements of relationship control phobia sound familiar to you? If so, which elements?

What behaviors on the part of your parents, other family members, or other caregivers may have affected your ability to love or trust other people? What problems related to issues of control can you recall from your early family life?

Recovery Exercise 6.2: Taking Control of RCP—Trust

Objective

To further enhance understanding of relationship control phobia by specifically considering how issues related to trust can contribute to a life sentence in the Borderline Zone.

Background

A reasonable degree of trust (a balance between no trust and blind trust) in others is perhaps the most healthy way of relating to other people. Yet some people, particularly those in the Borderline Zone, seem to be "running on empty" when it comes to trust.

Expanded Awareness

Think about your own capacity for trust. How would you describe your capacity to trust other people? How would you describe how trustworthy you appear to other people? What factors are responsible for your distrust of other people? What factors are responsible for other people's distrust of you?

How much trust would you like ideally to place in others? How much trust would you like others to place in you? What kinds of things need to happen in order for these ideals to become a reality?

Recovery Exercise 6.3: Taking Control of RCP—Love

Objective

To further enhance understanding of relationship control phobia by specifically considering how issues related to love can contribute to a life sentence in the Borderline Zone.

Background

As with trust, life in the Borderline Zone may sometimes lead people to believe that they are "running on empty" when it comes to love. Yet, the need to receive and give love is a very human one.

Expanded Awareness

Think about your capacity for giving love. How would you describe that capacity? What factors do you see as responsible for this capacity?

Now, think about your capacity for receiving love. How would you describe that capacity? What factors do you see as responsible for this capacity?

Describe your ideal capacity for giving and receiving love. What are the obstacles to achieving this ideal? In what ways might you begin to overcome these obstacles?

Recovery Exercise 6.4: Taking Control of RCP—Control

Objective

To further enhance understanding of relationship control phobia by specifically considering how the issue of control has affected your relationships.

Background

Life in the Borderline Zone is characterized by many problems and issues related to control. These problems may be manifest in a fear of being controlled by others, or a compelling need to feel as if you are in total control of a relationship.

Expanded Awareness

Look back on your own experiences in various relationships. How has the issue of control played a part in the quality of those relationships? How has it played a role in intimate relationships? In employer-employee relationships? Family relationships?

Ideally, what kind of role should the issue of control play in these different types of relationships?

Think about these questions and then commit your thoughts to paper in an essay entitled, "On the Issue of Control in My Life."

Recovery Exercise 6.5: Mirror, Mirror

Objective

To examine your self-image and begin to work on changing it for the better.

Background

To know where you are going, you must know where you are. An accurate self-image helps you to better know where you are. Some people hold distorted images of themselves. The distorted image may be, among other things, of the inflated or deflated variety. With a deflated self-image, people minimize their abilities and self-worth, believing that they are incapable of achieving what they wish to achieve. An inflated self-image is accompanied by the belief that they are somehow better and more deserving than other people.

Expanded Awareness

Look in a mirror. Study yourself for a few minutes and reflect on who you are and what you have been through. Try to imagine the young child inside of you. Try to see how that child has grown into the person in the mirror. Then, write an essay entitled, "My Self-Image: Past and Present." Explain whom you think you are now, and whether or not you see your self-image as inflated, deflated, or both.

Continue your essay with some words about whom you would like to be ideally, how possible it is to achieve that ideal, and what needs to be done to achieve that ideal.

Recovery Exercise 6.6: The Many Faces of Diversion

Objective

To reflect on the many methods of diversion and distraction.

Background

To *divert* is to deflect, reroute, or distract. In a military context, a diversionary tactic is one that draws attention from a critical event. In the Borderline Zone, a diversionary tactic is one that draws attention away from something as well. Unfortunately, diversion is too often used in the Borderline Zone to distract attention away from serious conflicts or stresses that must be dealt with head-on.

Expanded Awareness

In the past, how have you diverted attention from serious conflicts, stresses, or other problems that required attention? Have you used alcohol? Drugs? Self-injury?

What more adaptive ways might you use to divert attention from such problem areas? Ultimately, what tools will you need to transcend such problems, so that a diversion is no longer necessary?

7

A Skillful Exit from the Borderline Zone

And when I found myself totally overreacting to my toddler son, ready to beat him mercilessly, and I saw the fear in his eyes that I had in my own when I was a ravaged child—I simply snapped. I couldn't do what my parents had done—simply couldn't "pass on the legacy" ... From there the road to recovery ... began.

—Anonymous Internet Posting

I could have done and achieved so much more than I have, if only I learned at an earlier age what it was like to love and feel good about myself. It's finally starting to happen and I'm saying to myself, "What the hell have I been waiting for?" This feels good and it is only making me a stronger person. I have to stop wondering about the past, and what I left behind, and who I hurt. It's time to move on and to learn how to trust and to feel good about what I'm becoming. Like everyone out there, I have no idea what is ahead of me, but I feel more confident than ever. I've always felt like I had no say about my destiny, it was just about going with the flow. But now I certainly do have a greater sense of the control needed to continue down this rocky road.

Your dysfunctional childhood "stole" the freedom to choose your own destiny. It is time to take back your right to choose who and what you will be. The pain your heart carries and your mind feels does not have to be feared. Your journal writing helps to manage your feelings by putting them into words. Once a feeling, regardless of how terrible it feels, is put into words, its power to harm you is greatly reduced. Mastering what you have been made to feel means expressing those feelings in nondestructive ways. Until now, you often express yourself in destructive ways. This book is showing you that better methods of expression are possible.

We've stayed together for a hundred pages now, some of those pages have been pretty difficult ones. I honor and respect your trust, knowing as I do how very tough trusting anyone can be.

> *Trust, as we all know, is a very important aspect of any relationship. To unconditionally trust and have faith in someone is much harder than we think. Yes, it's easy to say I trust you, but do we really trust anyone? Trust is like love, you have to trust and have faith in yourself before you can feel this for anyone else. Everyone has their opinions of what it is, or should I say, what it is to them, and that's fine. But I know from firsthand experience that trust is a feeling that is felt deep inside. There are no questions of trust for me when it comes to a few people in my life. I've earned their trust and they've earned mine, and this all stems from love. Let me tell you this, it wasn't easy gaining their trust and even less so, trusting them. It's really a difficult subject to discuss. Think about me writing for this book, telling you about my problems, and how very hard all of this is I have to humble myself every time I sit down to my computer. I'm trusting you, and I don't even know who you are, but that's okay with me because I trust myself. Finally, it has happened, and it feels great.*

I hope that you feel enough trust in me to take the next step in your recovery. My task now is to share the skills that can help you to take better control of your destiny. These skills will help you compensate for the effects of psychotraumatization. The skills in this chapter can help you

- Overcome the fear of close relationships

- Overcome self-hatred

- Moderate sensitivity to stress

- Reduce dependency on impulsive gratification

Each of the skills described in this chapter will contribute toward achieving a better way of life.

Earlier in the book, I introduced one of these skills—positive affirmations. The other skills make their debut here. The skills are organized by an acronym: SACRED. I call the whole approach the SACRED Road out of the Borderline Zone.

The SACRED Road

Soothing

Affirmation

Control

Reinforcement

Equality

Determination

Each SACRED skill is described in detail in this chapter, along with how and when to practice them, and what they empower you to do. The chapter covers all six sets of skills, so it is a fairly long chapter. You should learn the skills in the order presented and focus on mastering one skill at a time. The Soothing skills are the foundation for all of the other skills and should be mastered first. With this in mind, then, most of your time should be spent on mastering the three Soothing skills before going on to the other skills.

Soothing Myself at Will

There are four skills in this set: *relaxing* (deep breathing), *objectifying* your problem or stress, *visualizing* your solution, and *obtaining* the results you visualize and want. Together they are called ROVO.

IMPACT!

Do I have to learn these @%&^@$ skills?!

The simple answer is NO! You don't have to learn anything you don't want to learn.

The skills presented here can help you exit the Borderline Zone. You are free to accept or reject them as you see fit. You know better than anyone about your life and your capabilities. You know what will work for you, and what will not. You have the wisdom to design your own skills. This is simply a course of action that I know has worked for others. But, ultimately, you know best.

Why Is It Important?

Life outside the Borderline Zone requires that you learn how to calm your emotions *without* depending on addictive activities.

How Long Will It Take to Learn?

Practice is everything. Plan on at least thirty minutes of daily practice five days per week for about two months to master all three skills in this set. The average person spends more time than this daydreaming, so most people have little trouble finding the time to practice. The real hurdle is your willingness to practice, but if you have read this far you are probably really into what we are saying. If you can't spare thirty minutes, then try starting out with five minutes.

The easiest of the ROVO Soothing skills to learn is Slow Deep Breathing (SDB). The hardest skills to master are Objectifying and Obtaining. Visualizing falls somewhere in between. The good news is that SDB will help you to master the three other skills in the Soothing set.

How Is it Done?

Relaxing. Learning to relax your body and your thoughts is a wonderful skill to master. If you can do this, you will feel incredibly relaxed and safely remain on the SACRED road to recovery. There are many methods of relaxation that range from meditation to biofeedback. But the relaxation method that is the easiest to learn is SDB.

Your objective is to develop the ability to calm your mind as soon as you feel your thoughts starting to race or as soon as you feel your anger starting to build. It is necessary that you practice SDB nearly every day for about fifteen to thirty minutes (five minutes is the minimum) until you can calm yourself on demand.

The basic instructions for learning SDB are in the Self-Help Skill on the following page.

Done properly, SDB will shut down the part of your nervous system that reacts with tension, mental agony, and negative emotions to stressors (both external and internal in origin). This technique is highly effective. It has been used, in various forms, by millions of people worldwide to manage tension. You can learn it in about eight to twelve sessions. However, it is very important that you pair a key phrase such as "I am calm" to your relaxed state of mind and body. You can select any short phrase you like. Other effective possibilities are: "Safe," "One," "At Peace," "Calm and relaxed," "Warm and safe," and so on. Write your key phrase in the space that follows:

My Key Phrase is _____

SDB and your key phrase can be used as soon as you start to encounter a stressful situation. To use SDB at just the right moment, you need to get in touch with your hourly stress level. If you wait until your stress level exceeds a rating of 4 or 5, you will probably not want to use

Self-Help Skill: Slow Deep Breathing (SDB)

1. Find a quiet place where you will not be interrupted for about fifteen minutes. Turn the phone off. Rate your stress level on a 0-to-10 scale where 0 means totally calm and stress-free and 10 means totally stressed out.

Prepractice Relax Rating

          0 1 2 3 4 5 6 7 8 9 10
Total Calm   Total Stress

2. Sit in a comfortable chair with your feet flat on the floor. Place your hands palms down on or near your knees.

3. Close your eyes and listen to all of the sounds in your environment for a few moments. Try to focus your thoughts on what you hear. Ignore all other thoughts. If your thoughts wander, gently squeeze your knees and return your attention to a sound.

4. After a minute or two turn your attention to your breathing. Now, as slowly as you can, breathe in through your nose to a count of 1, 2, 3, 4, 5, 6, 7, 8, 9, 10. Try to make your inhale last until you reach 10. Try to fill your lower abdominal area with air first, then your midsection, and finally your chest. Try to really expand your lungs as much as possible. It may make you feel uncomfortable at first; this will be especially so if you smoke cigarettes or pot. However, with a little practice your ability to do expand your lungs will increase.

5. After you have fully inhaled, hold your breath for a count of 1, 2, 3.

6. Then exhale slowly to a count of 10, 9, 8, 7, 6, 5, 4, 3, 2, 1. As you exhale, think, "I am calm" over and over again. Try to see these words light up in your mind as clearly as you can.

7. Repeat the SDB cycle for about ten to fifteen minutes or until you feel noticeably calmer. Concentrate on your breathing. Ignore all other thoughts. You will find it difficult to do this. But each time your thoughts drift, just squeeze your knees gently and refocus on "I am calm" and the rising and falling of your breathing. Once you get into a SDB rhythm, you can stop counting and just breathe.

8. After you feel calmer, open your eyes and rate your stress level again. How much calmer do you feel?

9. Remember to rate your stress levels pre- and postpractice. A rating, after practice, of 3 or less on the 0-to-10 relax scale is your goal.

Postpractice Relax Rating

          0 1 2 3 4 5 6 7 8 9 10
Total Calm   Total Stress

SDB. You will probably fall back on old addictive behaviors. Try to rate your stress levels every two hours or so (keep your ratings on an index card with the date and time of each rating). This will help you get more in touch with your hourly stress level.

Here are three typical BZ stress situations where SDB can make a major difference:

Use it to calm your mental agony. Once you have paired your key phrase with SDB relaxation, you can use your key phrase to calm yourself by simply repeating it to yourself during a stressful moment. Then, after a few minutes of SDB, you will feel more in control of yourself and of the situation. But remember, SDB will work best if you start using it *before* your stress levels go above 4 or 5.

Use it when writing in your journal. If you are writing in your journal and you start to feel overwhelmed by painful memories, just shift your thinking to your key phrase. Repeat it over and over again in time with your SDB and you will start to feel back in control. You will need to do at least five to ten minutes of continuous SDB to reach this goal.

Use it in tense interpersonal situations. Remember relationship control phobia? When you start to feel angry and misunderstood, instead of acting on impulse, focus your mind on your key phrase for a few moments. Take a brief time-out. Repeat your key phrase to yourself several times. Slow your breathing down a little. Remind yourself that you are in control. Try to understand the other person so that person can better understand you. Sometimes, you have to give a little to get a little.

Does using SDB seem impossible or ridiculous to you? Well, you *can* make this work for you. Hundreds of people in my treatment center have learned to use SDB to calm themselves and stay in control. And so can you. *Trust it and do it!*

Objectifying. Objectifying is a skill that empowers a person to look at a situation, and the emotions, thoughts, and impulses that go with it, with full awareness and choice. Objectifying is the opposite of impulsive reaction or gratification. It is a soothing skill because, like SDB, it will help keep you calm and safe.

Your objective is to focus your awareness on the stressful situation, and the emotions, thoughts, and impulses that go with it, while describing what is happening to you, what you are feeling, and what you are thinking, as a TV reporter might do. That is, describe it as if you were observing everything from the outside. Your job is to report everything without reacting. Remember, objectifying means describing what is happening without reacting to it.

This skill is harder to develop than SDB because it requires greater self-control. To learn it you need to describe what you are feeling as you are feeling it. This is a tough thing for you to do because of your psychotraumatic experiences (your instinct is to numb, deny, forget, or stuff stressful feelings). However, the combination of your journal writing, reading Samuel's writings, and learning SDB can help. This combination can empower you to objectively describe what you are feeling and thinking without acting on your emotions until, with full awareness and choice, you consciously decide to do so.

Each of the Soothing skills forms a foundation for the other skills. Mastering one skill will help you to master other skills. Objectifying is one skill that will take longer to master, but that's okay. Recovery from what you've been through takes time. But it is time spent on nurturing a new you, and that is time well spent.

See the following Self-Help Skill box to learn how to practice objectifying.

Objectifying is used together with SDB to prevent you from impulsively reacting in a self-injurious way to stressors. The two practice exercises will help you to get a feel for what objectifying means.

Visualizing. When visualizing, you use your imagination to create a powerful motivating image in your mind's eye. Imagination is an ability that everyone has, though few of us make full use of its enormous potential. Many people, however, use their imaginations to think up all the horrible things that could happen. They catastrophize about what could happen and in doing so conjure all of the negative emotions that accompany the imaginary disasters.

Using Visualization, you can harness the power of your imagination to guide yourself toward well-thought-out actions that keep you safe and improve the quality of your life.

Your objective is to visualize yourself engaged in positive action scenes in place of self-destructive, impulsive reactions to stressors. A well-visualized scene acts as a model for your behavior to follow. It motivates you to match your behavior to that model. It also helps you to confront your tendency toward negative thinking, which is one of the consequences of the distorted self-image conditioned by your psychotraumatization. In fact, the main obstacle that you need to overcome in order to employ visualization is your tendency toward negative thinking. Negative thinking leads you to expect the worst, even though you may say otherwise to yourself and others. Negative thinking says, "I can never learn this!" and "It won't work anyway, it's stupid!" Negative thinking has one purpose only: to keep you trapped in the Borderline Zone.

Visualization puts the behavioral principles of modeling and correspondence training to work for you. Visualization is a behavioral model to which you match (or correspond) your actions. This means that you do what your visualization model says you will do. When you execute the visualized action successfully, your success positively reinforces your use of the Visualization technique. This will automatically strengthen your desire to use this technique again. The more you use visualization the less impulsive and unpredictable your actions become. As you may have

Self-Help Skill: Objectifying

Practice Exercise 1: Observing Confusion

1. Go to a room where you have a TV, radio, and stereo. Put on a TV show, a station on the radio, and a tape or CD of your choice all at the same time. Set an alarm clock or a timer to go off in fifteen minutes.

2. Sit in the middle of all this confusion. Close your eyes and describe to yourself what is going on around you and how it is making you feel. Remember, just sit there with your eyes closed and try to describe your feelings and the situation you just created. What impulses are coming to mind? Do not act on them, just observe and describe them as if you were a TV reporter.

3. Continue until the alarm goes off. After the exercise write your observations in the "current day" section of your journal. Repeat this exercise until you can do it for thirty minutes without acting on an impulse to end the session before the alarm goes off.

Practice Exercise 2: Awareness without Emotion

1. Get a tape recorder and record some of your traumatic memories from your journal on a tape (if desired, you can erase the tape as soon as you have completed the exercise). Select passages that still evoke some feelings in you.

2. Play your tape through headphones with the volume on low. Put the TV on. Sit in a comfortable chair and start doing your SDB while repeating your key phrase. Ignore both the TV and the tape.

3. If you start to feel emotional stress, try to focus on the source of the emotions within your body. Is it centered in your stomach, neck, shoulders, head, brain, etc.? Then, try to describe how it feels with neutral words. Remember, you are a TV reporter whose job is to describe the events being experienced. Identify the trigger for the feelings (Was it something on your tape?). Become aware of any impulsive actions that come to mind. Remember, you are being objective, so you will not act on any of these impulses.

4. If the feelings or impulses are too overwhelming, STOP the exercise and get a soda or something to snack on to distract yourself. Otherwise, continue the exercise until the tape is over and you feel satisfied with your performance. Your objective is to listen to the entire tape without allowing your emotions or impulses to reach an uncomfortable level. When you can do this you have successfully completed this exercise.

Self-Help Skill: The Basic Steps of Visualization

1. Close your eyes.

2. Begin your SDB routine while using your key phrase. Continue until your stress level drops below 4 on your scale.

3. Now imagine yourself executing a series of actions that produces a desirable outcome. Imagine as much detail as possible. See yourself doing the actions. See where you are. See who you are with. Hear the sounds. Smell the odors. See what you are wearing.

4. As negative thoughts enter your mind, squeeze your knees, say your key phrase, and return to your visualization.

5. Once you have imagined all of the details of your action sequence, assign it a "trigger word," such as "Project Jump Start." You will use this trigger word to get yourself started on executing the action sequence once the time comes.

6. Close your visualization session with five repetitions of the positive affirmation "I want it; do it!"

guessed, visualization will help you become a more consistent person. Do the practice exercises in the preceding and following Self-Help Skills to hone your Visualization skills.

Practice makes better, but never perfect. Be aware that the exercises increase in psychological difficulty. This helps to strengthen you for the greater challenges ahead. Recovery doesn't just happen, it is a learning process that is with you for the rest of your life.

Obtaining. *Obtaining* is the final ROVO Soothing skill. It means putting into action the plan that you visualized and getting the results you want. Obtaining means focused action that gets desired results. It requires a clear vision of what you want; a sound, thoughtful decision to act; and execution of your decision with determination.

Putting the Soothing Skills Together

1. Use SDB and your key phrase to calm you emotions and impulses.

2. Use Objectifying to identify your stressors. Use it to describe the emotions and body locations of the emotions the stressors trigger. Use it to identify the action impulses the stressors trigger. Use it to describe the disruptive effects the stressors are having on your thought process. Use simple sentences and neutral words to Objectify what is happening to you.

Self-Help Skill: Visualization Practice Exercises

Practice Exercise 1: A Simple Visualization-to-Action Sequence

1. In a quiet room, sit in a comfortable chair and close your eyes. Do your SDB routine until your stress level is below 4.

2. Now visualize yourself getting out of the chair and picking up an object from one side of the room (for example, a book), bringing that object to the other side of the room, and placing a second object on top of it.

3. Get a clear picture of yourself doing just that in your mind. Once you have done this end the visualization with five repetitions of the positive affirmation "I want it; do it!"

4. Open your eyes and, without delay, do exactly what you visualized yourself doing. After you have completed the action sequence, praise yourself for matching your actions to your visualization (do not criticize yourself in any way!).

Practice Exercise 2: A Complex Visualization

1. In a quiet room, sit in a comfortable chair and close your eyes. Do your SDB routine until your stress level is below 3.

2. Think of someone close to you who you have not spoken to in a while that you would like to call. Imagine what it will be like hearing that person's voice. Imagine what you will say when you greet the person. Think about what you will talk about, and how the conversation will be a pleasant one. Think about the person's phone number; repeat it to yourself. See it in your mind. Think about where the person is living and what he is she is doing in life. Once you have done this end the visualization with five repetitions of the positive affirmation "I want it; do it!"

3. Open your eyes and, without delay, do exactly what you visualized yourself doing. After you have completed the action sequence, praise yourself for matching your actions to your visualization (do not criticize yourself in any way!). If the person is not home on the first call, keep calling until you reach him or her.

Practice Exercise 3: Visualizing Self-Control

1. In a quiet room, sit in a comfortable chair and close your eyes. Do your SDB routine until your stress level is below 3.

2. Think about an addictive activity that is harmful to you. Perhaps drinking alcohol, cutting yourself, speeding, using pot or cocaine, going into rages, or having unprotected sex with strangers.

3. Imagine yourself not doing the activity for the next _____ day(s) (you decide: one to seven days). Imagine what your schedule will be during those days and what you will be doing that will help you avoid doing your chosen addictive activity. Imagine how you will manage desires to do the activity (perhaps you'll use SDB). Imagine who can help you meet your goal. Imagine how happy you will feel to see yourself succeed in avoiding your addiction for your chosen number of days.

4. Open your eyes and, without delay, begin to obtain exactly what you visualized yourself wanting. After you have completed each day of the action sequence, praise yourself for matching your actions to your visualization (do not criticize yourself in any way!).

5. Repeat steps 3 and 4 each day of your chosen number of addiction-free days.

6. After you have completed the chosen number of days reward yourself with something healthy (not with your addictive activity), such as a movie, meal out, book, CD, etc. And remember to feel proud of yourself.

---

3. Focus on the source of the stress. Identify it as clearly as you can. Is it in the environment? Or is it coming from within your mind? Once you have identified it, describe it in simple words. Then identify the effect the stressor is having on you. What emotions are you feelings? What action impulses are you experiencing? Are your thoughts racing? Are your thoughts confused? Are you experiencing a flood of emotions and thoughts? Describe whatever is happening in simple sentences. Use neutral, not emotional, words. For example, "My boyfriend just said that he likes redheads (stressor). Since I have blonde hair I felt anger (emotion). The anger started in my face in the form of tension (body location of the emotion). I want to yell at him for insulting me (action impulse). My thoughts are speeding up (effect on thought process)."

4. Use the positive affirmations "I am in control" and "I think before acting" to help you avoid reacting impulsively and to prompt yourself to stay out of the Borderline Zone.

5. *Visualize* a healthy course of action. Make your vision as clear and as attractive as possible in your mind's eye. Repeat to yourself, "I want it, do it!".

6. Open your eyes and take control by executing your visualized action sequence. *Obtain* the results you want.

7. Ignore all negative thinking. Stay in the Recovery Zone.

Soothe Yourself with ROVO!
Relax—Objectify—Visualize—Obtain

Affirming Who I'm Becoming

Why Is It Important?

The next SACRED skill is *Affirmation*, which you are already familiar
with. Positive affirmations help to counteract the distorted self-image that
was conditioned by your psychotraumatic history. How many times during your childhood did your parents, siblings, peers, or other caregivers
feed you "negatives"? How many times did they emphasize what was
wrong with you? How often were they abusive? How often did they act
as a negative role model? How many times did they reinforce a negative
self-image?

Your answers to these questions explain why Affirmation is so important. What was done to you, you now do to yourself. Affirmation can
break this part of the cycle.

But here is the rub: People in the Borderline Zone reject praise from
others and resist realistically praising themselves. Self-hatred creates this
resistance: you feel unworthy of accepting anything healthy or good. Understanding this point as clearly as possible will help you to sidestep
this resistance barrier.

How Long Will It Take to Learn?

Affirmation is easily learned in a single day since it involves the
simple repetition of meaningful sentences. Getting into a routine of using
Positive Affirmations on a daily basis takes a week or two.

How Is It Done?

The Positive Affirmation practice routine from chapter 1 follows. If
you have been using this Positive Affirmation routine regularly, you are
in a better position to understand how useful this skill is. If you haven't
been able to do so, then this is your chance to get started.

The transformational healing power of Positive Affirmation is rooted
in the power of words to manipulate reality. Now this is something most
people rarely think about. But Marshall McLuhan, a noted professor and
thinker about communication media, thought long and hard about this
very concept. In his 1964 book, *Understanding Media*, he wrote about the
power of words. He said,

> The spoken word was the first technology by which man
> was able to let go of his environment in order to grasp it in

Self-Help Skill: Positive Affirmation Practice

Here is your Positive Affirmation practice routine. Twice daily, once in the morning just after you wake up and once at night, sit down in a comfortable place where you will not be disturbed. Take several slow deep breaths to calm yourself. Then close your eyes and repeat each PA ten times. After you have repeated all of them, say to yourself, "I believe in who I am and what I think." Repeat this ten times and take several slow deep breaths.

Repeat ten times each:

1. I am not to blame for being the way that I was.

2. I am responsible for changing myself.

3. I want to change.

4. I feel better when I face my inner pain.

5. I can change. I will change. I will never, never, never, never give up!

6. I am a good person and I will prevail.

Then take several slow deep breaths.

---

a new way. . . . Words are complex systems of metaphors and symbols that translate experience. . . . By means of translation of immediate sense experience into vocal symbols, the entire world can be evoked and retrieved at an instant.

What this means for your recovery is that by properly using *Positive Affirmation Slogans* (PAS) you can construct a new mental image of your behavior and of yourself—images that you can then retrieve on demand.

In short, PASes are advertisements for the mind. As you probably know, billions upon billions of dollars are spent annually on the development and communication of advertisements.

Why are such huge sums of money spent on ads? Because advertisement is effective. You can apply the same technology to develop a strong, healthy self-image and behavior pattern for yourself.

Positive Affirmation Slogans become effective through repetition and through the pairing of the PAS with pleasant experiences and feelings. A good PAS is worded in a simple but catchy fashion, for example, Nike's slogan "Just Do It!" It should evoke a positive emotional image that does not need to be fully conscious to be effective. It should be easy to remember, and it should be paired with action(s) that you want to take. Finally, you need to repeatedly expose yourself to your PAS throughout the day.

Designing Your Own PAS. You need about a dozen PASes to counteract the effects of the four borderline behavior patterns discussed in chapter 6—relationship control phobia, distorted self-image, hypersensitivity to stress, and excessive need for impulsive gratification.

Each PAS should be between five and ten words in length. The words should be emotionally powerful enough to evoke an attractive mental image. You should design at least two PASes for each of the borderline behavior sets listed above. Each PAS should be easy to remember. You should actually create an advertisement to illustrate each PAS by including pictures and images from magazines or photos, or, perhaps, drawing something to illustrate the meaning of your PAS. Mount each of your PAS ads on an 8½-by-11-inch piece of paper. The process of developing your PAS ads helps to condition their meaning into your mind. This is, of course, critically important to their ultimate effectiveness. The PAS suggestions I offer on the following page are just that, suggestions, to get you started. Feel free to use them in any way you desire.

Counteracting relationship control phobia. The major psychological objective of your PAS for RCP is to encourage trust and love of others so that your close relationships will become less stormy and more satisfying. Your fear is being abused and exploited. You can be jealous and envious of what others have that you do not have. This creates an undertow of anger and resentment that further strains your close relationships. Elements to include in your PAS are acceptance of love, trust as the means to overcome loneliness, your willingness to take a chance, and your resolve not to exploit others or to allow yourself to enter into relationships with those who would exploit you. Some suggested PASes are

- I can trust without fear.

- Feeling loved fills me with joy.

- I am worthy of being loved.

- All my resentments are fading away.

- Love and trust replace fear and envy.

- I can trust without fear; I can love without envy.

- I can protect myself from harm.

- I am safe. I am secure. I am good.

- I can love without being hurt.

Try your hand at developing your own PAS to counteract RCP.

Counteracting distorted self-image. The psychological objective of your Self-Image PAS is to overcome feelings of self-hatred and grandiosity. This means accepting yourself as you are and unconditionally loving and trusting yourself. You do not have to be a perfect person to love yourself. Your past, regardless of how bad it was or how awful you were, is gone! You need to find the courage now to be apart from what you were. When you look at yourself in the mirror, see someone who you love very much, someone who you trust and want to care for very, very much. See the person you can be; allow the person you were to fade away. Some suggested PASes are

- I love me.

- I can be real and pretend no more.

- I want to soothe and care for me.

- I am real; I love my life.

- My hurtful past is fading away.

- Love is healing my pain.

Using these as models, you will be able to design PASes that work well for you.

Counteracting hypersensitivity to stress. The psychological objective is to calm your anger, tension, and fear. You need to reduce your physiological response to stressors: keep your breathing, heart rate, and muscle tension in a calm range. You need to be able to cue yourself at the earliest signs of stress to kick back and relax. Of course, SDB practice is an essential component of managing your stress response. In fact, your SDB key phrase is a PAS. Some suggested PASes for stress hypersensitivity are

- I am calm and relaxed.

- I float above stress.

- I will not fear; I will face my fear.

- I will let fear pass over me and through me.

- I am protected.

- I see beyond the stress.

- Stress is only temporary; I will prevail.

- I am free of the old me.

The main theme to explore is that you are tougher than the stress; you can outlast it, or as Arnold Schwarzenegger said in *The Terminator,* "I'll be back."

Counteracting impulsive gratification. The psychological objective is to persuade yourself that you can live better without self-inflicted pain or self-injurious pleasure seeking. You need to see that you can enjoy life without crutches. Some suggested PASes are

- I will not hurt myself.

- I will care for myself.

- I will keep my body and my mind healthy.
- I do not obey my impulses.
- I love my life.
- I am free of alcohol.
- I am free of drugs.
- Stop my impulses.
- Addiction is death.

How and When to Use Your PAS. Write one PAS from each of the borderline behavior patterns on a three-by-five-inch index card. Carry the card with you throughout your day. Read your card several times during the day, and repeat each PAS several times. Try to visualize what each PAS really means. Pair your reading of your PAS card with pleasant feelings. For example, read your cards after an enjoyable meal, after a good exercise workout, after an SDB session, or when you are outside on an absolutely beautiful day. Pair your PAS with as many positive life experiences as you can. Doing this builds stronger recovery momentum. By the same token, avoid reading them when your mood is negative (that is, until you have fully memorized and absorbed them in which case you can use them to turn your mood around). Reviewing all of your PASes just prior to going to sleep can also be helpful. Here is a sample PAS index card:

PAS Reminder Card

Relationship control phobia:	I can trust without fear; I can love without envy.
Hypersensitivity to stress:	I float above stress.
Distorted self-image:	I am real; I love my life.
Impulsive gratification:	I do not obey my impulses.

Make Your Own Ad. Create a PAS advertisement for your most meaningful positive affirmation slogans. Post the ads in places where you will see them frequently. Copy key PASes on self-sticking notepaper and post them in places where you will find them. For example, place them on the bottom of your sock drawer, in your car, on the refrigerator—anywhere you will "discover" them. Think creatively about how you can surprise yourself with PASes you want to make a part of your personality.

The more you repeat and interact with your PASes, the more effective they will be. Gradually, your PASes will push aside the negative affirmations you learned as a child. As they fade away, it will become easier for you to enjoy healthy relationships, think of yourself as a stable and good person, and manage stress without feeling emotionally overwhelmed. You can accomplish all of this, but it will take energy, focus, and time. What is the alternative? Remaining trapped in the Borderline Zone.

Controlling the Decisions That Shape My Life

Why Is It Important?

Control (that is, true control) over your decisions is the next skill. Most of us think we are in control of our actions and lives. Few of us think of ourselves as being "out of control" even when we really are. My definition of being in control of your life is this:

> You are in control of your life to the extent that you can create a lifestyle for yourself that you feel pretty good about most of the time, which allows you to accomplish meaningful things that do no harm to others and do not put your life or health in danger without a meaningful reason for doing so.

To what extent does your current lifestyle meet the requirements of this definition?

As long as you operate in the Borderline Zone, you endanger your life, you have difficulty finding meaningful activities for work and play, and you do not feel even pretty good about your lifestyle. Getting out of the Zone means understanding how you got there. Once you've done that, you can learn to soothe yourself, to feed your head with Positive Affirmations, and to take control by making good decisions about what to do and what not to do. Making good decisions means understanding, *before* you act, the possible consequences (good and bad) of each of your choices and knowing when the timing is right to make a decision and when it is right to defer making any decision at all. This is a skill that takes considerable practice and experience to learn. Actually, it is a skill that, if you are tuned into the need to do so, you'll learn to do better and better over the course of your life. Your early psychotraumatic experiences blocked the normal development of this skill. It is now time to put your learning curve on the right track.

You use decisions to build your lifestyle in the same way a mason uses bricks to build a house. A solid lifestyle rests on a foundation of solid decisions. Decisions select your environments. They give you access to situations that, in turn, influence your behavior. Bad decisions can haunt you, and good decisions can delight you. Some decisions can affect your life for years to come (who to marry, what career to enter, whether to use addictive activities), some decisions have immediate effects that are good and delayed effects that are bad (for example, drug use), and some decision are made in a split second but can have lasting consequences (for example, cutting yourself or running a red light). Any way you look at it, the decisions you make control your life. If you do not know how to make good decisions, then you life is not yours to control.

How Long Will It Take to Learn?

Learning how to better control your life is a lifelong project. It will take you a couple of weeks to learn the decision-making steps outlined here. It will takes months of practice to see improved results.

How Is It Done?

Once you become aware that you need to make a decision about something, you should follow as many of these steps as possible. The more important the decision, the more time and effort you should put into making it. Remember, a good decision is one that is not impulsive or emotional. Follow these decision-making steps:

1. Be aware of and, if necessary, calm all of your emotions and needs (use SDB). Don't jump from the frying pan into the fire. Objectify the situation.

2. Find out how much time you really have to make your decision.

3. Identify all of your choices; even the ones that are not immediately obvious.

4. Think through the consequences, both good and bad and immediate and delayed, for each of your choices. Write them down, so you can think them through more clearly. The following table can be photocopied for this purpose:

	Good Results	Bad Results
I M M E D I A T E		
D E L A Y E D		

5. Never make any decision while you are intoxicated, feeling ill, or are emotionally upset. Defer making the decision if any of these things are affecting you.

6. Be prepared to accept full responsibility for your decision and its consequences (remember the Existential Paradox). Do not make a decision for which you cannot accept the full responsibility for all of its results—good and bad, immediate and delayed.

7. Rank your choices from most to least favorable.

8. Determine for each choice whether the consequences you expect will have a net positive, negative, or neutral effect on you and your lifestyle.

9. Ask yourself if you are depending on someone to bail you out if you make a choice that will hurt you in the long run. In other words, are you depending on an enabler to help you choose what is bad for you?

10. Decide on your best choice (most benefits, fewest costs, no danger to you, and no enabler to bail you out).

11. Determine the actions (an action plan) you need to take to implement your decision.

12. Are you capable of implementing those actions at the level of effort and for the duration required?

13. Determine if the timing is right to implement your decision and its action plan. In order to delay the timing of your decision, you must learn to tolerate the uncertainty associated with waiting to execute a decision. Uncertainty creates stress, but it does not need to be viewed as "bad stress." It can be visualized as a combination of anticipation and wisdom.

14. Once the timing is right, implement your decision and stay on track with its action plan.

15. Evaluate the actual results of your decision against the results you expected. Are you pleased with the actual results? If you are not, make some adjustments in your action plan or reevaluate your decision. Even well-thought-out decisions will go wrong at times.

This is quite a list of steps, isn't it? As I said, the control skill is pretty complex, and it will take time to master. Remember your decisions select the environments that influence your behavior. The environments that you expose yourself to exert strong control over what you do and feel. If you expose yourself to a party where drugs are being used, you are much more likely to use drugs. If you go to visit your mother and get into a fight, you are more likely to want to hurt yourself. Decisions filter and organize your lifestyle. This is why it is so important to learn how to make good decisions. Try practicing with the following two examples.

Going to See Mom. A woman in her twenties, we'll call her Sally, lives in the BZ. She grew up in a psychotraumatic family environment (Level IV on the PTES). Her mother was self-centered and fixated on all of her own medical problems. Sally's worst behaviors included a bad temper, getting drunk and sleeping with any guy who wanted her, and occasionally cutting herself. She couldn't hold a job. She had little desire to go to school. Sally wasn't living at home. She was seeing a therapist. Periodically, Sally decided to go home and visit her mom. Inevitably, they would fight with each other and Sally would storm out of the house, get drunk or high, and sleep with a guy. Sally couldn't seem to get control of herself.

How can you apply the decision-making steps to Sally's situation? The numbers here refer to the corresponding decision-making step.

1. The first step asks Sally to figure out what feelings and needs she is experiencing. The need she wasn't in touch with was her need for her mother to be a different kind of mom, one who could give her what she needed. Sally's feelings included sadness, emptiness, and anger.

2. Sally always believed that she had to see her mother. Actually, there wasn't any rush to make that decision.

3. Sally's choices were to see her mother, talk to her on the phone, write her a letter, or have no contact with her. Sally never took the time to consider all of her options.

4. Sally didn't consider the consequences of her different choices. When Sally visited her mother, they almost always got into a fight. Rarely did they enjoy their visits together. Sally wanted her mother to express love and caring toward her. She wanted her to admit to the hurt she caused Sally. She wanted her mother to drop all of her defenses and open up to her. This wasn't likely to happen, but Sally held on to the fantasy that it would happen.

5. Sally did not see that she was very emotional about her mother. Simply talking about her would often get her angry or tearful. Sally often made her decision to visit her mother when she was feeling down.

6. Sally always blamed her mother for the bad visits. It was never Sally's fault even though she would provoke her mother. Sally was blinded by all the anger and resentment she felt toward her mother. This set Sally up for a fight with her mother.

7. If Sally ranked her options she would have found that her preferred option was to go see her mother, followed by calling her, writing her, and having no contact.

8. If Sally now assessed the net effect each option would have on her, she would have discovered that writing to her mother would be the least negative option. It would also allow her to approach her mother in a safe way about what she really wanted from her.

9. Sally depended on her therapist to absorb all of the anger and hurt she felt after one of these visits.

10. Had she followed these steps she would have found that the best options would have been writing or calling. The worst was visiting.

11. Sally never had an action plan for her visits with her mom. She did have a fantasy plan that never came about and always led to frustration.

12. Sally never assessed her ability to engage her mother in a meaningful dialogue. She expected her mother to be able to read her mind and initiate the process.

13–15. Timing was never considered. Sally based the timing of her visits on her emotional state. Sally always evaluated the visits in the same way: "Mom is a bitch and it's her fault." Then she would feel guilty about fighting with her mom and about letting strangers take advantage of her. She had a hard time connecting the fact that she was using sex as a substitute for the love she wanted from her mom. Sally also failed to realize that she used these sexual episodes to punish her mom by making her worry about Sally's safety. The coded message Sally sent her mom was: "Mom, you don't care about what happens to me!"

Getting High on a Dime. Consider Tom, he's twenty-five years old and has had a drug problem for about ten years. He also experiences depression and anxiety spells. The psychotraumatic level of his family environment was Level III. His drug of choice is pot and he has smoked it every day for the last couple of years. His mother tended to enable his drug use by providing him with financial support despite the fact that he failed to stay clean after over a dozen treatment attempts and despite his lies and stealing. He has been in numerous treatment centers and is now in another. He has not been able to hold a steady job or complete any college or vocational training. He also was arrested and placed on probation for drug possession. He has been drug-free for about four months (a record for him). He went on a few home visits and was able to stay clean, but he was starting to experience desires to get high. He kept this information from his therapist, and told him instead that everything was fine. The next time Tom went home, he got high for several consecutive days and did not want to return to the treatment center. Eventually, he did return after he had time to consider his options.

Tom made three decisions: lie to his therapist, get high, and return to treatment. Tom didn't follow the decision steps very closely. Had he done so he would have realized that the real value of his decision to lie to his therapist was a net negative value for him. Yes, he enjoyed his high, but later he felt like he threw away four months of being clean, put his probation in jeopardy, and he felt that he betrayed the trust his therapist placed in him to make good decisions.

Tom's major decision-making errors were

- He was not fully in touch with his need to get high (he thought he could control it). He didn't trust his therapist enough to be truthful.

- He did not figure out all of his options (he could have told his therapist, but he didn't trust him enough).

- He took advantage of his mother who enabled him (she wanted him to come on home visits).

- He did not evaluate the consequences (both immediate and delayed, good and bad) of each of his options. Getting high relaxed Tom (immediate and good consequences), but it has kept him from working and going to school and has gotten him in trouble with the law (delayed and bad consequences).

Tom was able to think through his options more in accordance with the decision-making steps after his drug binge. He chose to return to treatment instead of continuing to get high (Tom used the option of returning to treatment as an enabler).

Apply the remaining steps of the decision process to Tom's situation. What other observations can you make?

The most important step in the decision-making process is step 1. Do you know what you are feeling and what your needs are before you go further into the process? Most people trapped in the BZ have a great deal of difficulty with this step. This is why mastering the Soothing skills is so important. They will help you to feel comfortable with finding out what you are feeling and needing. Learn it, do it!

Reinforcing My New Skills

Why Is It Important?

Reinforcement of your new skills is essential. You can reinforce your new skills by monitoring your use of them and the kind of results they are producing for you, and, most important, by praising yourself for using them. All behavior is developed and maintained by the type and quantity of positive reinforcement it produces. Cut off all reinforcement, and the behaviors connected to it will start to fade away. Add back the reinforcement and the behaviors will start to return. If your boss told you that he really appreciated your work but from now on no one was going to be paid anymore, would you continue to work at that job? All behavior needs reinforcement, the tricky part is finding out what types of reinforcers the new behavior (such as one of the SACRED skills) is likely to produce. Once you know this, you can help the reinforcement process along by seeking out those reinforcers. Artificial reinforcers (reinforcers that are not directly produced by the behaviors themselves) can also help to strengthen new behavior.

How Long Will It Take to Learn?

Reading this section a few times should give the necessary understanding of what positive and negative reinforcement is. The basic tracking system can be implemented in a week. Getting comfortable with reinforcing yourself in a healthy way could take months, maybe longer.

How Is It Done?

All of us have a commonsense understanding of reinforcers and the effect they have on our behavior. In everyday talk we call reinforcers *rewards, incentives, paychecks, prizes, commendations, accomplishments,* and many other things. In chapter 6 I talked about how drugs, sex, alcohol, and other distractions can be very powerful positive reinforcers. I also mentioned potential negative reinforcers such as cutting one's body and reckless driving.

The difference between positive and negative reinforcers is the same as the difference between adding something and taking it away. A behavior that produces a positive reinforcer gets something for you (something you want or need). An example of a positive reinforcer is food or praise. A behavior that produces a negative reinforcer removes something from you (something that feels bad or dangerous). An example of a negative reinforcer is being caught in traffic (the negative) and then finding a way out of the traffic (the reinforcer) or hearing an annoyingly loud noise (the negative) and then finding a way to stop it (the reinforcer).

Cutting is a negative reinforcer because it usually takes away the mental agony that its user is feeling. Sex is a positive reinforcer because it gives its user a feeling of being desired and orgasmic pleasure. In the case of dangerous sex (prostitution, unprotected sex with a stranger, sadomasochism), a combination of positive and negative reinforcers is at work. Different combinations of being desired, feeling pain, escaping from danger, receiving money, getting relief from mental agony, and having orgasms reinforce these sexual behaviors.

Addictive behaviors always produce a combination of positive and negative reinforcers. It is this combination effect that creates an addiction.

Now how can you put this bit of knowledge to use in strengthening your SACRED skills? First, you can track the reinforcers these skills will produce for you, and, second, you can set up behavior contracts with yourself to artificially reinforce skill practice with healthy positive reinforcers.

Tracking the Results. Tracking the results of your new skills is a simple task. You can use the Natural Reinforcer Chart on the next page to keep track of each time you observe one of the natural reinforcers associated with the SACRED skills. As you practice each skill, you will notice changes in how you feel and in what you are able to do. It is important that you pay careful attention to these changes. The Natural Reinforcer chart will help you to do this in a systematic fashion. It is a good idea to photocopy this chart ten times so you can keep a daily record for ten weeks. Start your tracking the week you first began to use each skill.

How to use the chart. Place a check in the "Day of the Week" column if you observe the listed natural reinforcer for the skill you are practicing. Of course, if you don't use the skill, you will not be observing the reinforcer. In the "Date First Seen" column, simply record the date you first observed the occurrence of the reinforcer. By keeping this record you will be able to chart your progress. As you identify each reinforcer, use Visualization to see yourself employing the skill and producing more of the same results. The more you sensitize your mind to these reinforcers, the stronger your skills will become. Your results will increase weekly, perhaps, by going from one or two observed reinforcers in the first two weeks to four or five by week four. By week ten you should see at least one result on a daily basis (that is, seven per week).

It is important that you remain patient and persistent. Everyone's rate of progress is different. One thing that is the same for everyone is that the initial rate of progress is slow. But with persistence and determination your rate of progress will gradually increase. Do not become discouraged. All good things take time to develop. You will prevail!

Behavior Contracting. Behavior contracting can increase your rate of progress. A behavior contract creates an artificial connection between a healthy pleasure (a positive reinforcer) and a target behaviors (skill) you want to do more often. When done properly this connection will strengthen your desire to use the target behavior.

Setting up a behavior contract. Begin by selecting the positive reinforcers you would like to use to strengthen your target behaviors. Select something that you enjoy, is neither harmful nor unhealthy, you can control your access to, and you can afford. For example, you might choose going out to a favorite restaurant, buying a new pair of jeans, getting a CD of a favorite group, or taking a day trip. Once you have selected a

Natural Reinforcer Chart

Skill	Natural Reinforcer	Date First Seen	S	M	T	W	T	F	S
Slow Deep Breathing	I felt inner calm and peace today.								
	I felt relief from mental agony today.								
	I was less angry today than yesterday.								
	I used SDB to reduce my stress level before it went above 4 today.								
Objectifying	I was able to figure out what was triggering my thoughts and feelings today.								
Visualizing	I was able to use my imagination to act according to my plans today.								
Positive Affirmations	I experienced positive thoughts popping into my mind today.								
	I used affirmations before I got too stressed today.								
Control Decisions	I stopped myself from acting impulsively today with decision making.								
	I was able to think of all of my options before taking actions today.								
All Skills Working Together	I did not use any drugs today.								
	I did not drink more than two alcoholic drinks today.								
	I did not have any alcoholic drinks today.								
	I did not cut or hurt my body today.								
	I did not abuse myself in any other way today.								

positive reinforcer, set a goal that you want to accomplish before you reward yourself with your reinforcer. Here are a few suggested goals:

- Doing SDB _____ days in a row

- Going without drinking an alcoholic beverage _____ days in a row

- Using objectifying _____ times this week

- Going without cutting myself _____ days in a row

- Visualizing and implementing _____ actions plans

- Creating _____ new PASes

- Using my PASes _____ times per day for _____ days in a row

- Using SDB and PASes to stop myself from overreacting to a stressful event _____ times in _____ weeks

- Writing _____ new pages in my journal and rereading them at least _____ times

- Using Objectifying to manage a stressful situation without reacting impulsively _____ times in _____ days

You can create a number of similar goals of your own. Your goal should mention a specific skill that you wish to target and how often you want to do it before rewarding yourself. You can also set a time limit for when you hope to accomplish the goal.

Once you have selected your reward and your goal, your final step is to write up your contract. You can use the following form to do that.

The start date is the date you propose to begin your contract. The renewal date is the date you will tear up your contract and revise it if you have not reached your goal. Enter your goal in the "My goal is" box. Enter your reward or rewards in the next box. In the last box, you can sign your contract. Finally, if you think it will help, you can enlist someone (perhaps a close friend or mentor) to witness your contract. A sample contract is on page 126.

When you meet your goal, schedule your reward celebration and enjoy it. Do not fall into the trap of thinking that you do not deserve your reward once you have met your goal. Also, be sure to avoid the opposite trap: cheating by enjoying the reward without achieving the goal. If you find yourself doing either of these two things, you will know that you are not being honest with yourself or with your recovery. If this occurs, you might try rereading the opening chapters of this book, or you might wish to contact me for some advice.

I suggest that you start using behavior contracting after you have been practicing SDB for at least two to four weeks. At that point you

---

SACRED Behavior Contract

Start Date: _____   Renewal Date: _____

My goal is: _____

_____

_____

_____

When I meet my goal, I will celebrate by rewarding myself with _____

_____

_____

_____

I promise not to enjoy the reward until I have met my goal.

Signed: _____

Witnessed: _____

---

should continue to use behavior contracting for at least ten weeks. If you find it helpful, continue using it beyond the ten-week mark. You can use behavior contracting to create excitement and interest that turbocharge the pace of your recovery.

Establishing Equality of Myself and Others

"We hold these truths to be self-evident, that all men are created equal, that they are endowed by their Creator with certain unalienable

Sample SACRED Behavior Contract

Start Date: _June 11, 1997_   Renewal Date: _July 11, 1997_

My goal is to _use SDB and positive affirmation to stop myself from_
overreacting to a stressful event five times in three weeks.

_____

_____

When I meet my goal, I will celebrate by rewarding myself with _____
dinner out with Tom at Margo's Fish House on a Friday night.

_____

_____

I promise not to enjoy the reward until I have met my goal.

Signed: _____

Witnessed: _____

Rights, that among them are Life, Liberty and the pursuit of Happiness
. . ." The forefathers of the United States wrote this in the Declaration of
Independence. They used these powerful words to start a revolution in
1776 that, more than two hundred years later, is still changing the face
of our planet. Are you ready to revolutionize how you measure your
own self-worth?

Why Is It Important?
Your past might make you feel inferior to other people. Your past
might also make you feel a false sense of superiority to others. You
are neither better nor worse than others. You are anyone's equal, as we
all are.

How Long Will It Take?

It will take many months, if not several years, for you to work out more self-esteem and a more positive self-image. Every skill and understanding this book has to offer is geared toward this goal.

How Is It Done?

There are two Equality skills: *Nurturing* yourself and *Asserting* yourself when necessary.

Nurturing. Nurturing yourself means taking good care of your physical and psychological well-being. It means eating properly; getting a proper amount of sleep; exercising; managing your finances so you can meet all of your expenses without undue distress; finding productive, challenging, and satisfying work to do; giving up addictive activities; protecting yourself from situations that in the past caused you harm; and avoiding the kinds of people who you allowed to hurt yourself in the past. Nurturing yourself also means taking care of yourself as a good parent takes care of his or her child. It means doing for you many of the good parenting things that were not done for you as a child. It means caring for your "inner child" as well as your "outer adult." Nurturing yourself means allowing yourself to feel good in healthy, not addictive, ways.

The next step is for you to develop a long-term plan that describes how you would like to Nurture yourself better. The plan need not be implemented right away. In fact, I suggest that you develop it, keep it at your bedside, and read it just before you go to sleep each night. Read it nightly until you can recall having a dream about some aspect of your plan. When you start to dream about your plan, that's your signal to implement it. However, if after two or three weeks of presleep reading you find that you cannot recall having any dreams about your plan, you should revise your plan until you do have a dream about it.

Once you have started to implement your Nurturing plan do so in a leisurely fashion. There is no time limit; this isn't a race. Don't criticize yourself because you can't get yourself to do some part of the plan. Do the easy parts first and the more challenging parts will become easier. You can use the Nurturing Chart on the following page to organize your plan. There is also a sample plan for you to examine.

Using the form. First, evaluate your needs according to the Nurturing areas listed on the left side of the form. Describe in "The Problem" column each problem that you would like to address. Then under the "Challenge Level" rank your nurturing problems from most challenging (1) to least challenging (10). If you find that several of your nurturing problems seem to be too challenging, then you can identify a few easier problems to tackle. This will make it easier for you to successfully Nurture yourself.

Next, you need to write clearly defined goals that can help you decide how much progress you are making in Nurturing yourself. They

The Nurturing Chart

Nurturing Area	The Problem	Challenge Level	My Goal	Progress Rating
Eating				
Sleeping				
Exercise				
Stress management				
Finances				
Negative situations or people				
People I've hurt or who have hurt me				
Addictions				

should be as clear as the goals you are using in your Behavior Contract (see page 125), but they do not need time limits.

Finally, rate your progress toward Nurturing yourself on a scale of 1 to 7, where a 7 indicates daily progress that pleases you, and 1 indicates minimal progress. Update your progress ratings on a weekly basis. Modify your goals once you have either achieved a goal or found that you cannot

Sample Nurturing Chart

Nurturing Area	The Problem	Challenge Level	My Goal	Progress Rating
Eating	*I'm eating too much and I weigh 20 pounds more than I want.*	4	*I'll eat more fruit and less junk food.*	
Sleeping				
Exercise	*I get out of breath when I run even short distances.*	6	*I will jog three times per week for 30 minutes.*	
Stress management	*I'm always over-reacting to my friend.*	5	*I will practice SDB and Visualize calming myself down.*	
Finances	*I can't pay my rent because I spend too much on partying.*	3	*I want to pay my rent with my first pay-check of the month.*	
Negative situations or people				
People I've hurt or who have hurt me	*I always fight with my father.*	2	*I want him to understand why I am angry with him. I will write him a letter.*	
Addictions	*I party too much and I'm tired, short-tempered and don't have enough money for what I need.*	1	*I will stop going to bars to drink.*	

accomplish it. In the latter case, you should make the goal less challenging or switch to another nurturing area you feel more positive about.

In this Sample Nurturing Chart, addiction was rated 1, the most challenging problem, and exercise was rated 6, the least challenging problem. It is best to begin Nurturing yourself by starting to do enjoyable exercise like, in this example, jogging. It is important to enjoy nurturing yourself. So, don't start with the most challenging problem; start with the easiest. And find creative ways to enjoy what you are doing. It is something you are doing for yourself. It is a cause for celebration and joy. You not denying yourself something; instead, you are giving yourself greater physical and psychological health.

Don't become frustrated if you forget all about your Nurturing plan for a while. You will come back to it again. It is not about being perfect; it's about being persistent. It's about coming back to it and, eventually, making it happen. "I want it; do it!"

Asserting. The second Equality skill is Asserting yourself when necessary. This means expressing your feelings (first to yourself and then, when appropriate, to others). It also means standing up for your rights when they are violated by others.

Asserting yourself falls in between being passive and being aggressive. When you are passive, you allow people to take advantage of you, and you end up feeling weak and ashamed. When you are aggressive, you intimidate others into doing what you want, but you tend to make enemies. When you are Assertive, you get your needs met and your feelings understood without shame and without making unnecessary enemies.

Body language is an important part of expressing yourself in an assertive fashion: good eye contact, strong gestures, balanced positioning, and steady breathing communicates strong intentions.

Two Assertiveness skills that come in handy when you are trying to say "No" to someone are Fogging and the Broken Record Technique. An Assertiveness skill you can use to express your needs is the Three-Part Statement.

Fogging. This technique is used when someone is making a request or demand that you do not want to go along with. A lot of people have a difficult time saying "No" to others. Some feel that they have to please people; for others, it is a matter of guilt and low self-esteem. They feel as if they don't have the right to say "No." Fogging makes it easier to do that. Let's say that someone wants you to pick them up after work, and you do not want to do this. But this person is very pushy and keeps asking. Using Fogging you might say, "I understand your need and I certainly would like to help. But I know that my afternoon will be very busy and I won't be in your area. I'm sure you understand that I can't do this." Fogging buries your "No" in a polite and long-winded explanation of how you would like to help but because of this and that you just can't. Fogging provides a polite but clear "No." I'm sure you can

Self-Help Skill: Fogging

The Fogging Formula

1. Explain how you really would like to help out or how you understand the other person's need.

2. Explain in a detailed fashion why you cannot do what the person wants you to do.

3. Close with a polite and clear refusal of the person's request/demand.

Practice Exercise

Write out Fogging statements for these demands:

- A friend wants you to get high with them and you don't.

- Your neighbor wants to borrow $20 and you can't afford to do that.

- Your father wants you to visit him, but you don't want to do so.

---

understand why fogging is so named; it delivers your "No" in a foggy mist of polite-sounding words.

Broken Record Technique. As its name suggests, the Broken Record Technique is the repetition of the same statement refusing a person's request or demand again and again and again until the person accepts your "No." It is very effective and simple to learn. You create one or two sentences to refuse the person's request; for example, you could repeat the sentence, "I'm really busy this weekend and I can't see you." Continue until the person accepts your "No." The strength of this technique is that, because you know what you are going to say, you can stop listening to all of the arguments and persuasion tactics the other person is using to

---

Self-Help Skill: Broken Record Technique

The Broken Record Formula

1. Create one or two sentences that clearly but politely refuse the other person's request or demand.

2. Stop listening to what the other person is saying. Hum to yourself or think of something else.

3. When the other person stops talking that is your cue to repeat your Broken Record statement word for word. Do not reply to any argument or persuasion the other person comes up with. Just stick to your Broken Record statement.

bend you in his or her direction. All you have to do is hum to yourself. As soon as the other person stops talking, just say your Broken Record statement. Keep it up until the other person gets the message.

If you are trying to stop drinking and you are out with a friend who keeps asking you to drink, you could say, "I'm not into drinking today." Repeat this as many times as your friend asks you to drink. Just say the exact same thing over and over again. Eventually, your friend will get the message. The magic of this technique is in the repetition. Do not argue. Do not explain yourself. Do not justify or excuse yourself. Just state the facts, again and again and again and again and again! It works like a charm.

The Three-Part Statement. You can use this technique to explain how you're feeling to another person in order to get the person to change his or her behavior toward you. It is harder to learn than the other two Assertiveness skills because it involves identifying how you feel (something everyone has a tough time doing). However, once you're able to do that, the rest is very straightforward.

The Three-Part Statement is better than arguing with someone. It is better than verbally attacking someone. It is better than saying nothing and feeling bad inside. The Three-Part Statement focuses on the other person's behavior, not on the person. Instead of saying, "You make me angry," you would say, "When you turn away from me while I am talking, I feel angry." The difference in meaning and effect between these two phrases is enormous! The Three-Part Statement tries to minimize hurting the other person's ego while still getting the point across. You want your message to get through. You don't want your message to trigger an angry exchange of harsh words that accomplishes nothing.

Try this technique out and see how it works for you. Expressing your feelings helps you to feel lighter and more in control of your life. It is very important that you reduce the bottled up feelings that you carry. As you read and work through this book, you are slowly releasing all the hurt feelings of your past, so it is imperative that you do not add any present hurts to replace your old ones. Your goal is to slowly release bottled up feelings while learning how to assert yourself when necessary.

Determination That I Will Never Give Up

Why Is It Important?

Winston Churchill, the prime minister of Great Britain during World War II, was one of the most determined people ever to live. Despite suffering from severe depression and excessive drinking, he was able to lead his nation at a time when it looked as if the "forces of evil," led by Adolf Hitler, were going to conquer his country. In a speech at the Harrow School on October 29, 1941, one of the darkest times during the war, Churchill said, ". . . this is the lesson: never give in, never give in, never,

Self-Help Skill: Three-Part Statement

The Three-Part Formula:
The Behavior + My Feelings + Action Request

1. Identify the behavior(s) of the other person that is the direct trigger for your feelings. Identify how the other person is making your feel. Do not say, "You made me feel this way." Say instead, "Your behavior made me feel this way." Behavior can be changed, but no one can change who they are.

2. Identify what you would like the other person to do differently so you will feel better.

3. Tell the person this directly and without anger or aggressiveness. Use good eye contact and strong posture.

4. If the other person tries to argue with you, repeat your Three-Part Statement and refocus the discussion on the person's behavior.

Here are a few sample Three-Part Statements:

- When you drink and we fight with each other (behavior), I feel very scared inside (my feelings). Could you seek help to stop drinking (action request)?

- When you use a sarcastic tone of voice with me (behavior), I feel like you are putting me down and then I feel angry (my feelings). Could you avoid using sarcasm when we talk (action request)?

- When you criticize me in front of my friends (behavior), I feel embarrassed (my feelings). Could you speak to me in private when giving me criticism (action request)?

---

never, never, never—in nothing great or small, large or petty—never give in except to convictions of honour and good sense."

How Long Will It Take to Learn?

Determination is more an attitude than a skill. It needs constant cultivation. Determination is built on our inborn instinct for survival; the survival instinct is at its core. If you consistently cultivate an attitude of determination, the results that you achieve will amply reinforce your efforts. Hope feeds determination. Determination and hope working together produce success, which is what your recovery is all about.

How Is It Done?

Determination is essential to successful recovery. In many respects you have already demonstrated a great deal of determination. You have survived the psychotraumatic events of your childhood. Even though your current lifestyle is painful, you are reading this book. These are signs of true determination. These are signs of someone who will never give up. To help you cultivate your attitude of determination, I have assembled some inspirational quotations and stories from a wide variety of sources. By reading and thinking about determination, hope, and success you will feed your own sense of them.

I suggest that you read all of these quotations and check off those that have special appeal for you. Meditate on those and try to incorporate their meaning into some of your own journal entries and daily experiences. Enjoy yourself!

Quotations about Determination, Hope, and Success

Failure is the opportunity to begin again, more intelligently.—Henry Ford

Do not be afraid of going slowly, be afraid of standing still.—Chinese proverb

I recommend you to take care of the minutes, for the hours will take care of themselves.—Lord Chesterfield

Failing doesn't make you a failure. Giving up, accepting your failure, refusing to try again, does!—Richard Exley

When the world says give up, Hope whispers, Try it one more time.—H. Jackson Brown, Jr.

It takes courage to live—courage and strength and hope and humor: And courage and strength and hope and humor have to be bought and paid for with pain and work and progress and tears.—Jerome P. Fleishman

You cannot escape the responsibility of tomorrow by evading it today.—Abraham Lincoln

Keep your face to the sunshine and you cannot see the shadows.—Helen Keller

Do what you can, with what you have, wherever you are.—Theodore Roosevelt

It's not over 'til it's over.—Yogi Berra

Only those who will risk going too far can possibly find out how far one can go.—T. S. Eliot

Things turn out best for people who make the best of the way things turn out.—Anonymous

By all means, don't say, "If I can;" say, "I will."—Abraham Lincoln

Remember, no one can make you feel inferior without your consent.—Eleanor Roosevelt

The key to everything is patience. You get the chicken by hatching the egg ... not by smashing it.—Arnold Glasow

When one door of happiness closes, another opens; but often we look so long at the closed door that we do not see the one that has been opened for us.
—Helen Keller

Even if you're on the right track, you'll get run over if you just sit there.
—Will Rogers

"One of these days is none of these days."—English proverb

Dost thou love life? Then do not squander time, for that is the stuff life is made of.—Benjamin Franklin

Experience is the name everyone gives to their mistakes.—Oscar Wilde

Unhappiness is in not knowing what we want and killing ourselves to get it.
—Don Herold

A crisis is composed of danger and opportunity.—Unknown

Success consists of a series of little daily efforts.
—Mamie McCullough

Success seems to be connected with action. Successful people keep moving. They make mistakes, but they don't quit.—Conrad Hilton

One of the greatest discoveries a man makes, one of his great surprises, is to find he can do what he was afraid he couldn't do.—Henry Ford

Nothing in the world can take the place of persistence. Talent will not, nothing is more common than unsuccessful men with talent. Genius will not; unrewarded genius is almost a proverb. Education will not; the world is full of educated derelicts. Persistence and determination alone are omnipotent.
—Calvin Coolidge

Knowing is not enough; we must apply. Willing is not enough; we must do.
—Goethe

The best way out of a difficult situation is through it!—Unknown

Select the inspirational quotations (or find some of your own) that appeal to you for use as one of your PASes or as the focal point of a Visualization. These quotations were taken from people who achieved great things by overcoming great obstacles. You have a great obstacle to overcome. It is an obstacle that is no less great than the obstacles the people quoted here had to overcome. So, as you overcome the obstacle of your psychotraumatic upbringing, you too will achieve a very great thing. And as Calvin Coolidge, president of the United States from 1923–29, said, "Persistence and determination alone are omnipotent."

Chapter Milestones

A tremendous amount of ground was covered in this chapter. As promised, it was a long one. I appreciate your persistence in getting through it and would love to hear your comments about this chapter. If you have any suggestions, especially on how it could be improved, you know how to contact me (see page 12).

1. No one can work on all of the skills covered in this chapter at the same time. This is a long journey. It begins with Soothing skills. You need to master SDB (slow deep breathing) first. Once you have done this you can master Objectifying, Visualizing, and using Positive Affirmation Slogans.

2. Once you have been using Soothing and Affirmation skills successfully for at least four to six weeks you can move into Controlling and decision making. During this phase of your recovery program, you need to use your Soothing and Affirmation skills to develop the correct mind-set for making better lifestyle decisions. During this period of time you can work on your Determination by thinking about the quotations in this chapter and trying to figure out how you can apply some of them to your lifestyle.

3. The final step is to begin to develop an inner sense of Equality. You can do this by nurturing yourself in important ways and by asserting yourself when necessary.

Positive Affirmation

The SACRED skills help me live outside the Borderline Zone.

Recovery Exercises

Recovery Exercise 7.1: Sacred Skill 1—Soothing

Objective

To focus attention on what you find soothing.

Background

The word *SACRED* is used on this book as an acronym for the words Soothing, Affirmation, Control, Reinforcement, Equality, and Determination—each an empowering skill to be employed for the benefit of oneself and others.

Exercises for learning about each of these skills are presented in the body of the chapter. Here, you will be asked to expand and amplify on your own personal meanings related to each of these terms.

Expanded Awareness

Too often, life in the Borderline Zone is filled with sad things, or things that can make you angry or otherwise upset. There are, however, other things that you may find soothing, relaxing, calming, and comforting. Focusing here only on socially appropriate ways of self-soothing, and not on inappropriate ways (such as those that involve the use of alcohol or other drugs), make a list of the things you personally find soothing.

Next to each item, explain how this activity has been soothing in the past, and how it can be used in socially appropriate ways in the future. In your essay, describe the ways that the good feelings obtained from such activities might be intensified.

Recovery Exercise 7.2: Sacred Skill 2—Affirmation

Objective
To draft one's own "declaration of independence."

Background
The Declaration of Independence is a document of pivotal importance in the history of the United States of America. It is a document in which the American colonists wrote out their thoughts about why they needed to be free from England. If you have reached this point in this book and have been diligently completing the exercises in sequence, you may be ready for a pivotal change in your own life—independence from the restraints of life in the Borderline Zone.

Expanded Awareness
Write out your own declaration of independence from life in the Borderline Zone. Declare about a dozen or so things or attitudes that you will be free of in the future. Think about how being free of these things or attitudes will change life for the better.

Recovery Exercise 7.3: Sacred Skill 3—Control

Objective
To revisit the issue of control and look at it in a new light.

Background

As noted in the last chapter, childhood events compel many people to feel as if they need to be controlling in their adult relationships. But are there any benefits to relinquishing control in adult relationships?

Expanded Awareness

Most of us are conditioned to believe that being in control is "good," while not being in control is "bad." For this reason, we strive to always be in control, if not controlling. However, sometimes it seems desirable to relinquish control to others. For example, if a patient is admitted to an inpatient program where everyone must follow the directions and orders of staff for the ultimate benefit of the patient, then it is good idea for the patient to relinquish control to the staff. Your task is to write an essay on any situations you can think of where it might be in your own self-interest to relinquish control to someone else.

Recovery Exercise 7.4: Sacred Skill 4—Reinforcement

Objective

To better acquaint yourself with the healthy kinds of things that you find rewarding.

Background

One form of reinforcement in the psychological sense has to do with things we find pleasurable or rewarding. In this exercise, you will be asked to make up your "Top 10" list of the ten most rewarding things you can think of.

Expanded Awareness

Beginning with 10 and working your way down to number 1, list your favorite ways of rewarding yourself. Limit yourself to only healthy rewards.

After making the list, write about ways you could use these favored activities as incentives for engaging in various types of socially appropriate behavior.

Recovery Exercise 7.5: Sacred Skill 5—Equality

Objective

To begin to think of yourself as no better or worse than other people in many key ways.

Background

All people, no matter who they are, come into the world and leave the world in very similar ways. People who are born into families of great wealth can find themselves in the depths of poverty and despair, and people who are born into poverty can find themselves with wealth and riches beyond their wildest dreams. In many cases, the only thing that can stop people from succeeding is themselves.

Expanded Awareness

Write a brief "newspaper" article entitled, "Similar Yet Unique." In that article, write about how you are similar to other people, as well as how you are unique. If you have had trouble believing that you are inwardly as good as other people, reflect on some of the conditions that may have led you to think that way. If you have had trouble believing that other people are as inwardly good as you, also reflect on some of the conditions that may have led you to think that way. Conclude your article with some inspirational thoughts regarding how you (and others like you) can break free of psychological and related obstacles that have kept you in the Borderline Zone.

Recovery Exercise 7.6: Sacred Skill 7—Determination

Objective

To fire up the determination to succeed, one step at a time.

Background

You are probably reading this book because you want a new, more adaptive, and more satisfying life for yourself. But how much do you *really* want it?

Expanded Awareness

Write a letter to yourself on the topic of "Yes, I Do Want It!" In it describe, in the most motivating terms possible, how and why it is important for you to trade in many of your dysfunctional ways of thinking, feeling, and behaving for new and more adaptive ways of thinking, feeling, and behaving. Be specific; be real, and let your true desire for change come through.

When you are satisfied with the letter, make three copies of it and mail each of the copies to yourself. Mail one copy each day for three consecutive days. Once you receive the copy of your letter, read it over and, if the spirit moves you, write and mail yourself a reply.

Recovery Exercise 7.7: The SACRED Self

Objective

To consider each of the six elements of the six SACRED skills in combination, and how developing them will lead to greater self-respect and a more fulfilling life.

Background

The word *sacred* is used with reference to things that are worthy of reverence or respect. Is it a term that you can apply to yourself?

Expanded Awareness

Write an essay entitled, "The SACRED Skills and the Sacred Self." In it describe how you will be using each of the SACRED skills to gain greater self-respect and a more fulfilling life. Describe how you are coming to see your inner self as a sacred reflection of who you really are.

Encouragement

These exercises require an awful lot of writing. Maybe you are thinking that this is too much to do. If this is the case, perhaps the following comments from Samuel will help you put the purpose for all of this soul-searching and writing into perspective:

I've always had the urges to better my life, but I never knew how to do so. While writing, I kept telling myself that the most important thing for me to do was to get in touch with those feelings that hurt the most. I would remind myself, "Don't get angry, feel the real feelings and deal with them in the right way, the way that will make me grow to be a good person, the opposite of how I was made to feel all my life." My writing has helped me in ways that I never imagined it could. It's a good thing—not an easy thing, just a good thing. I hope that as you are reading this you can say to yourself, "Yes, I do relate to this person, and, yes, I want to get and feel better." That's all my writing is for me, a passageway to feeling better and to living a healthy life. You, too, can think and act this way. Never give up!

> **Remember to write in your
> Recovery Journal today.**

8

Addictive Activities: At the Borderline between Pleasure and Pain

At a certain degree of lucid intoxication, lying late at night between two prostitutes and drained of all desire, hope ceases to be a torture, you see; the mind dominates the whole past, and the pain of living is over forever.

—Albert Camus, *The Fall*

Do you feel the way you hate
Do you hate the way you feel
Ever closest to the flame
Ever closer to the blade

—Bush, "The Greedy Fly"

An addictive activity is any reinforcer (positive or negative) that causes its user to lose control of the frequency of its use (that is, causes self-injury). To recap from earlier in this book, the definition of a positive reinforcer (for example, alcohol, gambling, sex, pot) is an activity or experience that produces pleasurable sensations. Negative reinforcers are more difficult to define. They affect your behavior by reducing the intensity of painful and/or fearful emotions, sensations, or experiences. Borderline behaviors that are strongly motivated by negative reinforcers include cutting, seeking out abuse, risking your life in trivial ways, and attempting suicide. Cutting reduces emotional pain and self-hate. Seeking out abuse often reduces guilt or self-hate. Risking your life in thrill-seeking activities reduces anxiety about the way your life is going. A decision to attempt suicide can promise an end to the pain of living.

Trapped

All of us want to feel good. We want to avoid people, places, and things that make us feel bad. We seek out people, places, and things that make us feel good. When the bad feelings in our lives come at us from our own minds, though, escape is difficult. We must either confront our feelings and work them out (which takes time and effort) or suppress them by turning to a "feel-good" thing (which is often a quick and easy, if temporary, way out of feeling rotten).

Now when you combine these two sources of motivation—seeking out pleasure and suppressing bad feelings—the stage is set for someone to become addicted.

In order for an activity to become an addiction it must produce both positive and negative reinforcement effects. For example, drinking produces a pleasant high (positive reinforcement). It also helps you to numb your negative emotions and be more sociable, but over time it creates withdrawal symptoms and lifestyle damage that make you feel worse. As a drinking habit progresses, further drinking is negatively reinforced by the prevention of withdrawal symptoms (negative reinforcement) and by reducing the anxiety (negative reinforcement) that comes from the knowledge that your drinking is damaging your lifestyle. If you are drunk, you won't feel withdrawal or anxiety. You will not care about how bad your life is getting until you sober up. And then you can get drunk again!

If you are a cutter, the act of cutting your body and bleeding reduces (negative reinforcement) your intense, and often wordless, emotional pain, but cutting often produces a narcotic-like high (positive reinforcement) as well.

Boozing, cutting, drugging, or sex can, thereby, create a vicious addictive cycle by combining both positive and negative reinforcement effects. You end up bouncing between the ecstasy and agony of your addictive activities as your lifestyle crumbles around you. Denial and minimization complete the picture. They help blind you to the damage you are doing to yourself and to your lifestyle. And so it goes, until you hit bottom, or you hit the end of it all.

Addiction was present in my life even before I picked up my first drink or drug. Both sets of parents had very addictive personalities and there wasn't a day that went by that my stepdad and mom did not drink. It's weird and upsetting that, when I was younger, I sat and watched my parents get drunk and hated everything about it. There were times when my brother, my sister, and I would literally beg my parents to stop. We would plead, "Please stop drinking, it's hurting you and making us fight!" The odd thing about it is that even after seeing what it did to my parents, I still got hooked. By age eleven, I had smoked my first joint and by age thirteen I was regularly getting drunk. My family life was so terrible that drugs and alcohol were my means of escape. Even knowing how bad the drugs and alcohol were for me, I still indulged to escape the mental agony that was bestowed upon me. By age fifteen I had already experimented with hallucinogens. At this time in my life my mother and stepfather were full-fledged alcoholics. My sister was a reclusive introvert. My brother and I were budding drug addicts and alcoholics. No wonder our family life was so fucked up. I think the saddest thing was that no one in my family was able to do a damn thing about it, even when they wanted to.

Self-Destroyer

Last year my stepfather died of a massive heart attack. This indeed hurt me very much, but on the other side of the fence I felt a sense of relief for him. Not to anyone's surprise, my stepfather had cirrhosis. Who really knew how long he had to live—a week, two months, ten years? I didn't know. My sense of relief came from the fact that he was no longer suffering. He wasn't a stupid man. He knew exactly what he was doing to himself. My stepfather had a death wish, and he got his wish. He had set his course, and there was nothing anyone could do. If there's one thing in my life now that is keeping me strong, it's the fact that I did make amends with him, and so did he with me. There was nothing one-sided about this, we both forgave each other for the past and moved on with life. As far as his drinking habits went, I was powerless and had no say, but the sadness that I felt for a long time seemed to fade away. The love I have for him never will. It is unconditional and forever.

My mother, on the other hand, has a trunkful of mixed-up emotions. She is so distraught and so hurt. She doesn't know what to do. She feels an overwhelming flow of guilt for leaving him. I really can't say I blame her for how she feels. The day she left him, he headed straight downhill. He was always on that downhill *slide, but never that bad. It was the best thing, though, that my mom could have done for herself. She had to escape the turmoil, or she would've gone down right along with him. As far as I can tell, my siblings are still caught up in the resentments they had for him and have not, and may never, touch, feel, or deal with their powerful emotions. For me this is sad, but it's also their choice. I've made many attempts to try and loosen their anger toward Pop. From what I gather, they just don't know how. It's not about not wanting to. They're both good people. It's just that their feelings of pain are woven deeply into their souls.*

Final outcomes can be scary. Few of us like to admit what addiction can do to us. And sometimes even when we know, like Samuel's stepfather knew, the hopelessness of our live renders that knowledge useless.

Self-Inflicted Violence

Some people find their addictions in activities that cause them more direct and immediate pain than a slow death from alcohol consumption. Self-inflicted violence can be found in some of the darker parts of the Borderline Zone. It is one of the major forms of pain addiction that psychotraumatized people use to manage their unmanageable feelings. This form of addiction was first introduced in chapter 6 under the topic of impulsive gratification. Only an "insider" could understand how such a painful activity could be sought out as a form of gratification. But, if the truths are told, cutting (or punching, burning, etc.) is a temporarily effective form of relief from the mental agony of life in the Borderline Zone. It can become as dangerous an obsession as crack, heroin, or alcohol. Self-inflicted violence endangers its users' lives, alienates them from loved ones, and ravages their lifestyles. A woman who cuts herself described her obsession as follows:

> Personally, I cut with a utility-knife blade, using Anbesol (toothache medicine that's 20 percent benzocaine in an alcohol base) for antiseptic and anesthesia. I start with a small cut, swab it with Anbesol, work the knife deeper, add more anesthetic, etc. I adopted this method because my primary purpose was bleeding, not pain.... I've lost as much as two-plus pints in a single session. During a two-week period in 1994, I lost a total of more than five pints.

This is a horrifying description for anyone other than those who have felt the acute mental agony of borderline living. The writer went on to say, "Why would any reasonable adult human being do these things? ... I seem a reasonable adult of well-above-average intelligence who's survived a great deal of *trauma* successfully."

A nineteen-year-old man from Australia wrote,

> Personally, I think cutting is a way of releasing emotions
> for people like me who have a lot of trouble crying and
> expressing emotional things like that. I personally find I'll
> cut if I'm feeling empty inside.... cutting is a simple way
> of feeling real and checking if you can still feel."

A young woman wrote this haunting passage as she struggled not to cut herself:

> Please stop following me. Hurt. Sad. Keep writing, scratch
> body. Cold blank. Why did it have to be this way? I would
> hide under my bed. Crash, crash, footsteps at the door;
> picture on the ground. Rocking, holding her, rocking. Keep
> writing ... I want him back. He used to always hit me in
> the head. Please I want to cut, cut, not cut, pain, hurt,
> blood, please. Tears bottled up inside. I can scream; yelling
> go away!

Pain that never goes away, emptiness and fear that even bleeding cannot drain, and an ever present sense of abnormality haunts the "pain user." Scarred bodies, hospital stays, involuntary hospital commitments, and brushes with death are the results the user achieves. The true problems, however, remain "safely" untouched.

The Common Addictive Link

All addictions, regardless of the subtype (pleasure and/or pain), share several common elements. Most fundamentally, they involve "dancing with death." They pleasure, terrify, hurt, thrill, and distract its users. They put the users on a "passive" road toward suicide. Users believe that if they overdose on their addiction, they will die, and all of their problems will die with them. This style of thinking relieves them of responsibility for their lives. *Subconsciously*, the users say to themselves, "I'm going to 'suicide' so what does it matter anyway? I can do anything I want to do." This belief gives users a false sense of absolute freedom from the control of others and from the control of society. It also enables them to hide an ugly truth from themselves: they do not control their lives; they are pathetic slaves to their addiction. If this sounds harsh, it is.

Addiction also allows users to punish those whom they feel wronged them. This is the most fundamental, often unconscious, motive of people caught in the BZ: Revenge! Revenge against those who hurt them. Revenge against their birth, and against their life. Revenge acted out by hurting themselves in order to hurt those who have hurt them.

Finally, all addictive activities temporarily relieve the users of their mental agony. Regardless of the form their mental agony takes—traumatic memories, depression, despair, anxiety, emptiness, loneliness, self-hatred, feelings of unreality, feeling overwhelmed, feeling numbed, reenacting the abuse of their childhood, intense anger, or a desperate need to take back control from "them"—their addictive activities produces relief, temporary relief from their very private forms of mental agony.

The bottom line: the borderline "drunk," the borderline "slut," the borderline "crackhead," and the borderline "cutter" share a common purpose: relief, revenge, and escape from mental agony.

Making a Choice

Giving up an addiction requires that *you* make a choice. It is a choice that involves more than just saying "no," but saying "no" is probably where you need to start. Remember the Existential Paradox: you are responsible for everything you say and do.

Addictive activities benefit users in the early stages by making them comfortably numb (a combination of positive and negative reinforcement effects) to their feelings. So, in order to make the choice to give up your addictive activities, you must give up the benefits you currently enjoy. You must also have a very clear picture of the benefits (a normal life, better health, more money, and so on) you will gain by giving up your addictive activities. These benefits include those that will come from no longer doing the addictive activities and those that will come from freeing you to pursue more productive and healthier activities.

Of course, the main reason for choosing to end your addictive activities is the negative impact it is having on your life. So you will need to list all of the negative consequences those activities are having on your mind, your body, your loved ones, and your lifestyle. The following chart will help you to summarize your reasons for thinking about stopping your addictive activities. After you've filled in the chart, under the section entitled "Negative Impacts on My Life," check off the *one* impact that is having the worst effect on you now.

Please complete this self-help chart before reading further. It may take a few minutes to complete, but doing so makes the remainder of the chapter more helpful. Objectify your use of addictive activities and write down what you observe.

Reflect upon your answers for a few minutes. After reading what you wrote, how do you feel about stopping your addictive activities? If you have decided that it is time to stop, will this be a difficult task? If you do not want to stop, are you willing to cut back on your addictive activities to reduce the harm they are having on your life? If you are not even willing to reduce your addictive activities, what or who do you think is preventing you from doing so? What or who is keeping your addictive activities appealing to you? Can you Objectify where your

Self-Help Skill:
Choosing to End My Addictive Activities

Benefits of Using _____ (addictive activity):

Negative Impacts on My Life:

Mind:

Body:

Loved Ones:

Lifestyle:

Benefits of Stopping:

---

addictive activities will take you? What is the endpoint of your addictive journey? Are you even willing to answer any of these questions?

Prochaska's *Recovery through Choice* Model

Seventy-five percent of ending an addictive activity is making up your mind to stop. This decision may be pushed on you by others (family, a judge, professionals), but regardless of how much other people pressure you, you must decide on your own, and for yourself, if you are going to stop.

The readiness to *begin* to think about stopping is the first step toward ending an addiction. A journey of a thousand miles always begins with a single step. A model for recovery through choice may help you think about your addictive activities in new and refreshing ways.

Dr. James Prochaska, a psychologist at the University of Rhode Island, has identified five stages that people who want to stop an addictive activity go through on their journey through the Recovery Zone (Prochaska et al. 1992). These stages are Precontemplation, Contemplation, Preparation, Action, and Maintenance. The most beautiful thing about Dr. Prochaska's model is that it allows for relapse and regression, and, in fact, views relapse as a natural and expected part of the recovery journey. Prochaska calls this the *spiral pattern of change.* People do not change in a straight-line fashion. They make some progress and then fall back. Sometimes they fall back to the beginning and sometimes they just fall a little bit. As time passes, they spiral forward in their journey toward more complete recovery.

As you read about each of these stages, try to figure out which stage you are in. What can you do to move yourself toward the next stage? How long do you think it might take for this to happen?

Typically, users will spend a considerable amount of time in stage 1, Precontemplation. It has been estimated that at any given time well over half of people with an addictive problem are in this stage. As long as a person is in this stage, treatment programs aimed at changing behavior will probably fail. People in this stage avoid being open with themselves or others about their problem. They also spend considerable amounts of energy hiding their addictive activities and arguing with others about their addictions. Loved ones tend to confront the users in this stage, and the users push them away, but some of this feedback does start to slip in.

During the Contemplation stage, what becomes helpful is getting information about the addictive activity, and the kinds of effects it can have on the user. It is also helpful to experience a bad consequence that is a direct result of an addictive activity episode *and* to talk about that experience in an open and expressive manner. In this stage, users are more open to reevaluating the effects their addictive activities are having on them, on their environment, and on the people they love. This evaluation process provides motivation to move toward the Preparation and Action stages.

Maintaining Support in All the Right Places

Progress during these first two stages (Precontemplation and Contemplation) is largely invisible to outsiders. Most of the progress takes place inside the user's head. Loved ones will hear a change in how you talk about your addictive activities, but they will have a hard

---

IMPACT!

Prochaska's Spiraling Steps of Change

1. *Precontemplation:* During this stage, people are unaware or only vaguely aware that they even have a problem. Others, however, see the problem and try to persuade them of their problem. If users seek help at this stage, they do so only under coercion. The likelihood of progress is low.

2. *Contemplation:* During this stage, users are aware of their problem and are seriously thinking about making a change. They know what they want to accomplish, but are not sure whether they are ready to take action yet. They often weigh the pros and cons of their addictive activities. They spend considerable thought on trying to decide whether what they are getting from their addiction and the effort it will take to give it up are worth what they will gain from being addiction-free. They are serious about doing something, but they are not ready to act.

3. *Preparation:* During this stage the user intends to take action in the next thirty days and may have already taken some small steps toward reducing their addictive activities (e.g., less drinking, more superficial cuts). They are not quite ready to take the plunge and end the addictive activities altogether. However, they are close to being ready to do so.

4. *Action:* During this stage, users have stopped or significantly reduced (by objective standards) their use of the addictive activities for one day to six months. They no longer drink; they no longer cut themselves; they no longer smoke crack. The most acceptable criterion is abstinence. However, for some addictive activities a large reduction, say 90 percent or higher, may qualify as an acceptable goal. The former users are expending a great deal of focused energy to make their effort succeed. In the action stage, the former users "walk their walk."

5. *Maintenance:* During this stage, former users are working hard to prevent relapses. To qualify for being for being in this stage, the former users must be free of the addictive activities for more than six consecutive months and must also be able to use coping behaviors to prevent relapses. During this period, the former users are actively repairing the lifestyle damage their addictive activities have caused. They are vigilant and prepared at all times. They realize just how easy it is to relapse if they allow themselves to take their success for granted. The maintenance stage lasts for an indefinite period of time— perhaps, even a lifetime.

time believing in your sincerity. They will recall how, in the past, you promised to change, but then only continued in your dysfunctional ways. This credibility gap between you and your loved ones will not be bridged by easy talk alone. Tough, no-nonsense action on your part will be required to convince them that this attempt is different. It is at this point, however, that a catch-22 arises. As I said earlier, overcoming addictive activities does *not* follow a straight-line path to success. Unfortunately, the odds say you will relapse. When you do, how will this affect your credibility with your loved ones? Will they relapse back into their old ways of perceiving you—as a liar, a manipulator, and a disappointment? And here is the core problem: Prochaska has found that users who successfully overcome an addictive activity do so because they, and at least one significant other (loved one), value the changes they are making. Without the dedicated support of loved ones, the transition to and through the Action and Maintenance stages will be extremely difficult.

How, then, do you maintain the support of loved ones even after you have relapsed? Here are five relapse-management rules to follow that will help prevent you from losing the support needed for your recovery efforts:

1. **Honesty.** Tell your supporters within twenty-four hours of a relapse that one occurred. The quicker you admit to what has happened, the more of your credibility you will preserve. Hiding the truth will destroy all of your credibility.

2. **Communication.** Give your supporters all the relapse details they ask for. Do not hold anything back. Be up-front, be truthful, be sincere. And most of all do not get angry when you talk to them. You made a mistake and you are ready to correct it. Do not get angry at yourself and then take it out on your supporters. This is a borderline behavior that you need to suppress. It will drive away those who you care about, and then you will be alone.

3. **Quick Recovery.** Figure out what went wrong. What caused your relapse? Overconfidence? Exposure to relapse triggers? Stress? Subconscious self-deception (talked yourself into relapsing)? Once you know how things went wrong, take steps to prevent a back-to-back (see number 5) relapse. Be sure that you tell your supporter what went wrong. Don't get angry, get well.

4. **Planning Ahead.** Avoid all possible triggers. Do not take any chances. Plan your daily schedule so that you are busy with productive or harmless activities. This way you will avoid going to places or seeing people you associate with previous addictive activity. Make a list of your triggers. It is also a good idea to follow any advice or help that your supporter has to offer. Find creative ways to avoid relapses.

5. **Self-Forgiveness.** The most critical rule for managing relapses is not to get so down on yourself that you say, "Fuck it!" and relapse again. You must avoid back-to-back relapses. A back-to-back relapse is a second relapse that occurs within seven days of the first one. If you allow your relapses to come back-to-back, their momentum will overrun you, and you will find yourself deep into your addictive activities once again.

If you allow yourself to follow these rules, you can maintain the support of those loved ones who sincerely desire to assist you. If you choose not to follow these rules, their support will most likely start to erode and eventually disappear.

The Choice to Stop or to Cut Back

Prochaska's model views relapse as a normal part of recovery and not as an all-or-nothing disaster. This may lead you to wonder, "What if I decide I do not want to totally stop my addictive activities?" This is a good question that does not have a simple answer.

Traditional approaches to addiction problems, especially for drug and alcohol use, have focused on total abstinence as the *only* appropriate method of treatment. Twelve-step programs such as Alcoholics Anonymous are entirely based upon this method. AA and its followers are totally committed to this method and do not accept the possibility that any other type of method could be effective. But other approaches have been suggested. Drs. Sobell and Sobell (1982) have proposed moderate drinking as a treatment method for alcoholics who are not physically dependent on alcohol and have not been drinking heavily for many years. When they first proposed this approach, they were severely, and unjustifiably, attacked by traditional-approach advocates. Today, research exists that supports the effectiveness of this approach.

Another approach, *harm reduction,* from the Netherlands, says that any movement toward better and more functional action or any reduction of harmful action is good even if it does not immediately eliminate the addictive activity. Someone who used to drink two six-packs of beer every day and reduced that to one six-pack per day is moving in the right direction. Of course, it would be better if it were only one beer per day. And, eventually, the person might not drink at all.

An AA member might say that one beer per day was just as bad as two six-packs because you are still boozing. However, if you can't completely stop drinking, it does make sense to cut back as much as possible.

The moderation and harm-reduction approaches do not apply to every type of addictive activity in equal measure. Moderating cocaine, heroin, or severe cutting habits are extremely difficult, and hard to justify. Harm-reduction methods could be applied to these addictive activities if the user was not ready to stop. For example, shared needles could be avoided, cocaine use could be limited to days off, and body cuts could be made more superficially. Harm reduction says that any movement toward reduced addictive activity is better than full-force activity.

The difference between harm reduction and moderation is in their final goals. Harm reduction seeks the ultimate elimination of the harmful activity while moderation seeks its permanent reduction to subharmful levels.

My purpose is to inform you of your options. You may be in a twelve-step program. You may have tried other approaches. The best approach is the one that you are ready to use. I encourage you to think about your addictive activities and their effects on your lifestyle, so you can decide what, if anything, you are prepared to do about them.

Where Are You Now?

At this point, it makes sense for you to place yourself in one of Prochaska's stages. Which stage do you fit into now, and which stage would you like to move into in the next thirty days?

Take one more look at how you have assessed yourself. Is your assessment as accurate as possible? Are you satisfied with it? If you are, you are ready to move on.

You will move through the Recovery Zone, to the threshold of the Free Zone, by overcoming your addictive activities. You cannot be free until you have accomplished this objective.

Self-Help Skill: Where Are You and Where Would You Like to Be?

Now	Next	Recovery Stage
☐	☐	**Precontemplation:** "I don't have a problem." Or, "I like my addictive activities."
☐	☐	**Contemplation:** "I don't like my addictive activities as much as I used to and maybe I need to do something about them."
☐	☐	**Preparation:** "It's time to start reducing my addictive activities."
☐	☐	**Action:** "I am eliminating my addictive activities or reducing them to harmless levels."
☐	☐	**Maintenance:** "I have stayed free of my addictive activities for more than six months."

Suggestions for Moving between Stages

From Precontemplation to Contemplation

If you are in the Precontemplation stage, you may have little interest in this part of the book. On the other hand, you may be hearing a lot of negative feedback from people you know. They may be telling you that you have a problem; and you may be telling them to go to hell. If you are beginning to think that there may be a problem, you can help focus your thinking by increasing the amount of information you have about your addictive activities. Of course, this may not be the term that you use. You may call them "vices," "good times," or your "secret." Perhaps you are finding that you are afraid that you can't pay the rent, or that you are HIV positive, or that you might cut a little too deep next time. Perhaps you are worried about the fact that you have to steal to pay for your habit. You might even owe your dealer some cash—maybe even too much cash. Perhaps you have noticed that your mood is getting worse. Maybe you can't hold down a job, or are often late for work. Maybe you are just starting to question whether your form of escape is worth what it is doing to you—and to those who still love you and haven't left you yet.

> Don't feel ashamed or embarrassed about your problems. It'll only stop you from getting better. Live up to it, deal with it, change it. It's right there in front of you; you just need to open your eyes and see it. That was probably the hardest part of my recovery— seeing that I needed to change. I needed to change the way I thought about things.

From Contemplation to Preparation

All good things, and bad things, must come to an end. If you are ready for a change, then it's time to think it through. The following Self-Help Skill contains questions that will help you do this.

These are tough questions to answer honestly. Once you have been able to answer them, you will know that you are in the Preparation stage. You can then begin to find little ways to reduce the harm your addictive activities are causing (and could cause) you.

Here are a few harm-reduction ideas for your consideration.

If you are a cutter

- Try scratching yourself instead of cutting and causing bleeding.

- Instead of cutting or scratching or punching yourself, use a red marker and "cut" with that; imagine that the red ink is blood.

- Try to feel the pain of your cutting; do not go into your usual trance. Tell yourself that it hurts!

Self-Help Skill:
Preparation—Am I Ready for a Change?

1. Why do I want to make a change?

2. Whom have I hurt in the past because of my addictive activities?

3. How have I hurt myself? What have I lost in people, opportunities, and possessions because of my addiction?

4. What things do I believe in? What values do I believe in? Whom do I trust and love?

5. How many close calls and brushes with death have I had because of my addictive activities?

6. How do I visualize a future where I am no longer using my addictive activities? How will I feel? What will I be doing for work? Where will I live?

7. What barriers separate me from where I want to go?

8. What will happen to me if I do not stop my addictive activities in the next six months? In the next year? Five years from now (how old will I be then)?

9. Who can I turn to for help? Why?

- Ask yourself if you would let someone else cut you.

- The next time you cut and bleed seek immediate medical attention—make what you are doing more real.

- Tell someone you trust that you are trying to stop. Seek out that person's help.

If your addictive activities involve alcohol and/or marijuana use

- Consider cutting back on certain days of the week, amount, where, and with whom you use these substances.

- Limit your drinking or smoking to Friday or Saturday.

- Do not drink and drive.

- Go from hard liquor to beer.

- Go from getting wasted to just having a few drinks.

- Go from daily pot-smoking to every other day and then once a week.

- Gradually reduce your use of these activities and/or reduce the harm potential of the circumstances in which you use them.

If your addictive activities include cocaine and/or heroin

- Improving your safety should be your first priority.

- Do not share needles.

- Do not go to dangerous neighborhoods to get what you think you still need.

- Put at least a few days between periods of use.

- Cut down on the amount you use per session.

- Tell someone you trust that you are trying to stop.

- Write and mail several letters to yourself telling yourself to stop now before it is too late.

If your addictive activity is sex

- Cut back on going where you go to find partners.

- Limit the number of different sexual partners to half as many per ninety-day period as before.

- Have as much sex as you desire, but with only one person—not several.

- Use protection (condoms) from sexually transmitted diseases such as herpes, HIV, and so on.

If your addictive activity is dangerous driving

- Go to a driver's education and safety course.

- Do not drive if you have lost your driver's license.

- Find out what your state's penalties are for driving without a license.

The preparation stage is a time when you begin to "put the brakes on" to slow your addictive activity level down. A traditional approach, such as a twelve-step program, does not allow for this type of preparation. However, as you will read, traditional support groups such as AA and NA can be helpful once you have entered the action stage.

By the end of the preparation stage you should be able to fully understand the following comments by Samuel:

> *When it came to my crack addiction, I had to completely change the way I thought. That's the biggest problem with addicts: their thought patterns. They think that getting high is okay, or that it'll help them deal with their problems. I know I was a crackhead and I remember what it was like. Part of me wishes that I didn't remember, but I know that it's good that I do, so I can learn from it. You need to dredge up those bad and painful feelings from the past and get in touch. Feel them, understand them, and know that*

*you can never go back. Brand this in your mind and never forget
this. This will be part of the solution needed to do this. The other
part is to follow through with your decision. No matter what,
stick to your guns.*

From Preparation to Action

Once in the Action stage you are ready to reduce your addictive
activities until they reach a zero or harmless level of use. Most addictive
activities require zero level use (abstinence) as a goal because of the motivational dynamics of even low levels of use. Strong drugs such as cocaine, heroin, and tranquilizers tend to motivate the user to higher and
higher levels of use. The need for higher doses (to get the same effect)
and the people and places that you need to encounter in order to get
the drugs are responsible for this effect. Addictive activities such as cutting also fit into this category: zero-level use is the only reasonable goal.

For some people, alcohol use may be reduced to harmless levels.
A harmless level is no more than two drinks in a twenty-four-hour period
and no more than three such twenty-four-hour periods per week. If you
can reach this goal and hold your drinking there without increasing its
frequency, then moderation is appropriate for you. If you cannot get
close to this goal, then zero-level use is probably going to be your preferred goal.

Moderation of sexual addiction is appropriate. The elimination of
the dangerous and excessive aspects of sexual activity should be your
goal. Sex with any willing stranger without protection and multiple partners each month can be considered a situation necessary for reduction
to zero-level use. For some people, a temporary period of zero-level use
may be required in order to gain control of their sexual activity.

In general, when in doubt, reduce your addictive activity to zero-
level use, then see how you feel and how your life changes.

Information Guide to Successful Action There are a number of
steps you can take to increase the odds that you will successfully reduce
or zero out your use of addictive activities. In this section I've included
information and techniques that can help.

Awareness of toxic and withdrawal effects. All addictive activities have
toxic effects from prolonged use; toxic effects include the physical, psychological, social, and legal consequences of an addictive activity. Some
addictive activities have *withdrawal effects* as well. The following table
summarizes some of the major toxic and withdrawal effects of the more
common addictive activities.

Which of the toxic effects in table 8.1 (page 158) are you experiencing? Write them down in your journal. Familiarize yourself with the toxic
effects of your addictive activities. Most users tend to minimize awareness

of the effects their activities are having on them. This reflects the state of denial that they are in. In the Action stage, denial is replaced by an awareness of the harm past addictive activities had on your person, loved ones, and lifestyle.

If you are coming off heavy alcohol use or heroin use, expect to experience strong withdrawal symptoms. It may be necessary for you to seek medical attention during this "detox" period. Most detox work can be done on an outpatient basis. You will also need reliable psychosocial support during this period. It is here that a close friend, loved one, or other supporter can be of great help to you. Your desire to use your addictive activity will be strong. If you do not have reliable sources of support, you should consider attending a self-help group such as AA, NA, or a mental health group. The yellow pages (look under the "Community Service Numbers" or the "Social and Human Services" sections) of your phone book or a call to your local mental health center or hospital will provide you with the number of a group you can call.

Proactive planning. Once you stop doing your addictive activities, you will need to reschedule the way you conduct your life. Large blocks of time will open up in your schedule. Where you once did your addictive activities, now there will be nothing. You need to reschedule this time with productive or interesting activities and with supportive people.

To accomplish this you will need an *Appointment Book* so that you can begin to proactively (that is, in advance) plan each day. You will also need to answer the following questions:

- What times of day and days of the week did you most often engage in your addictive activities?

- With whom did you engage in your addictive activities?

- Where in your home, at work, at school, in town, and so forth did you engage in your addictive activities?

- If your addictive activity required money, who or what were your sources of funds?

- Did your addictive activity required special equipment (pipe, spoon, knife, bong, and so on)? If so, gather all of this equipment that is in your possession and destroy it. Do not do this alone! Do this only with the help of a reliable, nonaddicted supporter or friend. If you attempt this on your own, exposure to the addictive equipment may trigger an overwhelming urge to use. Get help first.

- What are your weekly responsibilities (things that you must get done)? These might include going to work, doing your laundry, cleaning your house, writing out checks to pay the bills, going to school, doing the grocery shopping, and so forth. Make a

Table 8.1: Toxic and Withdrawal Effects

Substance/ Activity	Possible Toxic Effects	Possible Withdrawal Effects
Marijuana	Reduction in your ability to concentrate and remember things; paranoia; lack of motivation to achieve goals; daily use increases lung cancer risk	Increase in anxiety if you depend upon it for stress reduction; irritability and mild depression
Cocaine	Stealing to get the drug, which can lead to arrest and jail time; paranoia (peak and freak) and aggressiveness; overdose can produce heart attack, seizures, and death; irritated nasal passages; loss of self-respect; loss of loved ones; loss of employment and ability to be employed; financial ruin; nonexistent sex drive; emotional deadening; sleeplessness for days; easily exploited by others	Going through the "jones"; depression; intense cravings; anxiety; psychotic thoughts
Heroin	Reduced effectiveness of immune system; increased susceptibility to HIV/AIDS; stealing, arrest, and jail time; loss of ability to be employed; loss of loved ones and self-respect; overdose can produce convulsions, coma, and death; financial ruin; nonexistent sex drive; emotional deadening; easily exploited by others	Flu-like symptoms: watery eyes, runny nose, loss of appetite, tremors, panic feelings, chills, sweats, muscle cramps, elevated vital signs (blood pressure, pulse, tempera-ture, and respiration); strong urges to use; if untreated, seizures, death
Alcohol	Memory impairment; brain cell destruction; drunk-driving arrest, loss of license, and jail time; death in auto accident; vehicular manslaughter due to drunk driving; loss of employment; loss of loved ones and self-respect; financial problems; loss of sex drive; emotional deadening; aggressiveness	Heavy sweating, rapid pulse rate; hand tremors; insomnia; nausea and vomiting; visual, touch, or auditory hallucinations or illusions; anxiety and agitation; grand mal seizures and, if untreated, death
Ecstasy (MDMA)	Brain damage through nerve-ending degeneration and abnormal regrowth leading to mental impairments that may be irreversible; susceptibility to exploitation while high; wide variety of physical symptoms: paranoia, psychotic behavior, panic, depression, sleep problems and confusion	Possible mental haziness, confusion; largely unknown

Physical self-injury	Medical emergencies; physical disfiguration; scars; involuntary hospital confinement; suicide death	Strong urges to self-injure when stressed; panic feelings
Excessive sex	HIV/AIDS, other sexually transmitted diseases; rape, attack; loss of self-respect; exploitation by others	Strong urges to have sex; reduced sense of self-worth ("no one wants me"); more frequent masturbation
Fast, reckless driving	Auto accidents; injury or death; frequent traffic tickets, loss of driver's license; high insurance rates; loss of automobile transportation	Boredom while driving; strong urges to speed

complete list and, for each activity, estimate the amount of time it takes you to complete it.

Now that you have gathered all of this information you can begin to plan your days in three-day blocks of time as follows keep the following suggestions in mind.

- During at least the first four months after stopping your addictive activities, avoid meeting and interacting with people you did those activities with. Avoid going to those places where you did those activities. For example, if you drank and went to bars with Tom to do this, do not go to any bars even to drink a soda and do not call, see, or meet Tom for at least four months (and preferably much longer) from the day you stopped. If Tom calls you, tell him you have quit drinking and you are in recovery. Even if you consider Tom a friend, if he still drinks (or does coke, or makes you angry, or will sleep with you), avoid him completely. He will trigger your use of addictive activities. Be assured of that. For planning purposes, do not schedule yourself to be with anyone or at any place that falls into this category. A true friend is someone who does not enable you to participate in your addictive activities.

- Schedule in all of your responsibilities for the next three days. Include travel time to and from your activities. Schedule in work, chores, meals (including meal preparation), cleanup, sleep, and so forth. After you have done this, look over your schedule and identify those times where you have nothing scheduled. These are your high-risk times.

- Decide what activities you will schedule during those high-risk times. Where will you be, what will you be doing, and who will you be with? Create a list of healthy activities and healthy people. Select from this list to fill in your high-risk times.

- Each morning, review your schedule for the day. Make any changes required. Keep track of your schedule throughout the day. Check off scheduled items as you do them. Nightly, review your schedule for the next day. Every third night plan your schedule for the following three days.

- If unscheduled events come up, write them down on your schedule in red. If you engage in an addictive activity, write this in red and circle it. Follow the relapse-management rules from pages 150–151 to prevent back-to-back relapses.

- Use behavior contracting from chapter 7 to reward yourself for having X number of days free of any addictive activity.

If you find it difficult to use proactive planning *and* you find yourself engaging in addictive activity, then you are out of the Action stage and into a lower stage.

If you are using proactive planning but are still using addictive activities at a very reduced level, then you are spiraling between the Preparation and the Action stages.

If you are using proactive planning but your rate of addictive activity is not going down, then you are spiraling back to the Preparation stage.

If you have not even attempted to use proactive planning and are still using your addictive activities at a high level, you are probably still at the Precontemplation or Contemplation stage.

If you find yourself in a stage other than action, reread this chapter and seek out further information about your particular addictive activity.

Counterconditioning through imaginary exposure. An effective way for some people to confront their cravings for their addictive activity is through imaginary exposure to them. The people who can benefit from this are those who meet all of the following criteria:

- They have supporters
- They have been successful in reaching the action stage
- They have "stayed clean" (free of addictive activity) for at least ten weeks
- They have been practicing SDB from chapter 7

If you fall into this group please continue to read this section; otherwise, please skip ahead to the section on relapse management.

By practicing the following Self-Help Skill you can condition yourself to confront your urges with the reasons why you should not use. You can condition yourself to feel relaxed and calm in the face of urges.

This will strengthen your coping skills and help to minimize relapses. You should practice this once a day for twenty days. It is a good idea to use this skill with the help of a supporter who can be available in person or by phone while you are practicing. If, while practicing this, you feel such overwhelming urges to use that you believe you will do so, stop practicing this skill and contact your supporter immediately. If this happens more than four consecutive times or if you actually engage in your addictive activity, stop using this technique and consider joining an appropriate support group.

Self-Help Skill: Imaginary Exposure and Counterconditioning

1. On three-by-five-inch index cards write out how your addictive activities have harmed you or will harm you if you continue to use. Write out one reason on each card. Write out at least five cards.

2. In a quiet room free of distractions close your eyes and engage in SDB for five minutes.

3. After you feel calm, imagine that you are using your addictive activity. See yourself preparing and doing the activity. Continue to imagine this until your urges to do the activity intensify. When you feel them at a fairly strong level, open your eyes and read each index card to yourself until you feel your urges weakening. Keep rereading them until this happens. Repeat steps two and three again.

4. Finally, close your eyes again and do five minutes of SDB. Stop when you feel calm and free of any urges to use. Praise yourself. Use a PAS.

Relapse management. Most relapses begin inside your mind and can be predicted and prevented. The first principle to follow is that relapses are normal but preventable. The second principle is that you create almost all of your relapses through poor planning or self-deception.

You have already read about what you can do to keep your loved ones believing in you after a relapse (see page 150). If you value their assistance, these are important steps for you to follow.

Storyboard. Since most relapses start in your head, you need to learn how you mislead yourself into relapsing. One of the better ways of doing this is to write a *storyboard* that describes your next relapse. A storyboard is a series of drawings with captions that describes a sequence of actions. They are often used in the movie and TV industry. Draw, as best as you can, a sequence of events that leads up to you relapsing. Use stick figures if necessary. In each panel of the storyboard, write in an appropriate caption that describes what is happening. An eight-panel storyboard might look like one of those on the following two pages.

Once you have designed your storyboard (you can photocopy and use the blank storyboard on page 165), think about how you could intervene with yourself to abort the relapse. Where could you do something different, perhaps something suggested in this book, to stop yourself from using your addictive activities? Circle the panel where you could make a change and write in an alternative caption. Then redesign your storyboard to show a different outcome: an aborted relapse. This exercise should be repeated a couple of times, each with a different relapse storyboard. Doing this exercise will help you to uncover the ways in which you might try to deceive yourself into relapsing. It also will help you to recognize triggering events quickly enough to do something about them.

If people cause most of their own relapses, then the more you learn about how you persuade, manipulate, and deceive yourself into using, the more protected you will be against relapses.

Another relapse-management tool is SDB (see chapter 7). Managing the stress of everyday life without the "aid" of your addictive activities will require that you find replacement. SDB can help you to calm yourself as you find other ways of coping with stress. If you have given yourself the opportunity to develop your SDB skills, then you already know how helpful SDB can be. If you haven't yet given yourself this opportunity, then this is an excellent time to start using SDB.

Mentally managing relapse urges can be done in three related ways.

1. Dispute the expected benefits you receive from your addictive activity. As soon as you feel an urge to use your addictive activity, you need to turn on your self-protection machine and challenge the urge. Questions to ask yourself include

- How will I feel later if I give in now?

- What could happen to me, as far as negative consequences go, if I give in?

- How am I trying to sell myself to the urge?

- What bad things happened to me so far because of this addictive activity?

2. Distract your thinking with something totally unrelated to the urges. Once you have started to successfully dispute the urge, you can try to distract your thinking with something irrelevant. For example, count down from one hundred by threes; plan a really exciting vacation somewhere; go out and take a brisk walk; write a poem; call a supporter for help; think about your favorite movie star or hero. Imagine that you have been elected the president of the United States, what laws would you like to see passed? Now is the time to create a *Distractions List* that

Relapse Storyboard: Drug Use

Sitting home alone and feeling nervous and bored

Started to think about getting high

Called up Pete, who always has pot

Argued with myself about getting stoned

Left my house to go to Pete's

Pete hooked me up with a joint

We smoked it and I got high

When I came down, I felt lousy about relapsing

Relapse Storyboard: Cutting

My thoughts are racing and I feel horrible.

I cannot stand the way I feel.

I start to think about cutting myself. I know that works for me.

I don't want to cut. It makes me feel so abnormal.

I see something I can use to cut myself.

I feel better—the blood, the pain that is going away . . .

What have I done to myself? Oh no.

I'm trapped in something I can't stop.

My Relapse-Management Storyboard

you can carry with you and pull out in times of need. It is easy to do and a lot of fun. Be creative and enjoy yourself.

3. Reframe your ability to tolerate the urges. The final step is to reframe your ability to tolerate your urges. Instead of saying things like, "I can't stand it. They are too strong for me. This feels unbearable! I just have to give in!", you can place the urges in a completely different framework: Urges mean that you are in the Recovery Zone! They are proof positive of your commitment to take strong action on your own behalf to enjoy a better life. They reflect how strong a person you really are. They are not temptations. They are signs of courage and inner strength. Experiencing urges means that you are getting better! Convince yourself of this in your own words. In so doing you will greatly increase you ability to tolerate your urges.

Self-reinforcement (behavior contracts). This is something I described in chapter 7. It is also useful during this period of your recovery. I suggest that you set up a behavior contract to get the Action stage off to a good start. Appropriate goals for your behavior contract would include

- No drinking alcohol for ten consecutive days
- No cutting or any other type of physical injury for fourteen days
- No more than one drink in any forty-eight-hour period for three weeks
- No speeding tickets for ninety days
- No more than one sex partner in ninety days

Select your rewards and ask your supporter co-sign the contract. Once you have consistently met your goals for ninety days, you can try dispensing with the behavior contracts. If you falter, you can start using them again.

Medications might help. There are some medications available by prescription that may be of help to you in controlling your urges. For alcohol and opiate (for example, heroin) cravings there is Revia (naltrexone). To deter you from drinking alcohol there is Antabuse. Antabuse will make you ill if you drink while taking this drug. For sleep problems there are Ambien, trazadone, or, over the counter, melatonin. For depression that occurs after you fully stop using addictive activities, there are a variety of antidepressant medications (see chapter 10 for more information).

Support groups. Support groups such as Alcoholics Anonymous (AA) for alcohol and drug abuse, Narcotics Anonymous (NA) for drug abuse, Rational Recovery (RR) for alcohol and drug abuse, Gamblers Anonymous (GA) for gambling, Overeaters Anonymous (OA) for eating disorders, and similar groups can be helpful sources of social support for staying away from your addictive activities. Your local crisis intervention hotline can be a source of support during times of acute emotional distress. You can find support-group numbers in the Community Services section or the yellow or white pages of the phone book. You can find more information on support groups in chapter 10.

AA follows a strict, twelve-step approach that requires its members to adhere to zero-level use (abstinence). Traditional AA groups also require surrender to a "higher power" as the way the user admits to his or her utter helplessness in the face of addiction. AA does not support a harm-reduction approach to overcoming addictive activities. If you are a drug or alcohol user and you intend to set abstinence as your goal, AA or NA can be very helpful to you. Drop in on a meeting in your area to check it out. You can find the location of the nearest meeting by looking up AA or NA in your city's phone book.

If your addictive activities involve cutting or sex, you will need to call your local mental health association for the names of support groups in your area.

If your addictive activity is reckless driving, you can contact your local motor vehicle department for the locations of driver improvement courses.

Support groups cannot do the hard work for you, but they can provide you with the fellowship and emotional reinforcement to successfully remain in the Recovery Zone.

Final Stop: Maintenance

After you have been free of your addictive activity for *at least six months,* you have made it to the maintenance stage and to the border of the Free Zone.

During this stage you will experience strong feelings of emptiness and loneliness as you approach the Free Zone. This is your last test of determination to succeed. Once you have reduced or eliminated your addictive activities you may feel exposed, naked, and alone. You will have a great deal of free time on your hands. The time you formerly spent on your addictive activity—planning, acquiring, using, and recovering from it—will now need to be filled with lifestyle-enhancing activities. More importantly, your former source of stress reduction will no longer be available to you. As if this was not stressful enough, you may also start to experience strong flashbacks of psychotraumatic memories accompanied by feelings of profound loneliness and pain. Memories that you previously buried with addictive action will be fully experienced and you will feel alone. Many people falsely perceive the reemergence of their emotions and memories as addictive cravings. They are not cravings. They are your emotions. They feel strange because you buried them for a long time with addictive activities. Now that they are free to be felt, you are scared and want to run back to you-know-what. Feeling your emotions again could be viewed as a scary thing that must be avoided. It could also be viewed as the last hurdle you need to jump before you are free of your painful past. Which viewpoint appeals to you today?

> # Remember to write in your
> # Recovery Journal today.

The seven chapters that preceded this one did so because of this very reason: It is essential that the origins of borderline behavior be understood and that the work of confronting the pain of the past starts before you reach this point in your journey (the border of the Free Zone). Your journal writing is the key to this process and you should be doing it on a near-daily basis by now. Your journal and your mastery of the SACRED skills will empower you to make it through the loneliness and emptiness that exists between addiction and freedom. Keep your supporters close to you and your mind focused on where you want to go.

Right now things are pretty good in my life. I even pretty much quit smoking cigarettes. I've stopped virtually all drug intake. I only have a social drink. For me this is a great, yet extremely difficult, accomplishment. I've always been the person at the party looking for the next party. It never seemed to be enough for me. I always needed more. Don't get me wrong, I still feel this way at times but I've learned to control my urges. The single most difficult thing for me was to learn how to say no. No, I don't need to get fucked up and no, I'm not going to miss anything if I don't go out tonight. I always thought that if I didn't go out I would miss everything, well that's not true. What I was really saying was that if I don't go out I might feel lonely and insecure. I have always been afraid to be alone. That also was part of what I had to get over—being alone. I'm now okay with it. I can be at home and not think that I'm missing everything and feel insecure about it. I've learned to do other things with my time. I've learned to read a good book, watch some TV, and write my story.

It was hard to do this at first. I had to give up 95 percent of my peer group. In the beginning this immediately brought up feelings of loneliness. It was very weird for me. I thought that since I was doing something good for myself it would be easy. Well that ain't true, my friend. It was the hardest thing that I have ever encountered.

Almost a year and a half later it has gotten much easier for me. I don't get the overpowering urges to go out and party. I don't automatically feel lonely when I sit at home alone. I can say to myself that things are good and I'm a good person who deserves the best for himself. All of these things have allowed me to get this far, and there isn't anything that is going to stop me now.

Reinforcement, equality, and determination are your SACRED keys to making sure that nothing stops you.

Lifestyle Repair Work

Addictive activities, as you now know, damage and eventually destroy a user's lifestyle. Once you have overcome all of the issues you have read about, you will be positioned to start working on the task of repairing your lifestyle. A list of areas of possible damage follows on the next page, accompanied by a few suggestions on how to get the repair work started. In your Recovery Journal, write down the areas you need to repair and the specific actions you would like to take to do so. This section supplements the Equality skills from chapter 7 (see Nurturing section).

Chapter Milestones

1. Addictive activities are part of the way psychotraumatized people cope with life in the Borderline Zone. The specific addictive activity of choice is largely irrelevant. What is relevant is your readiness to do something about our own addictive choices.

2. The decision to quit an addictive activity may be pushed upon you by others, but no matter how much other people pressure you, the only way you'll stop is if the decision is your own.

3. You will pass through many stages in the Recovery Zone on your way to the Free Zone. Sometimes you may have to take a step back in order to move forward.

4. Above all else, when it comes to addiction, it is truly all in your head. It is your pain, your triggers, your choices. The keys to success are to choose with awareness, to choose wisely, and to choose decisively. And never, never, never give up!

Positive Affirmation

My recovery is a spiraling, step-by-step journey of choices that lead to freedom.

Self-Help Skill: Lifestyle Repair Checklist

Check	Area	Suggestions
	Finances	If you're in debt and you cannot meet your payments, you should consider consulting with a credit counseling service such as Credit Counseling Centers of America, Inc. at (800) 761-0061 for assistance on managing your bills. Put yourself on a budget.
	Driver's license	If you have lost your license or are near to doing so, find out whether you can take a driver's reeducation course. Many states offer these courses, and they can help you get a small discount on your insurance.
	Physical Health	Get a complete physical from a trusted physician. Find out whether your addictive activities have damaged your health. Don't stick your head in the sand on this one.
	Friends	Find new friends who can support your addiction-free lifestyle. Say goodbye to your "addictive friends."
	Loved ones who stood by you	Let them know that you love them and appreciate their support. It is very tough for a loved one to watch you hurt yourself. It is harder still to believe in your ultimate potential to get better even though all the signs look gloomy.
	Career	Reassess your career if you have one. Is this the career for you? Remember, you chose your line of work while you were still in the Borderline Zone. Now is a good time to reevaluate. If you don't have a career, it may be wise to seek out a career counselor for aptitude and interest testing to help guide your choices.
	School	Get as much education as you can. There is a wonderful world out there.

Recovery Exercises

Recovery Exercise 8.1: Freedom Bound

Objective

To foster thinking and new insights related to addiction, self-control, and personal freedom.

Background

Addiction involves a loss of control. Paradoxically, most people, in the course of a discussion about the subject, verbalize powerful sentiments against letting anyone or anything control them.

Expanded Awareness

Write an essay entitled, "Addiction, Self-Control, and Personal Freedom." In it, reflect on your own personal feelings about being controlled by anyone or anything. Try to distinguish between things you have done (in regard to your addiction) that have been outside of your control versus things that were a matter of personal choice.

Conclude your essay with thoughts about how self-control, especially with regard to your addictive activities, will ultimately lead to greater personal freedom.

Recovery Exercise 8.2: This Message Will Self-Destruct

Objective

To reflect on the meaning of suicidal and other varieties of self-injurious activities.

Background

Most people want to live their lives to the fullest. They seek out other people with whom they can relate in a meaningful and uniquely human way. They seek out activities that entertain, enrich, or otherwise reward. They have a general desire to eat nutritious food, exercise, and take care of themselves, even if they do not always do so. Most people hope to keep themselves healthy and active for as long as possible.

There are other people who exhibit behavior that stands in marked contrast to such life-affirming behaviors. They seem not to care very much about living a healthy and active life. In fact, at times they seem intent on self-destruction. They may gravitate to people capable of inflicting harm on them. They may involve themselves in activities and situations at which life and limb are placed at great risk. They may neglect themselves in many ways, including neglect in the areas of nutrition, exercise, and medical care. They may even intentionally hurt themselves on their own or by provoking others.

Often underlying such behavior is the hidden assumption that the worst that can happen is death. And death is not seen as such a horrible outcome, because it is viewed as bringing freedom with it. In reality, however, no one can say with certainty that death does, in fact, bring freedom. Perhaps the only thing we can say with certainty about what death brings is an end to living. And an end to living does not have the look of freedom.

Expanded Awareness

What kinds of self-destructive behaviors have you engaged in in the past? What is the "message" that comes to your mind to prompt such behaviors?

What kinds of things do you think in order to give yourself permission to engage in self-destructive behavior? What does your self-destructive behavior communicate to others about who you are?

In what less destructive ways might you be able to send the same or a similar message to others? What other, more constructive messages need to be sent to other people about who you are? What messages will help you to reverse your course toward a healthier life?

Recovery Exercise 8.3: Say It Isn't So

Objective

To consider the role of denial in addiction.

Background

When is being addicted not really being addicted? When addicts believe that they can stop their addictive activities whenever they really want to stop.

Expanded Awareness

In what ways would you describe yourself as an addict or as addicted?

In the past, how have you used denial to delude yourself or others? What benefits, if any, have you derived from denial of the true state of affairs?

What benefits, if any, might you derive from honest confrontation with your denied addiction?

Recovery Exercise 8.4: Sorting It Out

Objective

To reflect on the feelings and emotions that may be contributing to your addictive activities.

Background

The desire to seek out pleasurable feelings while suppressing the painful feelings is key to addiction. For many people, however, the pleasurable and painful feelings are hopelessly jumbled together. In such cases, sorting out feelings can be an important step in the recovery process.

Expanded Awareness

Divide a page into two columns, one labeled "Pleasurable Feelings" and the other labeled "Painful Feelings." Try to list a dozen or so types of feelings in each column.

Write an essay about which of your two lists holds greater power over your actions. Is it pleasure or is it pain? How can you begin to free yourself of their power? Do you want to take control?

Recovery Exercise 8.5: Moving Forward with a Look Backward

Objective

To consider how thinking about recovery as a five-stage process can help your recovery.

Background:

As discussed in this chapter, James Prochaska conceives of recovery as occurring in the following fives stages:

1. Precontemplation

2. Contemplation

3. Preparation

4. Action

5. Maintenance

Prochaska's model allows for relapse, and anticipates that most, if not all, people in recovery will occasionally fall back in their progress.

Expanded Awareness

Think about your own journey through the Recovery Zone. What obstacles are there to moving through these five steps? What kinds of circumstances do you anticipate might prompt a relapse?

Write your own behavioral prescription for a custom-designed, tailor-made "relapse inoculation" program; that is, a program that will help prevent relapses. In writing this program, feel free to use your own responses to other exercises in this chapter, including your Relapse-Management Storyboard.

Recovery Exercise 8.6: Top Ten Rules

Objective

To "know the rules" you must live by in order to achieve recovery and avoid relapse.

Background

This chapter contains a wealth of suggestions useful in recovery, and in developing an addiction-free lifestyle.

Expanded Awareness

After reviewing this chapter, write an essay entitled "The Top Ten Rules for My Recovery." Your essay should list and discuss ten rules in increasing order of importance. Rule 1 must be absolutely critical to the success of your recovery. The rules should be your own and you may include rules from any source you select.

Recovery Exercise 8.7: Feeling the Rules

Objective

To understand and appreciate the difference between "knowing the rules" and "feeling the rules."

Background

Reading about all of the rules and suggestions presented in this chapter will do little for your recovery if you do not feel, that is, *own*, the rules by making them your rules. People with a drinking addiction may be helped by rules such as, "No more than one drink in any forty-eight-hour period for three weeks"—but only if that rule makes sense to them both at an intellectual and emotional level.

Expanded Awareness

Critically examine the list of rules that you prepared in the previous exercise.

Then, write an essay entitled, "Feeling the Rules." In your essay, analyze each rule both from an intellectual level and an emotional level. Try to uncover your gut reaction to each of your ten rules.

Can you follow your rules with more success than failure? How will you make that happen? Are you willing to do anything it takes to live a healthier life?

9

Finding Support in the Recovery Zone

*No one can become fully aware of the very essence
of another human being unless he loves him. By the
spiritual act of love he is enabled to see the essential
traits and features in the beloved person; and even
more, he sees that which is potential in him, that which
is not yet actualized but yet ought to be actualized.
Furthermore, by his love, the loving person enables
the beloved person to actualize these potentialities.*

—Dr. Viktor Frankl, *Man's Search
for Meaning*

Help me. Teach me. Discipline me. Hold me. Love me. Support is an
essential part of life. I depend upon a support system of people who
help keep my life on track. So do you, and the other billions of us on
our planet. With the right kind of support, people can do wondrous
things. Daily evidence of this fact can be found all around. It is on TV,
in the street, at work, in school, in the papers and magazines, and even
on the Internet. Really, great and wondrous things do happen to real
people just like you! One way you can stay on track as you journey
through the Recovery Zone is to find a *supporter*, someone to watch over
you. Someone who is ready, willing, and able to help you. There are two
types of supporters you could find: *Mentors* and *Cheerleaders*.

Finding a Mentor

The road that leads out of the Borderline Zone and into the Recovery Zone is a rocky one at best. One way to make your task easier is to win the support of someone you think you can trust. This person could be a Mentor to you. A Mentor is someone who likes you and wants to get to know the *real* you. A Mentor is also interested in helping you make the kind of behavioral change you want. In other words, a Mentor is willing to get to know you as you *really* are and to help you to get where you would like to go. This can be a very cool thing.

Of course, if you decide that you do want a Mentor, you'll have to find one. Following these seven steps can help you do this:

1. A Mentor can be a family member, a friend, a co-worker, someone you met at a self-help group, someone from your church or temple, or a spouse. The first thing to do if you want to find someone to be your Mentor is to make a list of everyone that you know.

2. Once you have made your list, go through it name by name and cross out those who you cannot even imagine trusting with your real emotions.

3. Place a check mark next to the names of the people who have a strong character and an attitude of determination and optimism.

4. Put an X next to the names of those whom you admire in some way.

5. Circle any name on your list that is not crossed out, and has a check mark and an X next to it. Of these people, put a star next to the ones who you believe are strong enough to handle the intensity of your emotions; these are the people you can consider as a Mentor.

6. Ask each potential Mentor if he or she would be interested in helping you. Asking for help will require a major emotional commitment on your part. You will have to be prepared to explain your problem (you can use this book to do that), share your emotions, explain your objectives, and warn your potential Mentor of how difficult it will be, at times, for him or her to handle your emotions. You will also have to be prepared for rejection if the person declines to help you. If you feel that you cannot handle this kind of rejection, then you should hold off on seeking out a Mentor.

7. Once you are certain that you want to proceed, ask the people who are interested in helping you to read this chapter, as well as chapter 1. Once they have read it, engage each person in a discussion of his or her impressions of the chapters. If the discussion goes well and you have a positive gut feeling about the person,

ask why he or she would like to be your Mentor. If the answer seems sincere and straightforward, take a week to decide on whether you want that person as your Mentor. Use your Relaxation, Objectifying, and Visualization skills to imagine whether this person will be helpful to your cause. If you can visualize a successful relationship, then ask that person to be your Mentor.

How Your Mentor Can Help

You and your Mentor should work through the chapters of this book together. You should discuss the chapters and the feelings they stir up in you. You should review your journal writings and do some of the Recovery Exercises together. You and your Mentor should learn how best to apply the suggestions and exercises of this book to your daily life. Your Mentor can help you put into practice a plan that helps you to cut back, and then eliminate, addictive behaviors. He or she can also help you to practice SDB and the other SACRED skills. Your Mentor is your recovery partner who can help you stay focused and motivated as well as help you to confront your psychotraumatic feelings and memories.

The act of accepting help from a Mentor helps you to build your capacity to trust others. It brings you into closer contact with all of the reasons why you find it so difficult to trust another person. It helps you to see how quickly you tend to blame others for your "bad luck." It also helps you to realize how you go about pushing others away from you as you desperately try to hold on to them at the same time. The contradictions inherent in borderline behavior become crystal clear to you within the give and take of a Mentor relationship. However, these contradictions, and the powerful emotions they evoke, can also destroy the Mentor relationship if you allow them to do so. If you want your relationship to last, then you have to work to keep it going. You have to reinforce your Mentor's commitment to the relationship. You have to learn how to control your anger and impulses to lash out at others, or risk losing your Mentor. You have to learn how to give something to the relationship as well as taking what you need from it. And, most of all, you need to open your heart, with all of its pain and shame, to being cared for and loved by another. All of these demands may stress you out, but this type of stress can help you to heal your angry heart.

Advice to Mentors

Helping someone with borderline and addictive problems is a wonderful and overwhelming task. It will put your capacity to be fully human and compassionate through a stress test that very few experiences can match. It will pull out of you every fault, hidden pain, weakness, and vanity that you have carefully concealed from others and even those you have concealed from yourself. It will assault your emotions, arouse your anger, and break your patience. One Mentor wrote of the struggle into the Recovery Zone: "I tried. And I tried. And I tried. The more I tried, the more it hurt. The more his actions hurt me. His resentments. His anger. His lies. His manipulations. His failure to stay on a healthy course for more than even two weeks at a time."

People with BPD believe that they are bad. They do not know how to care about themselves. They reject being treated well by another person because they are ashamed of feeling good (it doesn't fit in with their childhood self-image of badness). So they will fight, manipulate, and test you until they break you or you accept them. But they will also secretly, at first, then more openly later on, appreciate what you are trying to do for them. The key for success is to help them to set very modest goals; to see beyond their anger to the hurt they feel inside; and to see beyond their deficiencies to the wonderful potential their borderline behavior is holding back. It is also very necessary that you set strict limits for yourself: you can help them but you cannot take responsibility for their actions. They, and only they, are responsible for what they do. Sometimes you need to allow them to fail so they can experience the consequences of their dysfunctional behavior. Just be there for them when they are ready to understand why things turned out so badly.

Helping people with borderline behavior is a thankless task at first, but if you believe in what you are doing, it will slowly, very slowly, bear fruit. And as you watch them grow out of their pain and self-destructive behavior patterns, you will come to know that you have made a difference in their life and in your own.

Choosing a Cheerleader

If you are not ready for a Mentor, or if you cannot locate one, you may be interested in finding people who can cheer you on your way through the Recovery Zone. Cheerleaders support your healthy behavior; they do not support your dysfunctional actions. Cheerleaders value what is good in you and they help you cope with the stresses and disappointments of your life. They can be found just about anywhere waiting to help out. Perhaps you have been a Cheerleader for someone else. It can be a very rewarding experience to be someone's Cheerleader. It's a great feeling to know that you are an important part of the life of another person.

Cheerleaders differ from Mentors in that they provide support but do not get deeply involved in understanding your painful emotions. In addition, the commitment you need to make to a Cheerleader is far less than that which you would make to a Mentor.

Cheerleaders are most helpful when they help you do one thing: stay drug-free, handle anger better, avoid negative contact with your parents, stay on a job, or express your feelings before they trigger self-destructive actions. For this reason, it can often be useful to have more than one Cheerleader. Each Cheerleader can then help you stay focused on one important change that you want to make.

If you are interested in finding one, Cheerleaders can be found through a variety of sources. One of the best sources is through a self-help group. The purpose of such groups is to help its members reach a specific goal. There are hundreds of different self-help groups. A list of self-help resources is available by calling the American Self-Help Clearinghouse at (201) 625-7101 (more on this in chapter 10). If one of your goals is to overcome feelings of depression and low self-esteem, you should contact a depression support group. If you drink or use drugs, then you could look to Alcoholics Anonymous or Narcotics Anonymous for a Cheerleader. If you overeat or starve yourself, you can look into Overeaters Anonymous. The purpose behind joining these groups is to find a sponsor who can serve as your Cheerleader—someone to urge you to keep trying to reach your goal, whatever that goal may be, when your optimism and energy are failing you or when your temptation to hurt yourself feels irresistible.

In addition to self-help groups, if you have a religious orientation, you can find your Cheerleader through your church or temple.

If you are a single parent, a Parents Without Partners' group can be a cheerleading source for you. If you are just plain single, then a singles group can be your source, not just for dates, but for some healthy support.

Once you have decided to seek out the support of others, you can search for cheerleading in many places. In a later chapter, we will discuss how you can even find support on the Internet. For now, know that if you want to find a Cheerleader, you will.

**Remember to write in your
Recovery Journal today.**

Designing a Support System

There are many things you can do to build a healthy support system even if you are not ready for a Mentor or Cheerleader. As you work on your SACRED skills, you will feel empowered to redesign the pieces of your life that, in the past, have encouraged you to harm and abuse yourself. Your journal writing can help you see how your past and present environments affect how you think, feel, and act. The suggestions that follow can increase the positive support you're getting from your environment and decrease the negatives. None of these suggestions are easily implemented, but they can help you to advance your cause by leaps and bounds.

Avoid negative contact with family members. When you're in the Recovery Zone you should avoid contact with family members who view you in negative terms and who have not acknowledged their responsibility for the psychotraumatic environment of your childhood. Contact with such family members can reignite traumatic memories and feelings and can increase the likelihood of self-injurious action. During recovery you need to protect yourself from contacts that could trigger such harmful actions. Confront your negative family members when your recovery is secure, when you feel strong and positive about yourself, and when your actions have become much more consistent. Read chapter 10 for more discussion of this topic.

Avoid negative exposure to peers, places, or things. This is only common sense. You must cut yourself off from everyone, everything, and every place that supported your former, self-injurious behavior. Exposure to old friends with whom you got high can trigger you to do the same. Exposure to old abusive romantic partners can, at a vulnerable moment, lead you to submit to their abuse for some affection. Leave those people, places, and things behind in the Borderline Zone. And do not look back!

Avoid taking on new and major responsibilities (for example, having a baby, marriage, demanding jobs) during your recovery period. Working your way through the Recovery Zone is a very stressful experience. Even though it is a healthy form of stress, it will consume a large amount of your psychological energy. New responsibilities will also put significant energy demands upon you. For this reason, they should be postponed until you feel yourself successfully exiting the Recovery Zone. A baby, a marriage, or a new high-pressure job might overload you and push you back into the Borderline Zone. It is better to be cautious. Protect your recovery and your future by staying focused and free from major, new demands.

Seek the company of positive role models, friends, and family. "Birds of a feather flock together." This is an old saying that by now should have new meaning for you. Cheerleaders, Mentors, true friends, and insightful family members are the people who will help you get through the Recovery Zone and into the Free Zone. The Free Zone is the psychological space that your self-help work will empower you to reach. Once there, you will know that you will never go back to being who and what you once were. Find positive people to reinforce your positive affirmations and your journey will be rewarded with joy and satisfaction.

Join a club or group that can help you develop a healthy interest or hobby. You will need to replace your self-injurious addictions and distractions with positive, self-esteem-building activities. There are thousands and thousands of clubs, hobbies, and sports that you can choose from. Your frustrated dreams and childhood dead ends can become your guide to a richer and healthier lifestyle. Seek them out and you will find what you need. Trust in your inner goodness.

Check out the Internet for support groups and chat groups. There'll be more on this in chapter 10, for now let's whet your appetite. The Internet is a fantastic way to connect with people who are struggling to exit the Borderline Zone. There are chat groups (people who talk by computer to each other), Web pages (designed by people, like Josh, (see chapter 10), who are working to exit the BZ), and information resources that you can use to further your own recovery. There's also a Web page designed for the readers of this book. This page will allow you to talk to Dr. Cohen, Samuel, and me and to other readers of *The Angry Heart*. Information on how to connect to the home page is in chapter 10.

Keep a journal of your progress. Make one short entry each day. Pick out what you did right in the day, not what went wrong. Start a section in your Recovery Journal entitled, "My Daily Success." Record only those things that you did right. Ignore the negatives. Focus on your successes—big and small. Enjoy them. Savor them. Rejoice in them. And allow them to guide you forward with confidence and grace.

Begin to reengineer your value system: value consistency, fairness, and self-discipline as your virtues. The "values" you learned in your childhood need to be rethought. This is the time to think about the values you would teach to your child. What would you want your child to hold dear? What would you want your child to believe in? Make these values part of your new life.

Take as much responsibility for your financial support as you can. If you depend on someone else or the government for your financial support, it is time to start thinking about taking over this responsibility. Caring for yourself in a financial way is part of recovery. Paying your own way means that you love your life and who you are. It is a true declaration of independence from the tyranny of past psychotraumatic events. It is part of living in the Free Zone.

Take excellent care of your physical appearance and health. How you look on the outside directly reflects what you feel on the inside. Caring for your appearance and health means that you are a good person. Start simply. Be consistent. Take pride in the results.

Putting Your Recovery into a Time Line

It is often helpful for people in the Recovery Zone to put major life events into a time line so they can see where they have come from and where they want to go. It is all too easy to become impatient with the pace of your recovery and to curse its every setback and hurdle. It is important that you understand that it took years for your emotions and behavior to undergo borderline conditioning. Unfortunately, it also will take time to recondition your behavior.

With this in mind, here is a time line that goes from birth to age seventy-five. (If you are older than seventy-five, forgive the oversight and good for you!) Photocopy it so you do not have to mark up your book. Then follow the steps below to complete your time line.

My Time Line

Birth	5	10	15	20	25	30	35	40	45	50	55	60	65	70	75

1. Mark a 1 under the age at which your psychotraumatic exposure began.

2. Mark an X under the age when all of your psychotraumatic exposure ended.

3. Mark a T under the age at which you first sought (or were taken for) treatment for your problems.

4. Mark an AH under the age at which you started to read *The Angry Heart*.

5. Mark an R under the age at which you believe that you entered the Recovery Zone.

6. Mark an F under the age at which you expect to be safely in the Free Zone.

On the following page is Samuel's completed time line for you to use as a guide to completing your own. Notice that his psychotraumatization began at about age one and ended at about age sixteen when he left home. He started therapy at about age eighteen, and began his involvement with this book at age twenty-three. He entered the Recovery Zone at age twenty-four. He expects to be safely in the Free Zone (without regression or relapse) by age twenty-nine. Notice that it took him about sixteen years to develop his problem (the duration of psychotraumatic exposure), and he expects that it will take five years to recover (the time from reading this book to being safely in the Free Zone). And even though it may take five years to recover, there are many more than five good years ahead for Samuel (given normal life expectancy).

Try being realistic with yourself. Expecting instant results will only lead to failure. You'll simply remain trapped in the BZ. If you are realistic, you will succeed in getting out.

Samuel's Time Line

Birth	5	10	15	20	25	30	35	40	45	50	55	60	65	70	75
1			X,T	AH	R	F									

Chapter Milestones

1. The right support is critical to a successful journey through the Recovery Zone and eventual passage into the Free Zone. It will take time for you to build a healthy support system and you will need to feel ready to reach out to others for help. You will know you are ready to reach out once you understand how you got stuck in the Borderline Zone.

2. Mentors, Cheerleaders, and other types of supporters can help you reach your goals if you allow them to do so. Remember, if you let others help, and show them that you appreciate their help, you will not have to do it alone.

3. Sometimes you won't be able to find supporters or be able to treat them well enough to keep them on your side. In this case it may be easier for you to think about seeking the help of a behavioral health professional. Combining the help of a trained professional with this book can make your journey faster and more successful. You will read more about this option in chapter 10.

Positive Affirmation

Positive support eases my journey.

Recovery Exercises

Recovery Exercise 9.1: Of Mentors and Mentos

Objective

To obtain new insights for dealing with familiar sources of frustration.

Background

Have you ever seen a commercial for Mentos candy? Many of these commercials tell short stories about situations that have great potential for frustration. Yet in each one of these commercials, a flash of insight and creativity (on the part of the person who happens to be eating the candy) brings a happy ending to what might have been an otherwise frustrating experience.

Expanded Awareness

Recall an incident that you found to be particularly frustrating. Now, act as your own Mentor and advise yourself as to how you might have handled the situation more effectively.

Finally, just for fun, write a script for your own Mentos commercial describing how you would avert frustration. The script should end on a high note as a result of your own brilliant flash of insight and creativity.

Recovery Exercise 9.2: The Making of a Mentor

Objective

To encourage thought about the ideal qualities of a Mentor.

Background

Some people have the intellectual resources required to be good Mentors but are lacking with regard to the personality attributes. Other people have the right personality but are not really intelligent or creative enough to be ideal Mentors. Moreover, different people, based on their own unique personalities and intellectual resources require different kinds of Mentors.

Expanded Awareness

Describe the person who could serve as the ideal Mentor for you; that is, a person who has the intellectual ability and personality that are right for providing advice and guidance upon which you can faithfully rely. What would this person look like? What would this person think like? Describe the person's personality. Describe how and why you think you would get along with this person. What sources of conflict do you foresee with this ideal Mentor? How might those conflicts typically be avoided?

In this chapter, you were provided with some guidelines for selecting a Mentor. If you have already selected one, discuss the ways that the person you selected differs from the ideal one that you described. Also, write about your plans for making the relationship with your real life Mentor work, regardless of any obstacles that may arise.

Recovery Exercise 9.3: Something to Cheer About

Objective

To enhance self-confidence as a prelude to accepting "cheers" from Cheerleaders.

Background

Some people have never sought out Cheerleaders for themselves; they do not cheer for themselves and would not expect anyone else to cheer for them either.

Expanded Awareness

Why are you worth rooting for? If you were going to "psych up" your personal cheering squad with words of inspiration before they began their cheerleading routines, what would you tell them about yourself as you are now? What would you tell them about the person you hope to be as you move through the Recovery Zone?

Recovery Exercise 9.4: Portrait of a Cheerleader

Objective

To visualize the ideal Cheerleader and explore the reasons that make such a person ideal for the role.

Background

Perhaps the most common and traditional images of a Cheerleader are that of some young, athletic female holding colorful pom-poms, or a young, athletic male holding a megaphone. However, when we think of personal Cheerleaders designed to help with recovery, entirely different images and attributes may come to mind.

Expanded Awareness

Describe a person who would be ideally suited to be a Cheerleader for you. Is this person a male or female? Young or old? Physically attractive or not? What personality and intellectual attributes would this person have? Instead of a megaphone, imagine that your Cheerleader is holding something significant in his or her hands; what is it? Why is it significant?

After you have described your ideal Cheerleader in as much detail as you can, think about how your description differs from your description of your ideal Mentor in exercise 9.2. What qualities do both of these people share? What qualities are different?

Recovery Exercise 9.5: A Wonderful Day in the Neighborhood

Objective

To think about how your interpersonal environment can be restructured.

Background

In this chapter, it was strongly recommended that you reevaluate the people you used to hang out with, and consider hanging out with "positive people to reinforce your positive affirmations." Stated succinctly, it is time, to the best of your ability, to make every passing day, a "wonderful day in the [interpersonal] neighborhood."

Expanded Awareness

Think about the people you used to hang out with. In retrospect, who do you think had a positive influence on you? Who do you think had a negative influence on you? Focusing just on one person who you thought had a negative influence on you, why do you think you continued to hang out with that person? How will you do things differently in the future?

Recovery Exercise 9.6: Lean on Me

Objective

To honestly monitor thoughts and feelings related to your Mentor or Cheerleader.

Background

A month or so after enlisting the support of a Mentor or Cheerleader, it might be a good idea to gauge how each of the people in the relationship (that is, you and your Mentor or Cheerleader) are thinking about the relationship, as well as the other person in it.

Expanded Awareness

Repeat exercise 9.1, this time with your Mentor or Cheerleader. After doing this, discuss what is going right about the relationship, as well as the ways, if any, that the relationship can be improved.

Recovery Exercise 9.7: My Ten Commandments

Objective

To identify the core values of your life.

Background

An important part of your support system is your values. Psychotraumatic experiences tend to distort one's value system. It is important to consciously review your own values as you move through the Recovery Zone.

Expanded Awareness

Think about what you believe in and hold true to. What would you give up your life to protect? How do you want others to remember you? Write out the "ten commandments" that you try to live your life by. Don't be afraid to revise them until you think you have gotten them just right.

10

Supercharging Your Recovery

It takes a special kind of wisdom to see change and redemption in another; most can only see what the person was, and not what he is now.

—*Babylon 5*, "The Hour of the Wolf,"

*You are young and life is long and there is time to kill today
And then one day you find ten years have got behind you
No one told you when to run, you missed the starting gun*

—Pink Floyd, "Breathe"

The first part of this chapter explores the "unconscious" motivators of life in the Borderline Zone. Do not expect this part to be easy reading. It was designed to hit hard so you can sort out your deeper feelings and motives.

The second part of the chapter provides you with resources to help you supercharge your passage through the Recovery Zone.

Part One: Advanced Awareness

What's Your Motive?

Tick Tock, Tick Tock

Time is our best friend and our worst enemy. Time is the great equalizer of people. Each of our days has exactly twenty-four hours in them. No one can buy, steal, or borrow more time than that—until death comes calling.

In our darkest moments, death can seem more attractive than life. In our brightest moments, we can become intoxicated with a wish for life ever lasting. In the in-between moments, however, our true character is measured.

One day in a flash of insight you will realize that time has been stolen from you. Stolen by the hurtful, painful things that happened to you. And when you see and accept this insight, you will feel incredibly sad. You will cry in a way that you have never cried before. You will sob from your soul. Your tears will pierce your body and feel as if they will never end because, finally, you will totally feel the pain that you so carefully buried.

But before you get there, you must intellectually see something else: "I was betrayed by people I trusted. I was deeply hurt. I learned to blame myself for what happened. In my heart of hearts I am angry about the guilt, shame, and hurt that was forced upon me. In the depths of my soul, safely 'hidden' from me, I know that I want *revenge*."

Hurt yourself. Hurt them. Hurt yourself. Hurt them. Hurt yourself. Hurt them. Hurt yourself. Hurt them. Hurt yourself. Chanting this mantra of revenge, you drive yourself to the borderline of self-destruction.

"Why am I hurting myself?" Because you seek revenge. *It* won't let you go, and *you* won't let it go.

What better way is there to punish those who hurt you than by hurting yourself? What better way is there to hide a motive for revenge than to become the target of the harm? Maybe if you hurt yourself enough, they will say it was all true. Maybe they will try to stop you. Maybe they will hold you, and love you. Maybe, they will even say they are sorry.

Maybe. But maybe it is time for you to look into the mirror of your soul and acknowledge your need for revenge before it claims you as its sole victim.

Tick tock, tick tock, tick . . .

Dead Ends

There are other motives that you need to become aware of. Though not as deep as the motive for revenge, they can still keep you trapped in the Borderline Zone for a very long time. The motives are *pleasing others, seeking out sympathy*, and *defeating others*. They cause dead-end behavior. Dead-end behavior, as the name implies, keeps you trapped in the Borderline Zone. On the surface such behavior may seem quite appropriate, but over time it becomes apparent that it is not.

Dead-end behaviors include blaming yourself, somatic distractions, fabricating stories about your life, pretending to dissociate, merging with your environment, becoming a "rebel without a clue," and playing mind games with professionals. It is rare for someone to be trapped in all of these behaviors, but it can happen.

Typically, people trapped in the Borderline Zone subconsciously use these behaviors to get their needs met or to avoid facing their pain. I bring these up so you can evaluate them for yourself and judge their role, if any, in your life.

Blaming yourself is a tricky behavior. Sometimes people in the BZ blame themselves for the failures of their lives by calling themselves losers. Sometimes they do this so they can "enjoy" feeling sorry for themselves or to get others (which is even better) to feel sorry for them. If reading this is making you angry, then you may very well be someone who does this.

At other times, people in the BZ fall into a depression (often after being rejected by someone close to them). While in this depression they blame themselves for everything and don't care about sympathy or pity from others. They become totally absorbed with their own badness. They believe that they are unloved by their parents and other significant people in their lives because they do not deserve to be loved. They use self-blame to deepen their depression and prevent change. If the depression gets deep enough, they may even attempt suicide.

Somatic distractions, physical symptoms that distract from coping with a more fundamental emotional issue, operate in two ways. One of the best times to get sympathy and positive attention from others is when we are feeling sick. Even psychotraumatizing caregivers respond favorably when their child has an illness; the child quickly learns that being sick or injured brings attention. Once this connection is made in the child's mind, the adult, now trapped in the Borderline Zone, often misinterprets bodily feelings as signs of an illness that isn't there to get a "safe" form of attention when he or she is feeling emotionally needy. Alternatively, the person may ignore bodily feelings when, in fact, they are signs of an illness that needs attention (a passive form of self-injury when the person is feeling really bad about him- or herself). In either case, the real emotional needs remain hidden from view by somatic distractions.

Fabrication is driven by the distorted self-image of the person trapped in the Borderline Zone. The tendency to fabricate stories is driven by low self-esteem and a need for some special attention. When people's self-esteem is damaged, they tend to become very eager to please or impress others. They want to be liked and, often, they will resort to making up stories about their lives that are simply false. Sometimes the stories brag of accomplishments and achievements that never happened. For example, you might tell people that you have a job that is more important and higher paying than it really is. In other cases, the person creates stories about a false illness to gain attention and sympathy. For example, a nineteen-year-old girl in a treatment program told everyone in her group therapy session that she had been tested and was HIV positive. When she was evaluated and retested she was found to be HIV negative. Later she admitted that she fabricated the entire story. Despite the negative implications of being HIV positive, this young girl fabricated this story to get attention and to distract her therapist from her real problem: living in the Borderline Zone.

Pretending to dissociate is a delicate problem. Dissociation is a psychological state in which people lose contact with their environment or identity for a period of time and may withdraw into their minds or into uncharacteristic behavior patterns. Their sense of themselves becomes disrupted. Typically, they do not clearly remember the dissociative episode and may even become unresponsive to external stimuli during the episode. In some cases, dissociation can become the prelude to a behavior pattern that reenacts past, often traumatic, events or to the development of multiple personalities (separate identities sometimes with their own names and lives). People who experienced early and severe psychotrauma are most susceptible to dissociative states. They learn to dissociate as a way of getting away from all the pain around them.

If you think you are experiencing involuntary states of dissociation, you should strongly consider consulting a behavioral health professional. A problem arises, however, when someone stuck in the BZ and unwilling to work to get out learns about dissociative states and mimics them to confuse loved ones or professionals. What unfolds is a cat-and-mouse game that distracts everyone involved from the genuine issues. Faking dissociative episodes is a dead end and will retard progress toward a better way of life. It should be avoided.

Merging with your environment is an acceptance-seeking and identity-seeking strategy. While in the Borderline Zone, people have a strong tendency to take on the behavior patterns of others. This is especially true when they associate with people who have other types of emotional problems. In these circumstances the person in the BZ will "catch" their symptoms. Such symptom-catching serves to distract the person with BPD from the true issues and, if he or she is in treatment, serves to mislead the therapist.

More positively, if a person in the BZ associates with healthier people, he or she tends to function much better. This is an important reason for developing the positive support system discussed in chapter 8. Positive thinking and positive support is also catching.

Many people caught in the Borderline Zone have a tough time figuring out their own preferences. They often find themselves adopting the preferences of others in order to be accepted. By becoming what others expect, they abandon their own points of view. Try as they may, they usually end up feeling like a square peg in a round hole. Blindly assuming the preferences of others becomes just another dead end.

The rebels without a clue rage against the machine without any idea of why. They are driven by anger to attack all symbols of authority and control. They do not understand (and act as if they do not want to understand) the causes of their rebellion. They numb their feelings with addictive activities, outrageous actions, and like-minded acquaintances. They dress to look the part of the rebel. They act cool and feel horrible. They blame others for all of the negative consequences their actions create. They live to rebel, and rebel to live. They want to be understood. They want to be loved. They want to stop, but they do not know how.

Playing mind games with professionals. People with BPD often only reluctantly seek professional therapy. Their reluctance comes from being pushed by others to get help or from their RCP. Without personal commitment and trust, psychotherapy has little chance of being helpful. It becomes another relationship lost in the emotional storms of the BZ.

Most people find it difficult to share painful experiences with a therapist. People stuck in the Borderline Zone are even more reluctant than most to do so.

During psychotherapy they tend to use defensive actions or mind games to maintain virtual walls that prevent them from openly conversing with the therapist. Typical mind games include threatening to harm themselves or emotionally punishing the therapist if the therapist does not do what they want. Other games include refusing to answer important questions, telling the therapist lies about their level of addictive activity, and telling the therapist what they believe the therapist wants to hear rather than the truth. Sometimes, the motive for playing mind games is power tripping. Disempowered by the BZ, it becomes tempting to exert control over others by deceiving and misleading them. In this way they can feel they got even with "them." For example, a woman in the BZ "got off on" getting doctors to diagnose the way she manipulated them to. She was good at doing this, but remains trapped in the BZ. Who is really in control, and who loses out?

Do these behaviors sound familiar? A skilled therapist can help you to get past these defenses by acting in a way that encourages you to gradually trust him or her (if you allow this to happen). You can help this process along by choosing to be in therapy and by choosing a therapist you can work with. (There's more on this in part 2 of this chapter.)

Defeat, failure, hopelessness, and selfishness—the cumulative impact of these dead ends is feeling trapped in a selfish and self-defeating cycle of failure. People stuck in this cycle might appear to be very selfish to those around them, because they are totally preoccupied, albeit in a negative way, with themselves.

Once you realize you are trapped, it is easy to lose all hope for a way out of the Borderline Zone. Fortunately, humans are fundamentally optimistic beings. It takes a long history of failure to reach the point of utter hopelessness. Having read this far, you are probably feeling positive enough to make it through the Recovery Zone to freedom.

The Psychotraumatizers: Villains or Victims, Too?

Are the psychotraumatizers (parents, caregivers, peers, teachers, strangers, or siblings) who hurt you villains or victims? It is a question that does not have a single or simple answer. Each person will need to answer this question in his or her own way. You will find that your answer will change as you recover. It may take many years before you are at peace with your "final" answer.

To illustrate the complexities of this question, review what Samuel wrote about his parents throughout the earlier chapters of this book.

When I was growing up, there wasn't a day that went by where I didn't wish that things were different. I loved my parents. I don't think I necessarily wanted different parents. I just wanted my parents to be different, to have different standards of conduct and different attitudes.

One of the things that really hurt me a lot is that my parents never said they were sorry for anything they did to me.

My parents yelled at me, beat me, ignored me, mocked my nervous facial tics, and taught me to feel like I was an unwanted piece of dirt. But we always said we loved each other.

My parents' alcoholism made me feel very sad. I really did love my parents a lot. I just hated what they became after just a few beers. Every day I felt completely powerless about what was going to happen between me and my family.

My parents still don't seem to understand what they put us kids through. When I think about it, I often feel the pain curdling in my stomach.

If there is one thing in my life now that is keeping me strong, it is the fact that I did make amends with [my stepfather], and so did he with me. There was nothing one-sided about this, we both forgave each other for the past and moved on with life.

For now, no longer is the hurt I feel from my parents going to dictate my life or my actions. I wish that I could say that I'm totally free of the pain and suffering, but, then, I'd be lying, and I've done enough of that.

Samuel did not want different parents. He wanted loving parents who would have created a secure, stable, and happy home. Samuel reveals the anger he feels toward his parents for what they did to him, but he also shares the fact that he loves them despite what happened. He longs for a reconciliation with his parents, but only managed to achieve this with his stepfather. He also realized that the way he was treated continues to cause him a lot of pain that, in the past, drove him to punish himself.

All people living in the Borderline Zone learn to punish themselves for the way their psychotraumatizers made them feel. They punish themselves because their trauma made them feel that they are bad, if not evil, people. They punish themselves to punish those who punished them. This is especially the case, if they were psychotraumatized as young children. Children learn to feel about themselves the way their parents, siblings, peers, and others treated them. If treated badly, they learn to feel that they are bad, and bad people deserve to be punished. So, as adolescents or adults living in the BZ, they seek to punish themselves with pleasure and pain to make their badness go away. The insight that you need to grasp is that *you are not bad. Your psychotraumatizer's actions were bad.* They treated you badly because of their own, perhaps overwhelming, problems; not because you were bad or evil. Chances are that your psychotraumatizers were psychotraumatized themselves. This was true for Samuel.

Those who hurt you are responsible for what they have done. They are as much subject to the Existential Paradox as you are. It is reasonable for you to expect them to admit to what they have done and to express sorrow for doing it. Unfortunately, they are often in denial about their responsibility and are, therefore, emotionally unwilling to own what they have done. For them to own what they have done, they will have to go through the same degree of pain and agony that you are going through now. This often prevents them from owning their responsibility for your psychotraumatization.

A man in his thirties was psychotraumatized by his father, a violently abusive alcoholic. As a child, he hid on the roof of his house to hide from his father's late-night, alcohol-induced rages. His father never acknowledged what happened until he was close to death from cancer. It was at that moment that he said to his son, "Don't do to your son what I did to you." This was the only thing this man's father could say to him.

The people who hurt you know what they did to you. Some will find the courage to admit their responsibility to you because they have improved the quality of their life enough to become strong enough to do so. Others will do so only when death is at their doorstep. But some will never admit to what they have done.

I would be lying if I said that it doesn't matter whether or not those who hurt you admit what they have done. It does matter. Such an admission can help to heal the hurt that both parties feel. You have three basic options in this regard: you can wait, you can confront, or you can open the door.

Waiting is self-explanatory. You focus on yourself. Work your way through the Recovery Zone and hope that the people you want to acknowledge their responsibilities will do so. Waiting is, perhaps, the most sensible approach if you are still living with or are dependent upon those who hurt you. Unless they are clearly ready to talk about the past, it is probably better to wait.

Confronting requires timing and preparation. You cannot productively confront those who hurt you until you are much stronger and healthier. You need to be in the Free Zone before you set up a confrontation. Once there you need to plan your confrontation.

If there are multiple people you wish to confront, select the person whom you believe to be most open to confrontation. You then need to write out the main points you would like to make. Avoid the use of provocative language. Your goal is mutual understanding and not revenge. For further guidance, review the assertiveness skills in chapter 8.

When you know what you want to say, plan a time and place for the encounter. If you are in therapy, you could ask the therapist to moderate the discussion. Make sure that it will be a private meeting free of eavesdroppers. Make sure you will feel safe there as well. Be sure you discuss your plans with someone in your support system prior to your meeting. You will need to talk with that person after the meeting as well. Expect the meeting to be emotionally draining.

The last step is to invite the person to a meeting with you to discuss the things that happened in the past. Be prepared for a "no" response. If the person is willing to meet with you, follow your outline and try to avoid getting too angry. Visualize the outcome you desire for several days prior to the meeting. Be prepared for follow-up meetings. One encounter will not be sufficient.

If the person refuses to come to a meeting with you, consider following the suggestions in the next section, or select another person from the list of people you need to confront and ask that person for a meeting.

Opening a Door involves preparing a letter or E-mail (don't use the phone) to send to those who psychotraumatized you. The goal of the letter is to explain how what they did (their actions) affected your life. The letter should not be angry in tone. It should not attack them personally. It should express your real feelings and explain how you are trying to recover from what happened. You can close the letter by asking for a *constructive* response, but ask them not to respond to you with anger. Emphasize that you seek healing, not blaming or revenge.

If they cannot handle their own feelings, ask them to ignore your letter. If they respond favorably to your letter, then the door is open for a face-to-face discussion. If they fail to respond, or respond with denial and anger, let things cool off for a while. Be sure to talk to someone in your support system about whatever type of response you receive.

Regardless of how things turn out in your attempt to get those who hurt you to acknowledge their responsibility, remember Samuel's comments: *For now, no longer is the hurt I feel from my parents going to dictate my life or my actions.*

Remember to write in your Recovery Journal today.

Environmental Exposure and Its Effect on Your Mood

One of the major symptoms of borderline disorder is *affective instability*. In the BZ, people tend to overreact to the things that happen to them. This tendency is discussed in chapter 7 under the topic of stress hypersensitivity. The effect I want to explore here is how exposure to particular environments can affect your mood without your awareness. Such exposure can make you feel depressed, angry, enraged, impulsive, hyper, or a combination thereof, and leave you puzzled about the cause.

A young man in a treatment program started to understand his psychotraumatic past as a result of reading this book. He experienced strong emotions and recollections. The staff who supported him helped him to work through these feelings. He started to feel a lot better about himself. In a phone call to his mother, he brought up his memories and feelings. She told him that they were all false memories and invalidated his feelings. The young man became confused and angry for days afterward.

The environment this young man was exposed to was the phone call with his mother. The effect was an increase in his "affective instability." Since his mother was part of his psychotraumatic past, her words had a powerful conditioned effect on him apart from their content. Her invalidation of his feelings, and denial of the reality of his past as he perceived it, triggered a period of emotional destabilization. If this young man had not been in a residential treatment program, he probably would have engaged in an addictive activity to cope with this exposure.

Caregivers who psychotraumatized their children tend to deny their responsibility for it by invalidating the perceptions, recollections, and feelings of their adult children. Their denial makes you doubt your own knowledge base. This stand-off contributes to keeping you stuck in the BZ.

Another young man who was successfully struggling through the Recovery Zone (living on his own and working) went for a holiday visit with his girlfriend to see his mother, who had assisted in his psychotraumatization. Having inherited a lot of money, his mother was doing well. The visit went well but when he asked his mother if he could borrow twenty dollars she refused. Her refusal triggered a chain reaction of negative feelings in him. He did not show these feelings right away, but within twenty-four hours, and for many weeks thereafter, he saw himself as a loser and a failure. He slipped into a depression. It took awhile for him to realize that he was angry at his mother for being unwilling to lend him just twenty dollars after she had inherited so much money. He felt rejected. He remembered the way she treated him as a young child, her anger and rage and drunkenness, and he wondered why she hated him so much. What did he do to her? Ironically, his girlfriend found his mother to be a fine person and didn't understand why he had gotten so upset.

This man also exposed himself to an environment (visit with mom) that triggered a period of emotional destabilization. Fortunately, he did not allow this to trigger a prolonged episode of addictive escape. He did get drunk once, but put a stop to this old behavior once he became aware of the true cause of his depression and self-hatred.

Psychotraumatization creates a conditioning history that can have powerful effects on your present behavior and feelings. This conditioning history is activated by environments containing *salient characteristics* that are the same or similar to those that existed in your original psychotraumatic environments. These characteristics include ten items: people, objects, activities, relationships, places, demands, needs, expectations, rewards, and punishments.

The most salient characteristic is the person (or persons) who created your original psychotraumatic environments. This person has the power to trigger confusing mixtures of feelings. If this person is a parent, caregiver, or sibling, he or she can trigger feelings as varied as love, hate, neediness, rage, fear, anger, and self-hate. Exposure to this person, even in adult life, can evoke such feelings especially if you are unaware of this conditioning effect.

The relationship control phobia I spoke of in earlier chapters is a product of this conditioning history. People who remind you of your psychotraumatizers in appearance, actions, or personal characteristics may evoke powerful reactions from you even though they may treat you with kindness. Often, this conditioned connection escapes your notice. Roles can also evoke powerful reactions as well. Roles that put you in submissive or vulnerable positions, such as a low-paying job, sexual activity, or separating from a friend, can produce emotional instability.

Awareness of the conditioning effects of psychotraumatization is an essential part of making it to the Free Zone. Learning how to run a *self-diagnostic* helps. Self-awareness is the antidote to impulsive, self-destructive actions. Learning to become aware of the causes of mood and behavior changes is a skill that you can develop and put to good use.

Doing a Self-Diagnostic. A self-diagnostic is a set of questions that you can use to overcome problems you might be having with putting your feelings into words. It can help you to determine what happened to cause your mood to change without warning.

Read each set of self-diagnostic questions that appear on the next page. If you can unequivocally answer *one* of the questions in each set with a "Yes," then check the "Any Yes" box for that set. Go through all of the questions and then total up the number of checked Any Yes boxes. Finally, rate the confidence you have in your answers on the scale provided. Rate it as "High" if you are very confident in your answers and do not have any doubts.

If you checked two or more Any Yes boxes or you checked the Any Yes box of "Conditioning check" and your confidence level was at least Medium, then you can assume that your recent environmental exposures caused your emotions to destablize.

If you have checked more than three boxes but rated a confidence level of low or very low, you are probably feeling confused because you are having difficulty reading or trusting your feelings.

If you have not checked any boxes and rated your confidence as Medium or higher, then you can assume that your recent environmental exposure is not causing your mood fluctuations. In this case, ask yourself whether you are anticipating some future events that may be worrying you or whether you are feeling physically uncomfortable or ill. If both of these things are negative, then consider discussing your feelings with a supporter or with a therapist.

Psychotraumatic memories of images, feelings, and actions that hurt you link past and present environments. When a present environment evokes an emotional response from you that exceeds that which a person free of a psychotraumatic past would experience, it does so because it has activated old memories. These memories may not be fully recalled. In many cases, people report only uncomfortable, disconnected emotions that make the present situation feel worse than it should. As discussed in earlier chapters, it is at these moments, when you are being "attacked" from within, that you are at greatest risk for impulsive action. Learning to perform a self-diagnostic (that is, Objectify) when you observe that your mood is changing for the worse will help prevent impulsive, self-destructive actions.

Self-Help Skill: Running a Self-Diagnostic

Whenever you find your mood changing without notice, run the following self-diagnostic to identify the environmental characteristics that caused the mood change. To do this you need to review what you have been exposed to since before you noticed a change in your mood and behavior. You may need to go back a few hours, days, or even weeks.

People check	Whom have I seen and interacted with? Anyone from my family? Anyone who hurt me in the past? Anyone who recently put me down? Anyone whom I had an argument with? Anyone that I hurt or misused? Any Yes [ ]
Location check	Have I been some place where I did addictive activities in past? Have I been somewhere that reminded me of my childhood? Have I been somewhere I felt confined or trapped? Any Yes [ ]
Needs check	Did I feel needy? Did I want, desire, or need something? Have my needs gone unmet? Any Yes [ ]
Demand check	Was I facing demands that stressed me? What were my responsibilities? Did these demands make me feel overwhelmed and likely to fail? Any Yes [ ]
Expectation check	What was expected of me by others? Did I know what was expected? Did I meet those expectations? Did I resent them? Did these expectations feel harsh or unfair? Any Yes [ ]
Reward check	Was someone using the promise of rewards to motivate me? Was I working to earn a reward? Any Yes [ ]
Punishment check	Was someone threatening me with consequences if I did not do what they wanted? Was I expecting to be punished for something that I did or did not do? Did I receive a punishment (for example, speeding tickets, loss of job, loss of relationship) because of my actions? Any Yes [ ]
Activity check	What types of activities was I engaged in (work, play, social, and so on)? Did I feel uneasy about doing these activities? Whom was I doing these activities with? Did I feel uneasy about being with them? Were the outcomes of these activities negative? Any Yes [ ]
Object check	What objects (tools, equipment, books, clothing, and so on) was I using during my activities? Was there anything unique or unusual about any of those objects? Did those objects make me feel uneasy? Any Yes [ ]
Conditioning check	Did anything remind me of my psychotraumatic past? Did I feel as if I were in a fog, as if a memory was "taking control" of me? Did I feel as if I was repeating past, negative actions? Did the situation feel as if it were from my dark past? Any Yes [ ]

Number of Any Yes answers _____ out of 10

Confidence Level: High   Medium   Low   Very low

Part Two: Resources That Can Help

There are wide variety of resources that can help you on your journey of recovery. These resources range from Web sites on the Internet and other self-help books to professional therapists, medications, and treatment programs.

You are the sole judge of whether any of the listed resources are of value. I have selected them based on my experiences and on the experiences of other people who have reported them to be of help. Feel free to pick and choose as you see fit.

The Internet

The Internet and the World Wide Web have become one of the hottest phenomenons of the 1990s. If you have surfed the Web then you know what I mean. There is a wide variety of informative and entertaining Web sites. I have selected several sites that relate to the issues of borderline, addictive, and psychotraumatic problems. These sites will put you in touch with helpful information and with fellow travelers who are also seeking the Free Zone.

If you lack experience with the Internet, you can get training through your local adult education center or at any number of stores that sell computers. If you do not own a computer, you can use a public library's computer or a computer at one of the computer cafés springing up across the country.

To access the Web you will need to join an Internet Service Provider (ISP) such as NetCom, America Online, MCI, or any of hundreds of small local providers. An ISP allows your computer to connect to the Internet through your telephone line. You can expect to pay about $9.95 to $19.95 per month for unlimited access to the Internet.

In addition to an ISP, you will need Web-browsing software. I recommend that you buy or download Netscape Navigator 3.0 (or the latest version) or Microsoft Explorer. They can be purchased at your local computer software store. Once you have your computer, a service provider, and browser software you are ready to surf the net.

I have organized the Web sites according to topic areas. For each site I give you the URL (Uniform Resource Locator), which is the Web address. You need to insert the URL address into the location field of your browser software and hit enter. You will then be electronically transported to that site. It is a lot of fun! Sometimes a site I reference in this book may become inaccessible. If this happens you may see a message that says, "The server you requested is unavailable." If that happens you can search for other sites by using a Web browser such as Yahoo (www.yahoo.com), Excite (www.excited.com), Lycos (www.lycos.com), or Hot Bot (www.hotbot.com). To use one of these, type in their URL and when you see their search screen, type in the key words Borderline Personality Disorder or Addiction. Then click the search key and you will receive a listing of all Web sites that contain these key words.

Borderline Sites

A good place to start is *Josh's Homepage*. This page is dedicated to issues facing people in the Borderline Zone. His URL is:

http://www.lookup.com/homepages/66733/home.html

You must enter the URL exactly the way it's printed here. If you add a space or character to the address, it will not work.

Josh's Homepage talks about himself and his experiences with borderline issues. It will also provide you with links (that is, URLs) to other related Web sites. From Josh's Homepage you can go to *Laura's Homepage* (http://www.huizen.dds.nl/~laura_d/) where she is doing a lot of thinking and writing about borderline problems. Laura has experience being in the Borderline Zone, too.

Through the Internet you will be able to make connections with hundreds of people who share your issues. This will provide a basis of support and information to help your recovery move along.

BPD Central located at

http://members.AOL.com/BPDCentral

is a clearinghouse of information about borderline personality disorder. It also has information about how you can join in on a weekly chat group (Saturday night at 10 P.M. EST) held through America Online for people interested in borderline issues. A chat group is an electronic conversation group where people type messages back and forth to each other.

A Canadian site that talks about a book called *Lost in the Mirror*, about borderline disorders, can be found at

http://www.golden.net/~soul/borderpd.html

Excerpts from this book can be found here as well as links to other relevant sites.

Self-Help and Support Sites

The *American Self-Help Clearinghouse* located at

http://www.cmhcsys.com/selfhelp/

provides a directory of self-help groups, organized by type of problem, that are active throughout the United States. The Clearinghouse phone number is (201) 625-7101. You can find a group in your area that deals with depression, drug abuse, alcohol abuse, sexual addiction, and so forth. Unfortunately, at this writing there are no groups that directly address borderline problems. However, the American Clearinghouse will provide you with guidance on how to start your own self-help group. Here are a few of the groups you can find on this site:

Group	Phone	Chapters	Founded
Sexaholics Anonymous	(615) 331-6901	700	1979
Sex Addictions Anonymous	(713) 869-4902	500	1977
Moderation Management (alcohol abuse)	(313) 677-6007	60	1993
Alcoholics Anonymous	(212) 870-3400	94,000	1935
Emotions Anonymous	(612) 647-9712	1300	1970

Emotions Anonymous is a good starting point for people who are actively working on their recovery. This group provides generic support for people with any type of emotional problem. The number listed here is their national number. Call them and they will help you locate the chapter that is nearest to you. Their Web site URL is

http://crusher.bev. net/health/EA.html

In addition to American Clearinghouse, there are two other self-help clearinghouses that can help you find support for your recovery: National Mental Health Consumers Self-Help Clearinghouse, (800) 553-4KEY, and National Empowerment Center, (508) 685-1518.

Addiction Sites

The *National Families in Action* site provides information on drug and alcohol abuse and can be found at

http://www.emory.edu/NFIA/DRUG_INFO

National Families in Action Online provides a wide range of information on drugs and their effects and dangers. It also has numerous links to other helpful sites.

Dr. Robert Westermeyer has a site that describes the Prochaska model of change I talked about in chapter 8. His site is located at

http://www.cts.com/~habtsmrt

He has several pages of information and suggestions about how to cope with urges. It is well worth reading and downloading for reference. There are many more addiction sites and the ones I have suggested can lead you to them.

The Angry Heart

The Angry Heart Web site is your interactive companion to this book. It is located at

http://www.slshealth.com

At this site you can post comments about the book to other readers. You can read their comments and send replies. You can read excerpts from the book. You can send E-mails with your questions and comments. You can read about our Mentorship treatment program and about the latest treatment options. You can organize or find information about Angry Heart support groups. You can also order additional copies of the book.

Books

Besides *The Angry Heart*, there are several other books I can recommend to aid your recovery. The book recommendations are organized by problem.

General Introduction to Borderline Disorder

Kreisman, Jerold, and Hal Straus. 1991. *I Hate You, Don't Leave Me*. New York: Avon.
This is a very good, general, nonthreatening overview of borderline personality disorder. Good, easy reading for you and other people that you would like to educate about borderline problems. Available from Avon Books by calling (800) 238-0658.

Abuse/Trauma

Adams, Caren, and Jennifer Fay. 1989. *Free of the Shadows: Recovering from Sexual Violence*. Oakland, Calif.: New Harbinger.
Written for people whose lives have been affected by sexual violence. A very helpful book. Available through New Harbinger by calling (800) 748-6273.

Middleton-Moz, Jane. 1989. *Children of Trauma: Rediscovering Your Discarded Self*. Deerfield Beach, Fla.: Health Communications.
This book focuses on the effects of physical, sexual, and emotional abuse. It will help the reader to overcome the grief and sense of loss that accompany such abuse. Available from the Courage to Change catalog by calling (800) 440-4003.

Alcohol/Drug/Sex Addiction

Fanning, Patrick, and John T. O'Neill. 1996. *The Addiction Workbook*. Oakland, Calif.: New Harbinger.
This workbook provides information about addiction and offers step-by-step directions for quitting. Available through New Harbinger Publications by calling (800) 748-6237.

Carnes, Patrick. 1983. *Out of the Shadows: Understanding Sexual Addiction.*
Center City, Minn.: Hazelden Publishing and Education.
A twelve-step approach to coping with sexual addiction. Available
from Hazelden catalog by calling (800) 328-9000. Catalog number is
4289A.

Washton, Arnold, and Nannette Stone-Washton. 1991. *Step Zero: Getting
to Recovery.* Center City, Minn.: Hazelden Publishing and Education.
Explains the concept of step zero (Precontemplation stage) when we
drop our defenses and begin to admit our addiction. Available from
Hazelden catalog by calling (800) 328-9000. Catalog number is 5042A.

Self-Injury Addiction

Miller, Dusty. 1994. *Women Who Hurt Themselves: A Book of Hope and Understanding.* New York: Basic Books.
This book suggests that people who self-injure do so because they
are reenacting traumatic events. The author believes that the problem can be successfully overcome.

Alderman, Tracy. 1997. *The Scarred Soul: Understanding and Ending Self-Inflicted Violence.* Oakland, Calif.: New Harbinger Publications.
This book for victims of self-inflicted violence teaches people what
they can do to stop hurting themselves, either through psychotherapy or by taking steps to break the habit on their own.

Depression/Anger/Forgiveness

Copeland, Mary Ellen. 1992. *The Depression Workbook.* Oakland, Calif.:
New Harbinger.
Teaches readers how to understand depression and what to do to
empower themselves to overcome it. Available from New Harbinger
by calling (800) 748-6273.

Potter-Efron, Ron. 1994. *Angry All the Time.* Oakland, Calif.: New Harbinger.
A helpful book for working on controlling a bad temper. Provides
reader with eight steps for effective anger management. Available
from New Harbinger by calling (800) 748-6273.

Dayton, Tian. 1992. *Daily Affirmations for Forgiving and Moving On.* Deerfield Beach, Fla.: Health Communications.
This book offers positive affirmations to help readers move past
pain, grief, and resentment, and move on with life. Available from
the Courage to Change catalog by calling (800) 440-4003.

Assertiveness Training

Alberti, Robert, and Michael Emmons. 1995. *Your Perfect Right.* San Luis
Obispo, Calif.: Impact Publishers.
Available through Impact Publishers, PO Box 1094, San Luis Obispo,

CA 93406. This is one of the most frequently recommended books for learning assertiveness skills. It is easy reading and very helpful.

Stress Management

Davis, Martha, Elizabeth Eshelman, and Matthew McKay. 1995. *The Relaxation & Stress Reduction Workbook*, 4th ed. Oakland, Calif.: New Harbinger.

This best-selling book teaches methods for managing stress through the use of relaxation, visualization, thought stopping, time management, and other methods. It is a comprehensive and understandable guide. We highly recommend it. It is available from New Harbinger by calling (800) 748-6273.

Starting a Self-Help Group

Common Concern: A Program for Forming and Enhancing Self-Help Groups.

This program can turn a group of five to ten people with a common concern into a fully functioning support group. Available from New Harbinger by calling (800) 748-6273.

Therapy

Overcoming borderline and addictive problems and making it all the way to the Free Zone is a difficult task for a number of reasons. The most important of which is the tremendous amount of emotional energy required to become aware of your inner pain. For this reason, supporters are required. As you work you way through this book you will come to see how carefully selected professional therapist can be very helpful.

It is perhaps too widely known that many behavioral health professionals view people with BPD to be "difficult patients." Many professionals will avoid treating people with these problems. The reason for this centers on the fact that, until recently, a clear understanding of the origins of this problem was not available. This made treatment difficult. The development of Dr. Linehan's Dialectical Behavior Therapy (DBT) (1993) and the development of our Mentorship Self-Help Therapy (MST), has brought new understanding and methods of treatment to people in the Borderline Zone.

Finding a Therapist

The selection of a therapist should be made in a systematic fashion. You can obtain a list of recommendations from your family doctor, your HMO or insurance company provider panel, the yellow pages of the phone book (under psychologist, counselor, clinic, or social worker), or from a friend.

It is important that you interview prospective therapists to determine who best matches your needs. The very process of interviewing therapists and asking them questions about their ability to help you will

screen out those who are uncomfortable with being challenged. Such individuals would be relatively ineffective therapists and should be
dropped from your list. Consider asking the following questions to all
prospective therapists who are willing to be questioned:

1. *How many people with BPD have you treated in the last year?*

You want to avoid therapists who have not had a lot of experience with
borderline problems.

2. *In your opinion, what causes borderline behaviors or symptoms?*

If their explanation differs significantly from the one described in this
book, consider another therapist.

3. *What is your policy on between-session phone contact?*

You want a therapist who will allow a certain amount of between-session
contact. Limits are okay, but no contact is bad.

4. *Would you be willing to give me as references former patients
of yours after you have contacted them and asked their permission
to use them as references?*

This is pushing things a bit, but it is a measure of how proud therapists
are of their work. Confidentiality may make most therapists unwilling
to do this, but if they ask their patient's permission, it can be done.

5. *What is the prognosis for someone who has borderline
symptoms?*

What you want to hear is reasonable optimism. No one can give you a
guarantee (if they do, skip them). If they hedge their bets too much, it
is probably better to move on to someone else.

6. *Are you willing to make use of* The Angry Heart *as part of
therapy?*

If you find this book helpful, therapists should be willing to make use
of it. If they are absolutely against doing this, it means they want to
overcontrol the therapy and it would be better to move on.

Do the therapists share your value system? Are they too conservative
or too liberal for you? Are they very formal and proper or very casual
and relaxed? Do they see you as a disease entity or as a person? Do you
prefer a doctor-knows-best approach or a more interactive style? Know
what your own values and preferences are. If you can't tolerate a doctor-knows-best approach, then stay away from those therapists. On the
other hand, if supercasual therapists aren't going to be able to handle
your games, then avoid them. Be honest with yourself and your prospective therapist.

The personality of the therapist is also an important consideration.
What you should look for is someone who is "down to earth"; not clinically distant or all-knowing. Your therapist should be someone who com-

municates interest in you as a person. Your therapist should make you feel as if he or she cares about seeing you get better. Your therapist should communicate strength and determination. Your therapist should talk in everyday, nontechnical language and should communicate respect for you and a willingness to be straight and honest with you. You should feel as if you could, with time, trust this person.

Your therapist can be a licensed psychologist, psychiatrist, or social worker. The degree matters less than the person's willingness to work with you and make you feel comfortable and safe. Therapy is not magic. Therapy is two people working as a team to help one person function better. It is important for you to respect your therapist as much as it is for your therapist to respect you. You will need to allow this person to push you to experience some very painful things. This will make you angry. You may even "hate" your therapist at times. However, as long as you respect and trust your therapist, you can tolerate his or her demands because you will see those demands are made to help you feel better.

The financial cost of therapy is always a factor. If you have health insurance and can convince your insurance company that your treatment is medically necessary you can get the cost covered. If you do not have insurance or your insurance company denies the need for treatment, you will have to decide how much a healthier life is worth to you. If you pay for your own treatment, you will be more likely to work hard at it. Mind games are an expensive luxury when you are paying the bill.

Once you think you have found the right therapist, schedule three trial sessions. At the end of the three sessions you will know whether you chose wisely. If, after three sessions, you feel good about your choice, stick with your therapist. If you don't, simply look for another therapist. However, do not expect to be cured in three sessions. In fact, you may feel worse. Base your judgment on how well you and the therapist are *working together*, not on your emotional state. In particular ask yourself, how well do the two of you handle conflict? Does your therapist understand your issues? Are you feeling a little afraid that your therapist will get you to feel what you need to feel (if you are, that is a good sign)? Are you trusting your therapist more? Add up your impressions and make you best judgment, then take action accordingly.

Once again, please remember that therapy is a team effort. A good therapist can only empower you to make changes that will help you live and feel better. Good therapy involves feeling a wide range of real emotions, some of which will be very painful and embarrassing. This is why it is important to respect, trust, and feel safe with the person you choose as your therapist. It is okay to get angry and yell at your therapist. This is part of doing therapy in the Borderline Zone. However, when you calm down, feel free to tell your therapist that you appreciate his or her concern for you. True, your therapist is being paid, but your words of kindness and appreciation will help you and your therapist to work as a team and get the best results possible.

Medication

Can medications be helpful in your quest for freedom from border-line and addictive behavior? Regardless of which type of BPD you have (Factor I or II), the proper type of medication taken for a limited period of time can be helpful. Medication, however, cannot cure borderline or addictive problems. Medication can help you

- Reduce your level of tension and anxiety so you can read and use this book and work more productively with your therapist
- Reduce the impulse to self-mutilate
- Decrease a severe depression

There are three rules of thumb to follow concerning the duration and amount of medication:

1. Use the smallest dosage of medication necessary to help you use your self-help book and work with your therapist.

2. Start decreasing the medication as soon as you make it halfway through the Recovery Zone (chapter 12 will show you how to measure this).

3. Don't use medication to bury your bad feelings (that is, don't use it as a substitute for addictive activities). Feeling bad is part of getting better. The longer you postpone this process, the longer you will remain in the Borderline Zone. However, if this book is stimulating feelings that are too intense for you to handle, then a small dose of medication may help to moderate your feelings.

The medication suggestions that follow should be discussed with a physician you trust. A decision to use medication should be made by both you and your physician.

Severe Depression

There are many medications available for depression. The newest ones belong to a class of medications called SSRIs (selective serotonin reuptake inhibitors). Serotonin is a chemical messenger that transfers information between nerve cells. It is one of many neurotransmitters that perform this function in the brain. Serotonin levels are thought to decline as a person becomes depressed. SSRI medications such as Prozac, Zoloft, or Paxil increase the amount of serotonin acting as messengers. Another class of antidepressant medication is called TCAs (tricyclic antidepressants), which act on a different neurotransmitter called norepinephrine. Some TCAs act on both neurotransmitters (such as, Pamelor and Tofranil). Depression can be treated with either type of antidepressant. Sometimes both types are combined. A typical dosage of 20 to 80 mg per day of Prozac or 75 to 125 mg of Pamelor is prescribed. It usually takes a few weeks before maximum improvement is experienced. Low doses of SSRIs (such as 30 mg of Prozac) sometimes work for a few weeks and then "poop out" in their effectiveness. If this happens, a higher dose is often needed.

Anxiety

Anxiety management should be done through the use of SDB (slow deep breathing), because this will increase your sense of self-control. If your level of anxiety becomes too overwhelming for you to handle, there are a variety of medications that can be prescribed on an as-needed basis to help you. Medications such as Ativan, Xanax, Buspar, Klonopin, and Valium are used for this purpose. With the exception of Buspar, all of these medications are potentially addictive. Many doctors are reluctant to prescribe them to people who engage in addictive activities for that reason. I recommend that you avoid using them. If serious and constant anxiety is a problem, try a low dose of Risperdal or Zyprexa. These are typically used to reduce psychotic thinking, but are also helpful for the management of severe anxiety. They are not addictive and because they have some side effects they encourage use only when truly necessary. A low dose for Risperdal is 1 to 2 mg per day and up to 5 mg per day for Zyprexa.

Self-Injury

Self-injury is a very serious behavior. If you are cutting yourself deeply and frequently or if you are engaging in other forms of physically damaging activity you should seek immediate professional therapy. Part of that therapy may include the use of medication for a period of time. My approach involves using medication until progress is being made with the book and then to gradually reduce the medication to zero. There are three types of medications you should consider. The medications are SSRI antidepressants (such as Prozac, Zoloft), Clozaril (an atypical anti-psychotic medication), and naltrexone (also know as Revia).

Recently a number of reports have come out suggesting that high dosages of SSRIs can help to reduce self-injury. This is based on research that has documented a connection between low serotonin levels and aggressive behavior toward others or toward self, such as self-injury (de Vegvar et al. 1994). This research theorizes that one of the physiological consequences of psychotraumatization may be a reduction in available serotonin in the brain. Prozac and Zoloft, among other drugs, increase the level of serotonin in some parts of the brain. Hence, Prozac or Zoloft may be helpful. The dosage you need to take is higher than that typically prescribed for depression. For example, if taking Prozac, the dose would be 80 mg, which is the upper limit of its dosage range.

In the treatment program I run, we have successfully used Clozaril at doses of 100 to 600 mg to reduce self-mutilation by up to 90 percent. In a few cases the behavior was totally reduced. Clozaril affects dopamine (another chemical messenger) and serotonin levels in the brain. The people using this medication reported that it was easier for them to think clearly, that they felt less anxiety, and had fewer urges to cut. Clozaril has a potential fatal side effect, however, which, while very rare, must be monitored for. People taking this medication require weekly blood tests to measure their white blood cell count. If their white count drops below normal, medication intake must be immediately discontinued. This means that Clozaril should be used only when the self-injury is serious and other methods of reducing it have failed or can be expected to fail.

Naltrexone is an opiate blocker that some have suggested can block the positive reinforcement effects of addictive activities such as heroin use, alcohol use, and self-mutilation. While taking naltrexone (the brand name is Revia), cutting yourself may become less reinforcing and, therefore, less attractive. Some people have reported that they even feel pain while cutting. A dose of about 150 mg of naltrexone may be needed to achieve this effect. In a study (Rubey 1995) of five people, four were able to significantly reduce their self-mutilation with naltrexone.

Comments on the "Borderline Cocktail"

The simultaneous combination of an antipsychotic (e.g., Risperdal, Haldol, Thorazine), an antimanic (e.g., Depakote, Tegretol), and an antidepressant (e.g., Prozac, Pamelor, or Paxil) is what I call the "Borderline Cocktail." It is frequently prescribed for people in the BZ. I believe that its actual effectiveness is not in line with its purported effectiveness. I base this judgment on the clinical experience I have had at the treatment program I direct. I have found that

1. The combination does not make the person feel significantly better, and my objective behavioral data generally does not support the efficacy of the regime when compared to a medication-free baseline.

2. When it appears effective it is hard to determine which medication is most effective.

3. The side effects of these medications can be quite uncomfortable.

4. Compliance with taking all of these pills is difficult.

5. Taking all of these medications often distracts the person from facing his or her BZ problems in psychotherapy.

Use this combination of medications only after you have tried solo medication trials targeting a clearly defined set of behavioral and emotional symptoms (for example, outbursts of anger, cutting yourself, or severe depression).

Suggested Medication Strategy

The following medication suggestions are based on the clinical experience of my staff of psychiatrists as prescribed in the residential program I direct. My medication strategy is to use *one medication* to reduce the intensity of the one set of emotions or behavior that you cannot tolerate. Once started, the medication should be used only as long as it takes you to make progress with the book and to learn to effectively use the SACRED skills. Once this occurs the medication should be gradually discontinued. If symptoms return and if you cannot manage them otherwise, you can restart the medication. The use of more than one medication at a time should be avoided.

The following box summarizes my suggestions for medications. If you decide to try medication, be sure you select your doctor carefully.

If you have Factor II BPD, it is important that you consult a behavioral health professional to evaluate whether you have bi-polar disorder

Table 10.1: Medication Strategies

Problem	Medications	Comments
Severe depression	Prozac, Zoloft, Pamelor, Effexor, Wellbutrin	Temporary or mild feelings of depression should not be medicated. Prozac is the preferred starting point.
Self-Injury	High dosage of Prozac, Clozaril, or Naltrexone	If the problem is severe, try Clozaril first.
Intolerable anxiety, cognitive confusion, alexithymia	Low dosages of Risperdal; Ativan or Valium if no history of drug/alcohol addictive activity	Use SDB and positive affirmations before trying any of these medications. Use the medications on an as needed basis and always use SDB *before* taking the medication. If taking medication on an as needed schedule is ineffective, try a low (2 mg) daily dose of Risperdal.
Hard-to-control temper outbursts or rages	Depakote or tegretol	Combine with SDB, positive affirmations, assertiveness skills.

(severe mood swings are the major symptom), attention deficit disorder (difficulty concentrating on nonpreferred tasks), or atypical depression (depression associated with extreme sensitivity to rejection). If you have any of these problems, medications other than those discussed in this section may be of help to you.

If you feel that medication could help you, consult your doctor or therapist for a referral to a psychiatrist who is willing to work with you. Use the same questions that you would use to screen potential therapists for screening a psychiatrist.

For additional information on the use of medications that can assist in the treatment of BPD read Carl Salzman's (1996) article in the *Harvard Mental Health Letter* or visit Glen Gabbard's Web page at

http://www.mhsource.com/edu/psytimes/p960424.html

Medication can assist you in reaching the Free Zone, but it cannot get you there in a quick or painless fashion. Its combination with self-help, this book (or its equivalent), support, a trusted therapist, and psychotherapy are your best bets for doing that.

Treatment Programs

If you feel that you may need a more intensive form of treatment than outpatient psychotherapy, there are a number of hospital, residential, or intensive outpatient programs that you can consider. Contact your local mental health provider or insurance company for the names of programs in your area. You may also contact us at (914) 279-5994 for assistance in locating a program.

SLS Health System's Mentorship Program. SLS Health System was founded in 1986. One of the programs we offer is the Mentorship Program for the treatment of borderline and addictive disorders. This program is available in a residential and intensive outpatient format. The program uses this book as its core treatment approach. Each member of the program has an individual therapist and a psychiatrist (if medication is desired). The ideal residential program duration is 45 to 120 days. The intensive outpatient version ideally requires three three-hour-long group sessions per week plus two individual sessions per week (tapering off sessions over a six- to twelve-month period as progress is made).

The residential program is more appropriate for those with severe addictive activity problems (cutting, cocaine, heroin, and so on) and those who feel suicidal. The intensive outpatient program is appropriate for those who work or who are attending school.

For more information about the Mentorship program contact me at 1-888-8CARE-4U. The program is located in Brewster, New York, which is sixty minutes north of New York City.

Chapter Milestones

1. There are several advanced forms of awareness that you need to develop to supercharge your recovery.

2. Facing all the darker motives that maintain and provoke border-line action is essential. As you master the SACRED skills, doing this will become an easier task.

3. Relying on your support system will also help you become aware of what you need to know.

4. There are many resources that you can make use of to help speed your recovery. The Internet, books, professional therapy, medications, and therapy programs can be accessed when you are ready.

5. Each of these resources can ease your journey through the Recovery Zone.

Positive Affirmation

I have the wisdom to use all the help I need.

**Remember to write in your
Recovery Journal today.**

Recovery Exercises

Recovery Exercise 10.1: Time Traveler

Objective

To see, feel, and experience the brightness of the Recovery Zone.

Background

A key part of advancing, if not "supercharging," your recovery, is being able to see a clear image of the "new you." It may be that the more clear and the more detailed this image of the future is today, the greater the possibility that it will actually come to pass tomorrow.

Expanded Awareness

Imagine yourself five years from today. How have you changed? How has the way you respond to frustration and stress changed? What new sources of joy and satisfaction are there in your life? How do you feel about those who are closest to you? How have your relationships with them changed? How do other people close to you see you now?

Recovery Exercise 10.2: I Hurt, Therefore I Am

Objective

To better understand the feelings felt and the images conjured up when you engage in self-injurious behavior.

Background

In the Borderline Zone, hurting yourself in any of various ways can be a means of experiencing feeling, especially when you feel numbed by thoughts and feelings. Hurting yourself may also be a way of seeking revenge; the thinking here may go something like, "They love me, so I will hurt what they love."

Expanded Awareness

Perhaps you have hurt yourself with the intent of arousing a particular reaction from people who love you. Write a brief essay entitled, "I Hurt, Therefore I Am." In this essay, explore the role of self-injurious behavior in your own life. Write about the effect it has on you, as well as its effect—and intended effect—on others.

Recovery Exercise 10.3: Fast Track to Nowhere

Objective

To recognize behavior that leads to dead ends—that is, nowhere.

Background

As discussed in this chapter, life in the Borderline Zone can involve many varieties of behavior that are thought to be goal-related, but are actually dead ends. The road out of the BZ is not by way of these dead ends, but rather expressways through Recovery.

Expanded Awareness

Blaming yourself. Somatic distractions. Fabrication. Pretending to dissociate. Merging with the environment. Being a "rebel without a clue." Playing mind games with professionals. Which of these dead ends have you been down? Write an essay about what you found at the end of each of your dead ends. As you write, reflect on such behavior in a way that is more honest and straightforward than you have ever been with yourself or anyone else.

Try to express as sincerely as possible your understanding of why these are truly dead ends.

Recovery Exercise 10.4: Letting Go

Objective
To revisit and explore sensitive and painful issues related to childhood trauma, with the objective of helping to minimize, if not eliminate, a need for revenge.

Background
People, who were traumatized in any number of different ways as children, may carry the resulting physical and psychological scars for life. Accompanying such scars are often a number of confusing feelings and questions about what happened and why. People may ask questions such as, "Was I hurt because I was bad or because the person hurting me was bad?"

Expanded Awareness
Can you find healthier ways to channel the anger and hurt you feel toward those who psychotraumatized you? Can you forgive those who hurt you?

Can you forgive yourself for hurting others? Can you let go and move on?

Write a short story that describes how, in a just world, you would go about doing this.

Recovery Exercise 10.5: The Letter

Objective
To write a letter to someone who has psychotraumatized you.

Background
It may be helpful to write a letter to someone who has hurt you. You may never send the letter, and they may never read it, but the act of writing out your feelings to a real person can release years of pent-up emotions.

Expanded Awareness
Draft a letter to a person who psychotraumatized and hurt you. In your letter express what you believe the person did to you and how it hurt. Discuss how the person's actions (or lack of action) has affected you since the trauma stopped. Discuss how you have attempted to recover from the trauma and its effects. Along the way, ask for a constructive response from this individual to help you better recover from the trauma.

Whether or not you ever mail the letter is a decision you can make with the members of your support system.

11

Recovery Snapshots

*You know, of course, where this other world lies hidden.
It is the world of your own soul that you seek. Only
within yourself exists that other reality for which you
long. I can give you nothing that has not already its
being within yourself ... All I can give you is the
opportunity, the impulse, the key. I can help you to
make your own world visible. That is all.*

—Herman Hesse, *Steppenwolf*

Choose your actions, or your actions will choose you.

—Anonymous

Each person's journey to the Free Zone follows a different route. This
journey is not an easy one. Periods of being stuck and losing your way
are the norm. Sometimes, family members provide little in the way of
support, and some even actively or passively undermine your efforts.

At first, successes are small and sometimes easily overlooked. Disappointments are plentiful. They can cause hours or days of depression
and self-hate. However, this self-help book, well-chosen support, and a
determined mind can help you complete this journey of recovery and
awakening.

Snapshots of Stops along the Way

Today, millions of children are being prepared for a life in the BZ. Millions of adolescents and adults are trapped in the Borderline Zone. The vast majority of them are trying to make it out. I would like to share the stories of a few of these people whom I have had the pleasure to know. (Names and all identifying information have been altered and some details are composites of more than one person's story.) Some of these people are making significant progress, others can't seem to stay out of the BZ. All of these people deserve as many chances as possible to make it. None of them caused their own initial psychotraumatization. By the same token, however, none are free of the responsibility for who they are and what they now do.

Peter: Slow, Steady Progress

Peter is in his early thirties. His childhood was difficult. His father was abusive and irresponsible and abandoned his two sons and their mother when they were young. He experienced Level IV psychotrauma. His mother was overwhelmed by her life and could not give to her sons the emotional nurturance they needed. Peter was plagued by periods of depression and suicidal thinking. He did some drinking and didn't do well in school. His mother felt he was "mentally ill." On a couple of occasions he attempted to hurt himself. He had been hospitalized several times before he came to our treatment program. After almost a year of treatment he was able to chart a new course for himself. He decided upon a career and went to school for the profession of his choice. His mother protested his choice. She told his therapist that he was setting Peter up for failure by encouraging him to go for his dream. With the help of his support system, Peter ignored her vote of no confidence and proceeded with his plans. Eventually, he even secured some assistance from her.

He entered school with determination. His girlfriend was his primary supporter and he depended upon her. School went well, but his reckless driving cost him his license, and his girlfriend eventually left him. He had to work for a full year to earn the money to pay his second year's tuition. He went through periods of mild depression, but he stayed on course. Things were never easy for Peter.

After three years of hard work and emotional ups and downs, he was set to graduate. On graduation day, a proud day for him, he was the only member of his family who attended the ceremony. Peter asked his former therapist to attend and he did. His mother could not take the day off from work. Peter understood, but quietly wished that it could have been otherwise.

Roger: A New Start

An alcoholic and violently abusive father tormented Roger and his mother for a number of years. Roger was exposed to Level IV psychotrauma. His mother was made into an emotional wreck. She took pills to calm her anxieties. She could not protect her son or herself. Roger became a "conduct problem" at home and in school. He tormented teachers and other people in authority. He used drugs and got drunk to make it all go away. When his parents got divorced, his father started a new life for himself and had little to do with Roger during his teen years. Roger was so out of control he had to be hospitalized a few times. Eventually, he came to our program. He fought everyone and everything until the day he started to feel his real pain. He took a chance and trusted his therapist. He worked out some of his anger in individual and group therapy. He was able to experience the hurt he carried inside and express through writing and talking. He started to think about himself in a more positive way. He was able to identify his strengths as a people person and a good talker. He learned to see that the future is not determined by the past; the future is a product of the choices he was now free to make.

When it was time to leave, he couldn't go home. His mother felt ambivalent about having him return home. She just couldn't take it. After a period of discussion and deliberation, he decided to move out of state and try his luck living on his own. He decided that it was time to learn about life in the real world.

Eventually, he got himself a good job and was able to make a bit of a life for himself. He couldn't say that he never used drugs or alcohol, but it wasn't like before. He reconciled things with his father. He is still struggling but has made a foothold for himself in the Free Zone.

Sarah: Severe Self-injury and Slow, Painful Growth

Sarah hated herself so much that she swallowed sharp objects, such as screws, to make this clear to everyone around her. Her parents were concerned and did not know what to do. They tried to help Sarah as best as they could, but found it hard to accept her as a person. Sarah was treated in many facilities. She was hospitalized over a dozen times. She gained a tremendous amount of weight, learned to hate herself more and more, and resorted to even more extreme forms of self-injury. Her parents became very angry with her. She wanted their approval and affection, but only knew how to provoke them with her borderline behaviors.

Sarah was exposed to Level III and, possibly, Level IV psychotrauma. Sarah's mother demanded perfection and, often, emotionally rejected Sarah. Sarah tried to live up to her mother's expectations, but always fell short. Eventually, she gave up meeting her mother's expectations and became, instead, a perfect failure.

When she came into our program, she was aggressive toward others, she swallowed objects to force people to take her to emergency rooms, and she hated herself so much that she could not even verbalize her own needs. With the help of some medication, a structured behavioral program to help her express her needs more directly, and time, she was able to decrease her self-injurious actions and talk more directly about her needs. She wasn't yet able to face her inner pain; it would have been too much for her at that time in her life. Her relationship with her family improved a little and she left to try out living on her own. She wasn't able to work but did manage to avoid the extreme borderline behaviors of the past. Sarah is in the Recovery Zone and she is satisfied with this for now.

Paul: Escape from the Pain

When his brother died accidentally on a camping trip, Paul woke up to life. All the drinking and drugging he was doing started to disgust him in a way it never did before. Paul was always the black sheep of his family. His two brothers were better at most things than he was. Paul had attention deficit problems. His brother who had died was his mother's favorite. Paul felt that he should have died in his brother's place. His mother even told him that (at least he thought she said that). After all, he was bad, and his brother was perfect.

His parents bitterly fought when Paul was young. His father cared about Paul, but could only express it in demanding and angry ways. His mother was controlling, rejecting, and intrusive. After his parents divorced, his mother felt she needed to find another man and Paul took a back seat to that task. Paul became hyperactive, anxious, easily confused, and prone to explosive outbursts of temper. He was hospitalized in his teen years several times and was given high doses of powerful tranquilizing drugs. They caused some serious side effects that scared him. His mother saw him as a very sick child and he saw himself as a worthless creature. Paul hated himself, and sometimes cut himself to prove it. Paul was exposed to sustained Level IV psychotrauma.

Paul came to the Mentorship program when he was nineteen and attacked everyone he could. He was angry. He was afraid. He hated himself more than anyone could imagine. He didn't trust his therapist. He manipulated him, but his therapist didn't treat him like a mental patient. His therapist trusted him and he told Paul when his actions were right and wrong. Gradually, Paul opened his heart. He spoke and felt much of the pain that was driving his anger. He was able to fully experience, within the safety of a therapy session, the full intensity of his self-hatred. With his therapist's help he was able to start loving himself by learning to reduce his rage and self-hatred. He started to think about his life in new ways.

At discharge he had nowhere safe to live. He wanted to live with his dad, but his dad's girlfriend wouldn't have it. His mom wanted him to live with her, but he wouldn't have it. His mom pushed for him to attend a special school. Paul didn't want any part of that either. He didn't want to be controlled anymore. He had learned to trust his therapist but wasn't ready to trust other authority figures. After much agonizing thought, he decided to move out of the country with a friend. A couple of years have past and he is surviving in a foreign country. He lives simply and by his wits, but in his mind he is free.

Andrea: So Much Hurt, So Young

As a little girl, Andrea would lie awake at night hoping her daddy would fall into a drug-induced sleep. Otherwise, he might storm into her room and terrorize her, hurt her, or worse. Her mother was also abused by her husband. She was battered and bruised inside and out. She couldn't protect her little girl or herself. She also tried to control everything Andrea did. Everyone lived in fear. Andrea was exposed to Level V psychotrauma.

Night after terrifying night this happened until one day when her dad finally stopped his drug abuse. Andrea, then a teenager, started to cut herself in a most brutal fashion. Her father was starting to treat her better, but the die was cast. Her career as a professional patient began. During one of her many hospitalizations and treatment episodes her dad died. Andrea didn't accept this and talked as if he were still alive, as if he were the greatest dad in the whole wide world.

When she came to our program, her body was terribly scarred from all the cutting she had done. She was skilled at getting objects to hurt herself with and despite our best precautions she was able to cut a long deep slice into her stomach. She stopped her incision only a few centimeters short of opening her belly. We lived through this horror with her. We helped her to get on Clozaril, which reduced her racing thoughts, severe anxiety, and urge to cut. Her cutting declined significantly.

Gradually, she began to trust one special staff person who was able to understand what she was going through better than anyone else. As Andrea felt more understood, her self-awareness expanded as her denial about her psychotraumatic past began to dissolve. She started to feel the buried emotional pain of her past. As she did, her attempts at cutting herself again became more frequent, but this time they were more superficial. Eventually, they dropped off to zero. Her mother started family therapy with her daughter and together they are trying to put together their life. The road is still dangerous, but Andrea is safely in the Recovery Zone.

Daniel: Searching for Self-Destruction

Not everyone is ready for recovery. For some people, the hurt is so deeply buried and walled off that they have few emotions left. Daniel was such a person. Superficially friendly and polite, Daniel was looking for thrills and self-destruction. An intelligent and handsome guy, he didn't trust anyone and used all of his skills to manipulate others. He was good at it; but not good enough to consistently survive. He was heavily addicted to drugs and sex. He dabbled with dealing and stealing. He was arrested and jailed. He was on probation. He alienated his adoptive parents. Daniel's considerable intellectual and interpersonal skills were put to dysfunctional use. This made it easy for him to find addictive activities to keep himself comfortably numb. It made it hard for Daniel to develop the level of awareness needed to exit the Borderline Zone.

He was adopted when he was three years old. His biological mother was a teenager, and, maybe, an addict. He stayed with her for a while, but then was removed from her home. He was in a foster home until he was adopted. He had attention deficit problems and he was exposed to Level III psychotrauma. No one knew exactly how he was treated as an infant or toddler. He didn't really remember much. In treatment programs he was cooperative as long as he was supervised. He trusted no one and shared little. In the pit of his stomach was a numbed-out zone of macho bravado. Sadly, we couldn't effectively communicate with him or help him to feel past his numbness. We tried for many months, but we failed. He left us and ended up first in jail, and then in a hospital, again.

Making It

Sometimes progress is difficult because old addictive activities are not easily given up. Though ultimately self-destructive, they do make the pain go away and, when all else fails, they can be tempting options. Real people are struggling with borderline and addictive behaviors. Most of them are succeeding enough to feel as if they are making a difference for themselves. Even though people who do not share your problem may ridicule your "slow rate of progress," you can counter their remarks by reminding yourself (and perhaps even them) that you have come a long way despite the pain inflicted upon you. As long as you remain determined, you will succeed regardless of how long it may take you to do it.

The next Impact! box summarizes findings from a book called *The Fate of Borderline Patients* (Stone 1990). As is the case with all studies, what is true for a sample of people may or may not be true for a given person. The results given should serve as a guide to what can happen, but should not be viewed as capable of predicting what will happen to any particular individual.

IMPACT!

Stats on Borderline Life

Dr. Michael Stone's study, reported in 1990, of three hundred people with BPD showed the following:

- 38 percent had suffered an early loss of parent, sibling
- 19 percent had suffered incest
- 11 percent had suffered parental brutality
- 13 percent of males and 7 percent of females committed suicide
- 90 percent of those with one or more positive factors (intelligence, attractiveness, etc.) and no negative factors (jailed, raped, incest) recovered
- People who never abuse substances showed an accelerated pattern of improvement
- People who did use substances only started to improve once they controlled their substance use
- People tended to improve as they got older, with peak improvement occurring in their late forties.

Chapter Milestones

1. There are many routes out of the Borderline Zone and no two people follow the same route.

2. Addiction, especially substance abuse and self-inflicted violence, must be controlled before real progress is possible.

Positive Affirmation

I am not alone.

Remember to write in your Recovery Journal today.

Recovery Exercises

Recovery Exercise 11.1: You're Not Alone

Objective

To look at your recovery process in relation to the recovery processes of others.

Background

This chapter contains brief case histories of a number of people. Sometimes it is helpful to compare the experiences of others to your own.

Expanded Awareness

Whose recovery story could you most closely identify with: Peter's, Roger's, Sarah's, Paul's, Andrea's, or Daniel's? What does your story and their story share? How is your story different?

What do you think is the hardest thing to overcome in order to successfully make it through to the Free Zone?

Recovery Exercise 11.2: Life One Year from Now

Objective

To think through your own outcomes.

Background

This chapter contains information about a study of the lives of people with BPD. The Impact! box that summarized the study presented statistics on outcomes that the people who participated in them experienced.

Expanded Awareness

Write an outcome summary with the following questions in mind:

What will your lifestyle look like one year from now? What will you be doing in the areas of work, education, living situation, recreation, and social life? How will you feel about yourself then?

How about five years from now? How will your life look? How will you feel looking back on today? What will you say was your greatest accomplishment?

12

Tracking Your Progress into the Free Zone

It is no use saying, "We are doing our best." You have got to succeed in doing what is necessary.

—Winston Churchill

You have got to learn to laugh. That will be required of you. You must apprehend the humor of life, its gallows-humor. But of course you are ready for everything in the world except what will be required of you ... As if there were not enough unhappiness in all you have designed already ... It is time to come to your senses. You are to live and to learn to laugh.

—Herman Hesse, *Steppenwolf*

Pain has its own sense of humor. One of the best measures of progress is our ability to laugh about where and who we have been. Our ability to laugh at past dysfunctional actions is a measure of the growth of our self-awareness. In this sense, laughter is more than just good medicine.

Human behavioral change proceeds in steps. Rarely does a person change in one massive, transformational leap. Behaviors start to change, results change, and then awareness changes. Changes in self-awareness can accelerate the pace of behavioral change just as a good coach can help an athlete to better learn a sport.

The Angry Heart Compass

The following behavioral compass (the Angry Heart Compass on page 228) can help you locate your position on the Angry Heart Map on page 227). You may remember the map and compass from the introduction. To locate your position on the map all you need to do is *honestly* check off each of the behavioral criteria on the compass that you believe accurately describes you as you are today. Do this for each of the three Zones in the compass.

Once you have checked off all applicable items, count the number of items you checked in each of the Zones and enter the number for each Zone in the Zone's box in the last section of the form, which is labeled "Your Location." Your score will then read "__ by__ by __." This is your location in psychological recovery space.

Make several photocopies of the Angry Heart Compass. Measure your position now, and then, again every few weeks or as often as you desire. Chart your scores to assess your progress. Don't expect rapid improvement in your scores. It will take many, many months for you to check even a single item in the Free Zone. It may take several years for you to be able to not check items in the Borderline Zone.

Try scoring yourself now. Compare this score to the one from chapter 1. How has it changed? On the page after the Angry Heart Compass there is a score interpretation chart that will help you understand what your current location indicates.

The Angry Heart Map

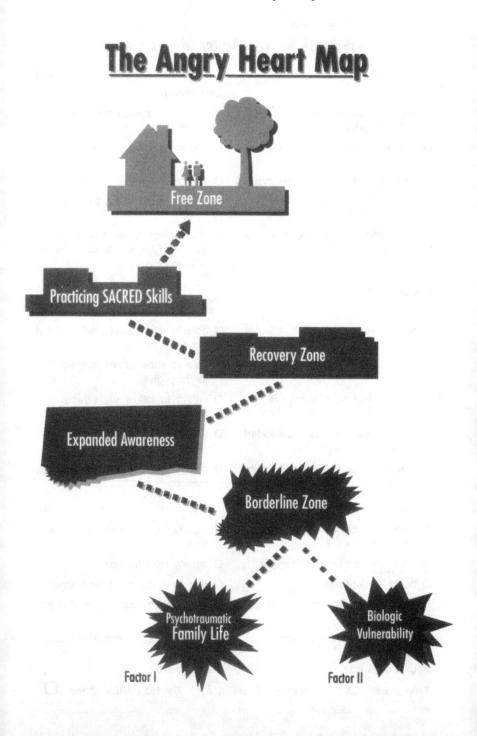

Self-Help Skill: The Angry Heart Compass

Free Zone
Score: /10

Early Stage

- [ ] able to openly talk about past pain with loved one
- [ ] able to hold on to close relationships
- [ ] able to hold steady employment
- [ ] able to tolerate stress without resorting to addictive activities
- [ ] comfortable being affectionate toward a loved one

Late Stage

- [ ] word and actions are more consistent
- [ ] you know what you want from life
- [ ] you can love another without fear
- [ ] able to laugh about the past
- [ ] you feel optimistic about the future and you are more at peace with the past

Recovery Zone
Score: /10

Early Stage

- [ ] able to write about pain
- [ ] able to cut short temper outbursts
- [ ] able to cut back addictive behaviors
- [ ] able to slow stress-accelerated mind
- [ ] able to accept your deficits without anger

Late Stage

- [ ] able to tolerate feedback without anger
- [ ] able to show others appreciation for help given
- [ ] willing to follow the advice of a mentor
- [ ] able to accept the help of a therapist
- [ ] the defensive "wall" is down more than up

Borderline Zone
Score: /10

- [ ] addictive activities used (drugs, sex, cutting, etc.)
- [ ] poor control over your temper
- [ ] bouts of depression
- [ ] suicidal thinking or suicidal actions
- [ ] angry, rebellious, inconsistent

- [ ] moods change a lot and you feel bad
- [ ] stormy relationships
- [ ] feel as if you can't trust anyone
- [ ] feel as if you don't know who you are
- [ ] racing thoughts, impulsive actions

Your Location:

Free Zone [ ]   Recovery Zone [ ]   By Borderline Zone [ ]

Self-Help Skill: Angry Heart Compass Guidelines

Score	Guidelines
Highest number: X by X by X	The highest number determines which Zone you are in. If it is the first then you are in the Free Zone, the second the Recovery Zone, and the third the Borderline Zone.
0 by 0 by 10	This is the starting point for most people in the Borderline Zone. Some will score less than 10 but few will score positive on the other two Zones.
0 by 2 by 7	After a couple of months of work you can expect a score similar to this.
0 by 5 by 5	After a solid year of work you can expect to be about here.
1 by 5 by 3	About a year and a half of work will get you here if you are using all of your resources.
5 by 7 by 3	More than two years of consistent work will get you to this point.
10 by 10 by 0	This position is your ultimate goal. It will take several years of consistent effort and toleration of setbacks to reach this point.

The guidelines in the chart are best-guess estimates. They are not based on a rigorous scientific study of the rate of progress made by people going through a healing process. I am just now beginning to conduct these studies and would welcome your participation. If you are interested in helping out, please contact me by E-mail, mail, or phone. As I gather more information, I will post the latest set of guidelines on the Web site. You can also request them by sending me an SASE (self-addressed stamped envelope) through regular mail.

The form on the next page can be used to keep your own log of your Angry Heart Compass locations. Feel free to photocopy it and keep it in your Recovery Journal.

If your journey is going at a slower pace than you would like or is slower than the pace suggested by the compass guidelines, then consider assessing the reasons for this by reading the items in the Borderline Zone of the Angry Heart Compass you checked on your last measurement. You can then use the chart on page 231 to help guide your search through the book to find the sections that can help you improve your rate of progress. Of course, you can ignore any and all of these suggestions as you see fit.

Self-Help Skill: Angry Heart Compass Location Log

Date	Map Location		Comments
	by	by	Chapter 1's Score
	by	by	
	by	by	
	by	by	
	by	by	
	by	by	
	by	by	
	by	by	
	by	by	
	by	by	
	by	by	
	by	by	
	by	by	
	by	by	
	by	by	
	by	by	
	by	by	
	by	by	
	by	by	
	by	by	
	by	by	
	by	by	
	by	by	
	by	by	
	by	by	
	by	by	
	by	by	
	by	by	
	by	by	
	by	by	
	by	by	

Self-Help Skill: Assessing Roadblocks to Progress

Borderline Zone Item Checked	Chapters/Skills to Work On
Addictive activities used	Reread chapter 8 and redo the exercises. Consider joining a support group. If your self-injury draws blood, consider seeking out medication to help weaken your urges to harm yourself.
Poor control over your temper	Review and use Slow Deep Breathing and Objectifying skills in chapter 7. Redo exercises in chapter 7.
Bouts of depression; suicidal thinking or actions	Face your pain more directly (reread chapters 1 through 4). Nurture yourself (chapter 7). Retake the PTES (chapter 6). Seek the support of others—going it alone is depressing in itself. Use positive affirmations several times per day. If you have strong suicidal urges consult a professional.
Angry, rebellious, inconsistent	Face your pain directly. Increase your journal writing. Visualize alternative behavior (chapter 7).
Moods change a lot and you feel bad; racing thoughts, impulsive actions	Reread stress hypersensitivity section in chapter 6. Practice SDB daily with positive affirmations.
Stormy relationships; feel as if you can't trust anyone	Reread Dr. Erickson's stages in chapter 1. Review RCP in chapter 6. Reread chapter 9 on support. Go on the Internet and join a chat group. Find a support group.
Feel as if you don't know who you are	Reread the section about distorted self-image in chapter 6. Reread your journal entries.

Remember, you need to *positively* reinforce the efforts of your Mentor and support system to maintain strong momentum. Let those who are helping you know that you appreciate them. Send them a card, a gift, or the like. When you are abusive or harsh toward them, apologize directly to them for acting that way. Be sincere in your apology. An apology is not an act of submission. It is a communicative action that clarifies misunderstanding and error. Do not let your setbacks become disasters by burning out your key supporters. I know that it is difficult to admit being wrong, but doing this is very therapeutic and sensible.

Plot your position on the Angry Heart Map regularly. Practicing the SCARED skills will help to move you out of the Recovery Zone and into the Free Zone. Failure to put them to positive use could lead you back into the Borderline Zone.

Chapter Milestones

1. Keeping your recovery on track requires both measurement of progress and motivational replenishment. Measurement and motivation will help you get where you want to go.

2. Your supporters need to feel your appreciation so they can support and motivate you in return.

3. You need to honestly measure your location in psychological recovery space so you will know how far you have come—and how close you are to the Free Zone.

Positive Affirmation

I seek to know the true location of my life.

**Remember to write in your
Recovery Journal today.**

Recovery Exercises
Recovery Exercise 12.1: Consistently Yours

Objective

To develop and measure your ability to be consistent in word and action that will help you to eliminate borderline behaviors from and introduce more productive actions to your daily routine.

Background

One of the keys to effectively living in the Free Zone is being viewed by others and by yourself as a consistent person who does what you say you will do. This attribute builds trust with others and its impairment is one of the primary negative consequences of being psychotraumatized by people and, especially, by people you trusted. Being able to trust others means that you must be able to trust yourself. Trusting yourself means being able to do the important things you say you are going to do most of the time.

Expanded Awareness

There are two parts to this exercise. The first is developing the ability to predict your most important behavior during a specified time period (for example, hour, day, week). The second involves planning a schedule and then completing at least 85 percent of it.

In your journal start a section called "Consistency." Select a short time, let's say one hour. Predict where you will be, whom you will be with, and what you will be doing in that one-hour period. Write your predictions in your journal. Then over the next hour see how accurate your predictions turned out to be. For example, you could predict that you will be at home, alone, and you will do some reading and TV watching. You might find that you were at home, alone, and watched TV and talked on the phone. In this case, your prediction would have been almost accurate. Practice this exercise a few times each day until you can predict an entire day's events with 85 percent accuracy. Use behavior contracting to reinforce your learning.

Now this may seem like a silly exercise to go through, but it isn't. It gets more interesting when you make the time period longer and when you go from predicting what you will do to committing yourself to carrying out planned activities.

When you can accurately predict a day's events, you are ready to move to part two of this exercise: doing what you intend.

Start with an entire day. Plan the key things that you want to accomplish that day. Include the self-help tasks and goals that you want to accomplish during the day such as no self-injury, no alcohol use, talking with one of your supporters, and so forth. Pay careful attention to any promises that you made to people. Make sure you plan your day with time available to do whatever it may take to keep your promise. Of course, you should only include healthy promises here.

Once you are able to accomplish 80 percent of what you plan or promise to do for a single day try to expand your time horizon to two days. Work up to being consistent for four- to six-day blocks of time.

This exercise is hard work and, for this reason, it may seem unappealing. However, without pain there is no gain. Developing the ability to be consistent in word and action is truly worth the effort.

Recovery Exercise 12.2: My Compass, My Guide

Objective

To foster thinking and imagery about movement within and between the various zones—Borderline, Recovery, and Free—described in this book.

Background

In this chapter, an Angry Heart Compass was presented as a tool to help you track your therapeutic progress. In this exercise, you will be challenged to think of ways you can use your compass to point you in the right direction.

Expanded Awareness

Examine your compass entries for the Borderline, Recovery, and Free Zones. Pay particular attention to how the numbers you entered differ from the numbers you would ideally like to have entered.

Now write a brief essay entitled, "My Compass, My Guide." In that essay, list how you intend to use what you have learned from your compass to constructively change the direction of your life.

Recovery Exercise 12.3: Mentor Surprise

Objective

To use creativity in planning a meaningful "thank you" to the Mentor who has been working with you.

Background

People like to be liked and appreciated. If you have had a Mentor working with you on your road to recovery and freedom, now might be a good time to express your gratitude to that person.

Expanded Awareness

Create a homemade greeting card to thank your Mentor for his or her efforts.

Beyond saying "thank you" in words, your card should impart a message that lets the Mentor know that you have truly learned something about who you are and all that you are capable of being. Your message will be the greatest "thank you" of all.

13

The Angry Heart Theory

We find ourselves in a bewildering world. We want to make sense of what we see around us and to ask: What is the nature of the universe? What is our place in it and where did it and we come from? Why is it the way it is?

—Stephen W. Hawking, *A Brief History of Time*

You can safely skip this chapter if whys do not interest you. This chapter is about the theory behind this book. It supplements the information presented in the introduction. It is a deceptively simple theory.

As we move into the twenty-first century, it is becoming fashionable to think that many human behavioral problems are caused by abnormal brain chemistry, and that the problems can be repaired by man-made chemicals. It is also fashionable to recognize the terrible harm that childhood economic stress, abuse, and neglect cause. The disintegration of the American family and the eroding of family values is a sound bite shared by nearly every political campaign. The plague of drugs and alcohol abuse claims new victims daily in every school yard, mall, factory, and office in our country. The prisons fill up, the politicians talk, the kids get high, their parents get divorced, people receive treatment, managed care companies control costs, and we all lament what is going on around us as if it were happening somewhere else.

But what happens if we realize that the somewhere else is here? If we accept this as fact, then we can ask, what is all of this doing to us, and to our children? Are we a chemically imbalanced society, or are we an environmentally imbalanced one? Should we all be taking Prozac, or is it time to clean house? Is there even a difference between these choices?

The Angry Heart Theory addresses some of these issues in the context of explaining what goes wrong in a child's world to cause borderline and addictive problems.

The Psychosocial Environment

The Angry Heart Theory uses the word *environment* to refer to more than just the physical environment. The theory talks about *psychosocial environments*—the environments that condition and channel behavior on a moment-to-moment basis. They are the environments that surround us, and "contain" our behavior. They are the environments with which you continuously interact: you affect them and they affect you. They reward you, they ignore you, and they punish you. They educate you, and they challenge you. You change them, and they change you. You control them, and they control you. Without the presence of active psychosocial environments, your behavioral output would decline to near zero levels.

Active psychosocial environments organize you and all the people, places, and things that define your lifestyle. They are composed of time, space, and *contingencies*. Time and space are familiar concepts, but contingencies are not. Active psychosocial environments organize the connections among their parts through, what psychologists call, contingencies. Contingencies connect behavior with environmental results and vice versa. For example, running a red light might connect you with an accident or ticket. Planting tomato seeds might connect you with ripe tomatoes for a salad. Playing a slot machine might connect you with a winning jackpot. Smiling warmly at a person might connect you with a new friend.

Contingencies connect actions to environmental results. Some results strengthen the actions that produced them. These results are called *positive* and *negative reinforcers* (I spoke about these in earlier chapters). Other results weaken the actions that produced them. These results are called *punishments*. Finally, the absence of a result tends to weaken the actions that failed to produce the expected or desired result. This is called *extinction* (or ignoring).

Contingencies can be thought of as the rules of the game. Each environment you enter has its own set of rules. Your effectiveness in an environment depends on your ability to analyze the environment and understand its contingencies or rules. If the contingencies of an environment change in unpredictable ways, are excessively harsh in their results, or make demands that exceed your behavioral capability, you feel ineffective and highly stressed. These types of contingencies can, under the right circumstances, have a psychotraumatic effect upon a person.

The Neural Environment

Inside your skin is another type of environment. It is a biochemical environment that creates, and then is managed by, your brain (neural environment). The brain is the organ of your body that uses chemical messengers, called *neurotransmitters*, to process the *contingency information* communicated by your psychosocial environment into behavioral action. The psychosocial environment then judges the "fit" of the behavioral actions the brain produces. It reinforces the ones it judges acceptable (says "yes") and ignores (says nothing) or punishes (says "no") the others.

The interaction between your psychosocial environment and your neural environment produces your *conscious self*. It is through your conscious self that you come to know who you are. The capacity for a conscious self enables humans to create something new: *self-aware behavioral action*. This capability has changed both human history and the face of our planet. It cast us out of the Garden of Eden and produced some of man's greatest achievements. Your ability to change your own life is also based on this capability. Without it, your behavioral actions would be an unconscious biochemical response (modified by the cyclic metabolic processes of your brain and body) to the contingencies organized by your psychosocial environments.

Self-aware action is the conceptual cornerstone of my approach to treating borderline and addictive problems. *The Angry Heart* will help you if and only if it expands your *self-awareness* enough to empower you to *take action* and make use of its skills and advice. An expansion of your self-awareness can only occur if you experience just enough painful feeling and knowledge (without numbing it) to fuel its growth. No pain, no gain. (Sorry.) But, too much pain, too quickly, and you will use addictive activities to run from the process.

With this background information out of the way, I can give you a thumbnail sketch of my conditioning theory of borderline and addictive problems.

The Angry Heart Theory

The heart of this theory (remember it applies to Factor I BPD) is based on a simple assumption: Psychotraumatic contingencies, in family and developmental environments, cause a disruption of a child's psychological and physical growth. This disruption can cause the child to develop *high levels of fear* (manifesting itself as anxiety, withdrawal, dependency, depression, anger) and *low levels of trust* (manifesting itself as anxious bonding, self-hatred, suspicion). This combined effect expands over time through the emergence of a relationship control phobia and a disruption of a child's neural environment (for example, reduction in serotonin levels). As these effects compound each other, the child becomes more hypersensitive to stress (causing the child to be angry, unstable, withdrawn, depressed, anxious) and develops a more distorted self-image (simultaneously grandiose and self-hating). The dysphoric (unhappy) moods and confusing thought processes, which are the result, motivate a trial-and-error search for effective forms of escape from these negative patterns of feeling and thinking. Impulsive action and gratification seeking (addictive activity) are, thereby, initiated and conditioned through the tandem effects of negative (reduction in bad feeling or thought) and positive (pleasure stimulation of addictive activity) reinforcement. The intensity and strength of these escape and avoidance (addictive activities) behaviors increase markedly during the adolescent years when greater opportunity and capability are present.

The theory also assumes that anyone (a friend, parent, grandparent) or anything (intelligence, attractiveness, talent, and so on) that mitigates or offsets the psychotraumatic effect on a child will reduce the severity of resultant borderline and addictive behaviors. The earlier a positive factor is present, the longer its duration, and more intense its impression, the greater is the reduction in the psychotraumatic conditioning effect.

The theory does *not* assume the existence of any necessary or specific genetic predisposition in the child for the psychotraumatic effect to occur. The presence, however, of any factor (genetic or otherwise) that would tend to make the child harder to raise (such as attention deficit disorder), independent of the psychotraumatic levels of the developmental environment, will exacerbate the effects of preexisting psychotraumatic contingencies by increasing the stress load on the people (parents, siblings, and so on) in the child's family environment.

As a psychotraumatized child moves through adolescence, his or her dysfunctional, behavioral repertoires organize into borderline functioning and, in the absence of therapeutic or supportive intervention, into borderline personality disorder (which simply means that the behavioral patterns become a more integral part of who the person is). The level and cumulative duration of psychotraumatic exposure, the presence of positive mitigating factors, and the average degree of support generated by a person's lifestyle environments determines the severity of the functional impairment experienced by that person.

Defining Psychotraumatization

Psychotraumatization is a core theoretical concept. The PTES scale in chapter 5 defines five levels of psychotraumatic exposure. Within each level are several types of exposure experiences. This catalog of psychotrauma is not complete. More study and research is needed to identify additional psychotraumatic experiences.

My definition of a psychotraumatic experience is an aversive event that triggers a fear response capable of causing a person to become concerned about his or her psychological or physical safety while effectively inhibiting the person's ability to protect him- or herself by terminating or escaping the aversive event. This concept includes abuse, neglect, and invalidation (Linehan 1993).

Concern about physical safety includes fear of death, torture, mutilation, injury, or exposure to deadly illness. Concern about psychological safety includes fear of being emotionally abandoned, fear of having your identity invaded by the overwhelming demands of another, and fear of having those whom you depend upon for survival hating you.

Here are a few specific examples of aversive events classified as psychotraumatic or not. The disciplinary use of a spanking, a reprimand, or a loss of privilege is not psychotraumatizing. The beating of a child because a parent is in a drunken rage is. The verbal humiliation of a child because the parent is in a bad mood is. The destruction of all of a child's possession because a parent is mentally ill is. The frequent physical abuse and taunting of a child by his or her peers is. The bombardment of a city is. The consistent manipulation of a child with the threat of loss of parental love is. Drug-testing a child is not. The torturing of a soldier is. Confinement in a concentration camp is. Making a child do his or her homework is not. The key defining characteristic of a psychotraumatic aversive event versus a nontraumatic aversive event is whether or not the child or adult behaved in a way indicating that his or her psychological or physical safety was threatened and he or she could not terminate or escape it.

Borderline Phases

As presented in the introduction, there are three major phases of borderline behavior. A direct self-harm phase, an indirect self-harm phase, and an inter-phase. People move between phases or can remain in a single phase for variable periods of time.

People in the direct self-harm phase are at higher risk for suicide than those in the indirect self-harm phase, who are at higher risk for

---

IMPACT!

Factor II BPD—Biological Vulnerability

In Factor II BPD, a biologic vulnerability that may include childhood bipolar disorder, attention deficit disorder, genetic defect, or intrauterine neuro-toxin exposure creates a child who is neurologically dysfunctional. This biologic dysfunction shapes hard-to-tolerate behavior in the child. The child's behaviors create high levels of stress within the family. Previously functional interaction patterns among family members begin to become dysfunctional. This has a negative effect on the child's aversive behaviors, making them worse. This feeds back, in turn, to the rest of the family, making them feel even more stressed. Progressively, the child's and parent's self-efficacy and self-esteem are affected by their failure to function effectively as a family. This interactive cycle continues until, in the absence of proper treatment, adolescence makes matters virtually impossible as a full-blown borderline behavior pattern emerges.

As this process unfolds the child, parents, and other family members are left feeling enraged, confused, helpless, hopeless, and guilty. All are punished.

---

accidental death or injury. Here are the behaviors seen in each of the three phases:

Direct Self-Harm Phase

- Physical self-injury (cutting, burning, bruising, and so on) addiction
- Suicidal thinking and gestures
- Frequently withdrawn and depressed mood

Indirect Self-Harm Phase

- Drug, alcohol, sex, reckless-driving addiction
- Explosive anger, moodiness, or inappropriately outgoing behavior
- Legal difficulties (loss of driver's license, drug arrests, and so on)

Inter-Phase

- More stability in behavior and feelings
- Acceptance seeking with sensitivity to rejection
- Transient mild depression and mild anger outbursts

Mentorship Self-Help Therapy (MST) Approach

If the cause of borderline and addictive problems is rooted largely in psychotraumatic conditioning, what is the therapy? The therapy needs to elicit and then extinguish the fear, pain, and anger caused by psychotraumatization; it needs to begin to desensitize the relationship control phobia and reduce the use of addictive activities. Once these three things are on an improving track, the reorganization and repair of the person's lifestyle needs to begin.

In Mentorship Self-Help Therapy, someone has to get your attention and initial trust to help you to want to get these things started. The paradox to be overcome is that you need to trust someone while being unable to trust anyone. However, it is only with your permission and with your self-help that change can take place. No one can mandate you to change. You can have your symptoms medicated with the most potent "borderline cocktail," but it will do nothing to get you out of the BZ unless the decision to use medication was a free choice made with expanded self-awareness. Otherwise, the medication becomes the equivalent of just another addictive activity. And the person giving it to you becomes just another controller (that is, an abuser or enabler) who must be defeated.

The person you allow to help you need not be a professional therapist. A caring and strong person who is willing to help another human being in need can initiate a process of healthy change. Many people receive support and help from spouses, lovers, and close friends. When you combine a supportive person with the information and suggestions contained in this self-help book, you can get things off to a good start. However, at some point, for people with higher levels of psychotraumatization or life-threatening addictive activity, professional assistance will be needed. By combining carefully chosen professional assistance and supportive people with this book (or its equivalent), you create a winning combination.

Chapter Milestones

1. The Angry Heart Theory has strong implications for social policy makers, families, schools, and nearly every institution of our society. As a society, we need to devote more resources to understanding what creates an optimal environment for raising children and what environments create psychotraumatic conditioning.

2. Borderline and addictive problems can reach epidemic proportions if the growth of psychotraumatic causes is not stopped.

3. Understanding the theory behind what you are doing may help to motivate you to accomplish your goals.

Positive Affirmation

I seek to understand how the society I live in affects me.

Recovery Exercises

Recovery Exercise 13.1: The Rules of the Game

Objective

To achieve greater insight into the contingencies operative in your life.

Background

A contingency is something that may occur as a result of your actions. In the board game *Monopoly*, many of the contingencies, such as whether or not you go to jail, operate more on the basis of chance than anything else; the fate of an individual player rests on the roll of a dice or the "chance card" that the player happens to draw. By contrast, in real life, you have much more control over the contingencies that operate . . . such as whether or not you go to jail.

Expanded Awareness

Explore in depth two significant "rules of the game" that seem to have been operative in your own life. The first of these rules will be a statement about how engaging in one type of behavior has typically resulted in something significantly positive in your life. The second of these rules will be a statement about how engaging in another type of behavior has typically resulted in something significantly negative in your life. For example, fill in the blanks below for each of the following statements:

1. In the past, when I _____ (fill in with a behavior), the result has been _____ (fill in with a significantly positive consequence that took place).

2. In the past, when I _____ (fill in a behavior), the result has been _____ (fill in with a significantly negative consequence that took place).

After you have written the two statements above, write a discussion of each statement that explores the whys behind what you wrote. That is, try to probe your own motivation for engaging in the behaviors you listed. Why do you think you engaged in such behaviors? Then, explore the consequences of your behaviors; how and why did they come about?

Finally, write two personally meaningful rules of the game that you can follow in the days ahead. The rules you write should reflect your desire to have more positive consequences and less negative consequences in your life in the Recovery Zone. The rules should also reflect your insight into why you did some of the things you did in your past.

Recovery Exercise 13.2: No Pain, No Gain

Objective

To foster self-growth by gaining insight into painful elements of the past.

Background

You read in this chapter that genuinely experiencing painful feelings from your past is essential to the task of expanding your self-awareness and to growing beyond what you are. Prior to reading this book, you may have avoided confronting emotionally painful thoughts through the use of drugs, emotional numbing, or any of several other means. Many of this book's Recovery Exercises were painful tasks. Hopefully, they have helped you to think more about and have expanded your understanding of who you are and the road you have traveled. Are you ready to share some of the pain you have "discovered" with someone else?

Expanded Awareness

Many people carry with them a private thought, feeling, or image that is troubling or painful. People may keep this thought, feeling, or image to themselves in the belief that if other people knew about it, they would think less of them or, even, reject them.

At some point in time, it will be therapeutic to share what hurts or troubles you with a therapist, in a therapy group, with a Mentor, or with a very close friend. Are you at that point in time now? If so, plan to share the thought, feeling, or image that hurts or troubles you in the interest of gaining greater insight into how it has been affecting your everyday existence. If you aren't ready to share the pain with people, consider explaining to them why you are not ready to share this with them at this time. Finally, think about the gains you may be able to make in your life as a result of experiencing—and resolving—some of the past pain.

14

The Freedom of a New Beginning

Breathe, breathe in the air
Don't be afraid to care
Leave but don't leave me
Look around and choose your own ground
For long you live and high you fly
And smiles you'll give and tears you'll cry
All you touch and all you see
Is all your life will ever be. . . .

—Pink Floyd, "Breathe"

There are no final results; no victory flags or parades; no shouts of congratulations. Just you knowing that it's gotten a whole lot better. Never perfect, just better. It all comes from inside. You feel better about yourself, others, prior situations, and possible situations. Actions and results will change.

New actions and better results. There is nothing better, although there is nothing easy about it. It's all about the reward. It's a big one. The reward is our freedom from, let's call it, the dark side. We all have one. The dark side is my pet name for it. It sounds so black and white, but it's really neither.

As the battle rages on, you will see the difference. It's a never ending battle—I know, because I'm still fighting this battle every day. It's been almost six years now that I have been trying to win this battle. I haven't won it yet, but, the most important thing is that I have not lost it either. And the casualties are certainly going way down. I'm not cured or suddenly immune to the dark side. I've just learned how to better manage and control my urges. Trust me, with time you will get stronger and start to see the differences that you are making. Then the people around you will notice the difference. They'll wonder what's happening, but they'll never ask. They'll simply accept it.

Hopefully, you also feel empowered to accept and change yourself. I know that the task ahead can appear overwhelming at times. It is, but it isn't. It really is all a matter of perspective. Those who spend their precious days lamenting the tragedy of their past are blinded to the possibilities of their future. Those who look to each day as a new opportunity for growth and enjoyment, for putting distance between themselves and what happened to them, make it to the Free Zone. It is all about perspective, and each of us are free to choose our own perspective.

Most readers agree that Samuel's writings help them to begin the task of feeling and resolving their psychotraumatic past. As Samuel has so clearly written, a person's psychotrauma extends both to the recent past (which unfortunately is self-generated) as well as to the distant past (which was generated by others). Starting to feel and to resolve all of your psychotraumatic exposures is the major hurdle that must be overcome before you can enter the Recovery Zone.

Most of the people who read this book also find the SACRED skills to be something of a drag to learn. Part of the resistance comes from being told that you should learn these skills. As we all know, people in the BZ resent with a passion being told what is good (and, especially, what is bad) for them. So, it is only natural to feel resistance to this outside demand to do something. Can you transform this "demand" into an inner desire to become a happier person?

The other part of the resistance often comes from believing that the SACRED skills will not help; that they are silly or demeaning to use ("If I use them, it means I'm sick"). People in the BZ often feel abnormal and sick. Anything that reminds them of this (such as learning a self-help skill) can turn them off. All I can suggest is to try one or two of the skills. Doing something new and healthy is essential to making it out of the Recovery Zone and into the Free Zone. If you are of the mind that the SACRED skills are bogus, then create some skills of your own. The act of doing so will help build your inner strength and determination to succeed. Self-initiating any form of healthy change will also unleash positive lifestyle momentum.

What were the changes, the differences you decided to make? Well, one change I know you made was reading this book. You need to get in touch with your actions and results. Talk about them. Write them down. Understand what you will do. One mistake is an accident, but more than one is a habit. Don't do what you have done in the past. This is a new you. It's time for new feelings, actions, and results.

Our time together is drawing to a close. Samuel, Dr. Cohen, and I wish you the very best of luck with all of your life's adventures. We know that if you have read this far you are indeed determined enough to succeed. Please feel free to contact us (or visit us on the Web) to share your comments, curses, and experiences. We'd love to hear from you. Once again from all of us a very big Good Luck!

I know I love myself and respect the life I'm living. Every day is important to me, and, in my own way, I make the best of each one. My higher power has given me a new lease on life.

There is nothing special about me. I'm your normal, everyday guy who got sick and tired of living the life of a loser and did something about it. You can do the same.

Be patient, be consistent, and don't be hard on yourself. Most importantly, do not lie to yourself. If it gets bad, and it may again and again, be honest. Know that you started to get it right, and that you will get back to getting it right as often as necessary!

Enjoy your victories—big and small. And never give up.

Take a chance, and free your heart of anger. You won't be disappointed.

Congratulations on your new beginning.

Positive Affirmation

Everything your life could ever be "is all your life will ever be."

Appendix

Positive Affirmation Summary

Chapter 1	I am a good person and I will prevail.
Chapter 2	Telling my story helps me ease my angry heart.
Chapter 3	Talking helps me feel better.
Chapter 4	"Ugly" truth heals better than "soothing" denial.
Chapter 5	I seek the safety of my own Recovery Zone.
Chapter 6	The power of choice frees me from life in the Borderline Zone.
Chapter 7	The SACRED skills help me live outside the Borderline Zone.
Chapter 8	Positive support eases my journey.
Chapter 9	My recovery is a spiraling, step-by-step journey of choices that lead to freedom.
Chapter 10	I have the wisdom to use all the help I need.
Chapter 11	I am not alone.
Chapter 12	I seek to know the true location of my life.
Chapter 13	I seek to understand how the society I live in effects me.
Chapter 14	Everything your life could ever be, "Is all your life will ever be."

Never Give Up!

References

American Psychiatric Press. 1994. *Diagnostic and Statistical Manual IV.* Washington, DC: American Psychiatric Press.

Bandura, A. 1997. Self-efficacy. *Harvard Mental Health Letter,* 13(9):4.

Biederman, J. 1997. Is there a childhood form of bi-polar disease? *Harvard Mental Health Letter,* 13(9), 8.

Camus, A. 1956; 1991. *The Fall.* New York: Vintage Books.

de Vegvar, M. L., L. J. Siever, and R. L. Trestman. 1994. Impulsivity and serotonin in borderline personality disorder. In K. R. Silk, ed., *Biological and Neurobehavioral Studies of Borderline Personality Disorder.* Washington, DC: American Psychiatric Press.

Dulit, R., M. R. Ryer, A. C. Lean, and B. S. Brodsky. Clinical correlates of self-mulitation in borderline personality disorder. 146th Meeting of the American Psychiatric Association (1993, San Francisco, California).

Erikson, E. 1950. *Childhood and Society.* New York: Norton & Company.

Famularo, R., R. Kinscherff, and T. Fenton. 1991. Posttraumatic stress disorder among children clinically diagnosed as borderline personality disorder. *Journal of Nervous & Mental Disease,* 179(7):428–431.

Favazza, A. R., and K. Conterio. 1988. The plight of chronic self-mutilators. *Community Mental Health Journal,* 24, 22–30.

Frankl, V. E. 1959. *Man's Search for Meaning.* New York: Pocket Books.

Gabbard, G. 1996. Integrated treatment of borderline personality disorder. Internet document: http://www.mhsource.com/edu/psytimes/p960424.html, 16 May 1997.

Harm Reduction: *A Work in Progress,* http://www.safeworks.org/Protocol/, Dec 1996.

Hawking, S. W. 1988. *A Brief History of Time.* New York: Bantam Books.

Hesse, Herman. 1963. *Steppenwolf.* New York: Bantam Books.

Jung, C. G. 1953. In J. Jacobi and R. F. C. Hull, eds. *Psychological Reflections.* Princeton, N. J.: Princeton University Press.

Kroll, J. 1988. *The Challenge of the Borderline Patient.* New York: Norton & Company.

Linehan, M. 1993. *Cognitive-Behavioral Treatment of Borderline Personality Disorder.* New York: Guilford Press.

McLuhan, M. 1964. *Understanding Media.* New York: McGraw-Hill.

Miller, F. T., T. Abrams, R. Dulit, and M. Fyer. 1993. Substance abuse in borderline personality disorder. *American Journal of Drug and Alcohol Abuse,* 19:491–497.

Miller, J. G. 1978. *Living Systems.* New York: McGraw-Hill.

Perry, B., R. Pollard, T. Blakley, W. Baker, and D. Vigilante. 1996. Childhood trauma, the neurobiology of adaptation and use-dependent development of the brain: How states become traits. In Press: *Infant Mental Health Journal.*

Prochaska, J. O., C. C. DiClemente, and J. C. Norcross. 1992. In search of how people change: Applications to addictive behavior. *American Psychologist,* 47(9):1101–1114.

Reiger, D., W. Narrow, D. Rae, R. Manderscheid, B. Locke, and F. Goodwin. 1993. The de facto US mental and addictive disorders service system: Epidemiologic catchment area prospective 1-year prevalence rates of disorders and services. *Archives of General Psychiatry,* 50:85–93.

Rubey, R. 1995. Naltrexone, opiates, and self-injurious behavior. Internet document: www.uhs.bsd.uchicago.edu/~bhsung/tips/tips.html.

Salzman, C. 1996. What drug treatments are available for borderline personality disorder? *Harvard Mental Health Letter*, 13(3):8.

Sartre, J. P. 1964. *Nausea*. New York: New Directions Publishing.

Silk, K. R. 1994. *Biological and Neurobehavioral Studies of Borderline Personality Disorder*. Washington, DC: American Psychiatric Press.

Silk, K. R., S. Lee, E. M. Hill, and N. E. Lohr. 1995. Borderline personality disorder symptoms and severity of sexual abuse. *American Journal of Psychiatry*, 152(7):1059–1064.

Sobell, M. B., and L. C. Sobell. 1982. Controlled drinking: A concept comes of age. In K. R. Blanstein and J. Polivy, eds., *Self-Control and the Self-Modification of Emotional Behavior*. New York: Plenum.

Sorge, R. 1991. Harm reduction: A new approach to drug services. *Health/PAC Bulletin*. Winter:70–75.

Stone, J. 1990. *The Fate of Borderline Patients*. New York: Guilford.

Teicher, M. H., Y. Ito, C. A. Glod, F. Schiffer, and H. A. Gelbard. 1994. Early abuse, limbic system dysfunction, and borderline personality disorder. In K. R. Silk, ed., *Biological and Neurobehavioral Studies of Borderline Personality Disorder*. Washington, DC: American Psychiatric Press.

Turner, J. S., and D. B. Helms. 1979. *Life Span Development*. Philadelphia: Saunders.

Wolman, B. B. 1973. *Dictionary of Behavioral Science*. New York: Van Nostrand Reinhold.

More New Harbinger Self-Help Titles

THE SCARRED SOUL
The first book written for the victims of self-inflicted violence helps readers explore the reasons behind the impulse to hurt themselves and take steps to overcome the psychological traps that lead to self-inflicted pain. *Paperback, $13.95*

THE ADDICTION WORKBOOK
This comprehensive guide explains the facts about addiction and provides simple, step-by-step directions for working through the stages of the quitting process. *Paperback, $17.95*

WHEN ANGER HURTS
A complete guide to changing habitual anger-generating thoughts while developing healthier, more effective ways of getting your needs met. *Paperback, $13.95*

CHOOSING TO LIVE
A step-by-step program for those who are considering suicide helps readers replace negative beliefs, feel better through coping, and develop alternative problem-solving skills. *Paperback, $12.95*

SELF-ESTEEM
The only book on the subject that uses proven cognitive techniques for improving self-esteem by talking back to the self-critical voice inside you. *Paperback, $13.95*

Call **toll-free 1-800-748-6273** to order. Have your Visa or Mastercard number ready. Or send a check for the titles you want to New Harbinger Publications, 5674 Shattuck Avenue, Oakland, CA 94609. Include $3.80 for the first book and 75¢ for each additional book to cover shipping and handling. (California residents please include appropriate sales tax.) Allow four to six weeks for delivery.

Prices subject to change without notice.

Some Other New Harbinger Self-Help Titles

Claiming Your Creative Self: True Stories from the Everyday Lives of Women, $15.95
Six Keys to Creating the Life You Desire, $19.95
Taking Control of TMJ, $13.95
What You Need to Know About Alzheimer's, $15.95
Winning Against Relapse: A Workbook of Action Plans for Recurring Health and Emotional Problems, $14.95
Facing 30: Women Talk About Constructing a Real Life and Other Scary Rites of Passage, $12.95
The Worry Control Workbook, $15.95
Wanting What You Have: A Self-Discovery Workbook, $18.95
When Perfect Isn't Good Enough: Strategies for Coping with Perfectionism, $13.95
The Endometriosis Survival Guide, $13.95
Earning Your Own Respect: A Handbook of Personal Responsibility, $12.95
High on Stress: A Woman's Guide to Optimizing the Stress in Her Life, $13.95
Infidelity: A Survival Guide, $13.95
Stop Walking on Eggshells, $14.95
Consumer's Guide to Psychiatric Drugs, $16.95
The Fibromyalgia Advocate: Getting the Support You Need to Cope with Fibromyalgia and Myofascial Pain, $18.95
Healing Fear: New Approaches to Overcoming Anxiety, $16.95
Working Anger: Preventing and Resolving Conflict on the Job, $12.95
Sex Smart: How Your Childhood Shaped Your Sexual Life and What to Do About It, $14.95
You Can Free Yourself From Alcohol & Drugs, $13.95
Amongst Ourselves: A Self-Help Guide to Living with Dissociative Identity Disorder, $14.95
Healthy Living with Diabetes, $13.95
Dr. Carl Robinson's Basic Baby Care, $10.95
Better Boundaries: Owning and Treasuring Your Life, $13.95
Goodbye Good Girl, $12.95
Being, Belonging, Doing, $10.95
Thoughts & Feelings, Second Edition, $18.95
Depression: How It Happens, How It's Healed, $14.95
Trust After Trauma, $15.95
The Chemotherapy & Radiation Survival Guide, Second Edition, $14.95
Surviving Childhood Cancer, $12.95
The Headache & Neck Pain Workbook, $14.95
Perimenopause, $16.95
The Self-Forgiveness Handbook, $12.95
A Woman's Guide to Overcoming Sexual Fear and Pain, $14.95
Don't Take It Personally, $12.95
Becoming a Wise Parent For Your Grown Child, $12.95
Clear Your Past, Change Your Future, $13.95
Preparing for Surgery, $17.95
The Power of Two, $15.95
It's Not OK Anymore, $13.95
The Daily Relaxer, $12.95
The Body Image Workbook, $17.95
Living with ADD, $17.95
When Anger Hurts Your Kids, $12.95
The Chronic Pain Control Workbook, Second Edition, $17.95
Fibromyalgia & Chronic Myofascial Pain Syndrome, $19.95
Kid Cooperation: How to Stop Yelling, Nagging & Pleading and Get Kids to Cooperate, $13.95
The Stop Smoking Workbook: Your Guide to Healthy Quitting, $17.95
Conquering Carpal Tunnel Syndrome and Other Repetitive Strain Injuries, $17.95
An End to Panic: Breakthrough Techniques for Overcoming Panic Disorder, Second Edition, $18.95
Letting Go of Anger: The 10 Most Common Anger Styles and What to Do About Them, $12.95
Messages: The Communication Skills Workbook, Second Edition, $15.95
Coping With Chronic Fatigue Syndrome: Nine Things You Can Do, $13.95
The Anxiety & Phobia Workbook, Second Edition, $18.95
The Relaxation & Stress Reduction Workbook, Fourth Edition, $17.95
Living Without Depression & Manic Depression: A Workbook for Maintaining Mood Stability, $18.95
Coping With Schizophrenia: A Guide For Families, $15.95
Visualization for Change, Second Edition, $15.95
Angry All the Time: An Emergency Guide to Anger Control, $12.95
Couple Skills: Making Your Relationship Work, $14.95
Self-Esteem, Second Edition, $13.95
I Can't Get Over It, A Handbook for Trauma Survivors, Second Edition, $16.95
Dying of Embarrassment: Help for Social Anxiety and Social Phobia, $13.95
The Depression Workbook: Living With Depression and Manic Depression, $17.95
Men & Grief: A Guide for Men Surviving the Death of a Loved One, $14.95
When Once Is Not Enough: Help for Obsessive Compulsives, $14.95
Beyond Grief: A Guide for Recovering from the Death of a Loved One, $14.95
Hypnosis for Change: A Manual of Proven Techniques, Third Edition, $15.95
When Anger Hurts, $13.95